Y0-CAX-306

HOUGHTON MIFFLIN

Spelling and Vocabulary

Senior Author
Shane Templeton

Consultants
Donald R. Bear
Rosa Maria Peña

HOUGHTON MIFFLIN

BOSTON

Acknowledgments

For each of the selections listed below, grateful acknowledgment is made for permission to excerpt and/or reprint original or copyrighted material as follows:

SCRABBLE® is a registered trademark of Hasbro Inc. Used by permission of Hasbro Inc. All rights reserved.

Select definitions in the Spelling Dictionary are adapted and reprinted by permission from the following Houghton Mifflin Company publications: Copyright © 1994 THE AMERICAN HERITAGE CHILDREN'S DICTIONARY. Copyright © 1994 THE AMERICAN HERITAGE STUDENT DICTIONARY.

Excerpt from "Adobe Way" in *Flights* from *Houghton Mifflin Reading,* by Durr et al. Copyright © 1986 by Houghton Mifflin Company. Reprinted by permission of Houghton Mifflin Company. All rights reserved.

Excerpt from *Charlotte's Web,* by E.B. White. Copyright 1952 by E.B. White. Text copyright renewed © 1980 by E.B. White. Illustrations copyright renewed © 1980 by Garth Williams. Adapted and reprinted by permission of HarperCollins Publishers and Hamish Hamilton Ltd.

Excerpt from "Hurdles," by Mary Blocksma with Esther Romero in *Flights* from *Houghton Mifflin Reading,* by Durr et al. Copyright © 1986 by Houghton Mifflin Company. Reprinted by permission of Houghton Mifflin Company. All rights reserved.

Excerpt from *The Once-a-Year Day*, by Eve Bunting. Copyright © 1974 by Eve Bunting. Reprinted by permission of the author.

Excerpt from *Seven True Elephant Stories,* by Barbara Williams. Copyright © 1978 by Hastings House. Adapted and reprinted by permission of the author.

Copyright © 2004 by Houghton Mifflin Company. All rights reserved.

No part of this work may be reproduced or transmitted in any form or by any means, electronic or mechanical, including photocopying and recording, or by any information storage or retrieval system without the prior written permission of Houghton Mifflin Company unless such copying is expressly permitted by federal copyright law. Address inquiries to School Permissions, Houghton Mifflin Company, 222 Berkeley Street, Boston, MA 02116.
Printed in U.S.A.

ISBN: 0-618-31168-8

3 4 5 6 7 8 9 10-B-11 10 09 08 07 06 05 04

Contents

|ĕ| |ē|
fresh   peach

mend + right =

end r might

Contents

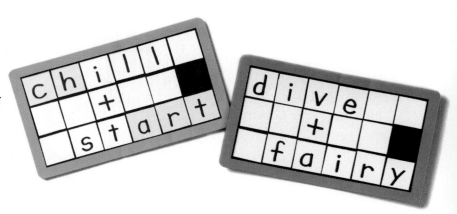

railroad

Contents

Contents

Contents

Contents

Student's Handbook

How to Study a Word

① Look at the word.

- What are the letters in the word?
- What does the word mean?
- Does it have more than one meaning?

② Say the word.

- What are the consonant sounds?
- What are the vowel sounds?

③ Think about the word.

- How is each sound spelled?
- Did you see any familiar spelling patterns?
- Did you note any prefixes, suffixes, or other word parts?

④ Write the word.

- Think about the sounds and the letters.
- Form the letters correctly.

⑤ Check the spelling.

- Did you spell the word the same way it is spelled on your word list?
- Do you need to write the word again?

9

Activities and Games

Word Sorts with Partners

1. Choose 15 to 20 Spelling Words that can be sorted into two or more categories.
2. Write each category on a slip of paper. Write each Spelling Word on a slip of paper.
3. Trade category cards and word cards with a partner. Try to sort each other's words into the correct category. Review and discuss each other's work.

CHALLENGE Have your partner try to guess your categories and sort the words. Discuss the word sort together.

Sorting Ideas

- by vowel sound (**Example:** short **a** from long **a**)
- by spelling patterns for one vowel sound (**Example: ay, ai,** and **a**-consonant-**e** for the long **a** sound)
- by the way -*ed* and -*ing* are added (**Example:** tan*ning* from dan*cing*)
- by prefix or suffix (**Example:** *re*read from *un*kind or color*ful* from care*less*)
- by syllable pattern (**Example:** VCCV from VCV)

Pattern Match

Players: Any number; one caller
You need: paper, pencils, list of Spelling Words

How to Play

1. Players choose a sound that has several patterns, such as the long *o* sound.
2. Each player draws a ticktacktoe grid and writes the sound above the grid and one pattern in each square. Each pattern must be used at least once. Players choose the patterns for the squares in their grids.
3. The caller reads a Spelling Word that matches the sound and one of its patterns. Each player tries to write the word correctly in a square that has the matching pattern.
4. The caller reads more Spelling Words, using words with different patterns in any order.
5. When a player writes three words across, down, or diagonally, the caller checks the words. If any words are spelled incorrectly, play continues until a correct ticktacktoe is made. The winner becomes the next caller.

Missing Letters Game

Players: 2 to 4
You need: a game board with 22 squares, 22 or more word cards with incomplete Spelling Words on one side and complete words on the back, game markers, spinner

How to Play

1. Shuffle the cards. Place them in a pile face up so that only the top card shows.
2. Player 1 picks up the top card and holds it so that another player can see the word on the back. The other player reads the word, and Player 1 tries to spell it aloud. If correct, Player 1 spins the spinner and moves the number of spaces shown.
3. Players take turns until one player passes *End*. Cards can be reshuffled and reused to finish the game.

front   back

cab_   cabin

_act   exact

Spelling |ă| and |ā|

Read and Say

Basic

READ the sentences. **SAY** each bold word.

|ă|
plant

|ā|
skate

1. skate — Did you **skate** on the pond?
2. blade — I will cut each **blade** of grass.
3. gain — Cars **gain** speed going down a hill.
4. safe — Have a **safe** trip.
5. drag — Lee will **drag** the ladder closer.
6. aid — The nurse will **aid** the hurt boy.
7. past — I have been sick for the **past** week.
8. gray — Her dirty white coat looks **gray**.
9. drain — Please fix the **drain** in the sink.
10. break — Don't **break** the cup.
11. jail — Was the robber sent to **jail**?
12. shape — The **shape** of a ball is round.
13. plant — The flowers on the **plant** are red.
14. hang — Jill will **hang** up her coat.
15. pray — He will **pray** for rain.
16. pain — She was in **pain** from her cut.
17. glass — The dish is made of **glass**.
18. shall — We **shall** be there.
19. sale — That store is having a **sale**.
20. steak — The dog likes to eat **steak**.

Think and Write

The short *a* sound is usually spelled *a* followed by a consonant sound.
The long *a* sound is often spelled *a*-consonant-*e* or with two letters.

> |ă| dr**a**g |ā| sk**ate**, g**ai**n, gr**ay**

• What is one spelling pattern for |ă|? What are three patterns for |ā|?
What is the spelling pattern for |ā| in the Elephant Words?

Now write each Basic Word under its vowel sound.

|ă| Sound	|ā| Sound

Review		**Challenge**	
21. last	23. clay	26. champion	28. athletic
22. stage	24. face	27. graceful	29. activity
	25. paint		30. relay

Independent Practice

Spelling Strategy   Remember that the |ă|
sound is usually spelled *a* followed by a consonant sound.
When you hear the |ā| sound, think of the patterns
a-consonant-*e*, *ai*, and *ay*.

Word Analysis/Phonics Complete the exercises with Basic Words.

1–2. The first sound in *ship* is shown as |sh|. Write the two words that
begin with the |sh| sound.

3–5. Write the three words that rhyme with *train*.

Vocabulary: Definitions Write the Basic Word that fits each
meaning.

6. a piece of meat
7. to crack
8. gone by
9. to glide on ice
10. a color that mixes black and white
11. to hope very much
12. to pull along
13. to give help to

Challenge Words Write the Challenge Word that fits each meaning.
Use your Spelling Dictionary.

14. a winner
15. good at sports
16. to pass along
17. showing beauty in movement
18. movement or action

Spelling-Meaning Connection

Can you see *safe* in these words: *safely, safety,
unsafe*? These words are all related in spelling
and meaning. **Think of this:** Following *safety*
rules will keep you *safe*.

19–20. Write *safety*. Then write the Basic Word that you
see in *safety*.

Review: Spelling Spree

Hidden Words Write the Basic or Review Word that you find in each row of letters. Do not let the other words fool you.

Example: l a **p r a y** a r d *pray*

1. l e s p a y s a f e e l
2. t r a s h o s t e a k
3. r i s k a t e a r
4. l e g a i n e a r l y
5. w a s h a l l e l s
6. l a s h a n g e r

7. f a l l a s t e l l
8. c a s t a g e a r
9. s o f a c e d a r
10. s a l e a p e d
11. w e b l a d e a r
12. g r a l s a i d o

Letter Math Write a Basic or Review Word by adding and subtracting letters from the words below.

Example: st + page − p = *stage*

13. br + steak − st =
14. gr + pray − pr =
15. cl + play − pl =
16. gl + class − cl =
17. pr + way − w =
18. j + pail − p =
19. p + train − tr =
20. p + fast − f =
21. p + faint − f =
22. pl + grant − gr =

23. sh + tape − t =
24. dr + main − m =
25. dr + sag − s =

✓ **How Are You Doing?**
Write your spelling words in ABC order. Practice any misspelled words with a family member.

br + steak − st

Proofreading and Writing

Proofread: Spelling and End Marks End every sentence with the correct mark.

STATEMENT: Grandfather works at the Sports Center.
COMMAND: Read this article about his store.
QUESTION: Do famous players shop there?
EXCLAMATION: What a great job that must be!

Find four misspelled Basic or Review Words and two missing end marks in this ad. Write the ad correctly.

Are your skates old and out of shap

Do you have a dull skate blad?

Does your sled need a new coat of pant?

Visit the Sports Center during our winter sal

Write a Personal Story

Write a paragraph telling about a good time that you had outdoors during the winter. What was the weather like? Who was with you? Why was this experience special? Try to use five spelling words.

Check that you used correct end marks. Proofread for one kind of error at a time.

Proofreading Tip

Dec.

Jan.

Feb.

Mar.

Basic

1. skate
2. blade
3. gain
4. safe
5. drag
6. aid
7. past
8. gray
9. drain
10. break
11. jail
12. shape
13. plant
14. hang
15. pray
16. pain
17. glass
18. shall
19. sale
20. steak

Review

21. last
22. stage
23. clay
24. face
25. paint

Challenge

26. champion
27. graceful
28. athletic
29. activity
30. relay

Proofreading Marks

¶ Indent
∧ Add
⊱ Delete
≡ Capital letter
/ Small letter

Expanding Vocabulary

Spelling Word Link

safe
break

Using a Thesaurus Where can you find words that say exactly what you mean? Look in a thesaurus. A **thesaurus** gives words that can be used in place of other words. This thesaurus entry gives *careful* and *protected* as words for *safe*.

part of speech   definition   sample sentence

main entry word ·····> **safe** *adj.* free from danger, risk, or harm. *This old bridge is not safe.*

subentries
careful taking the necessary caution. *My mother is a careful driver.*
protected covered or guarded from harm. *Wild animals are protected in this park.*

1–2. Read pages 253–254 to learn how to use your Thesaurus. Then look up *break* in your Thesaurus. Write the two subentries listed for *break*.

Work Together Work with a partner to write a caption for each picture strip. Use a subentry for *break* in each caption.

3.

4.

Real-World Connection

Recreation: Winter Sports All the words in the box relate to winter sports. Look up these words in your Spelling Dictionary. Then write the words to complete this part of a letter.

Spelling Word Link

skate

snowmobile
sledding
rink
toboggan
sleigh
parka
ski
gloves

Dear Grandma,

Every year our town has a Winter Weekend. Skiers from many towns __(1)__ in downhill races, and skaters perform in the ice __(2)__. You can hear the sounds of __(3)__ motors as people ride all over town. People also ride in a horse-drawn __(4)__. Everyone with a sled goes __(5)__. My brothers and I use a long, narrow sled called a __(6)__. I stay warm in my new red __(7)__ and matching __(8)__ for my hands. I love Winter Weekend!

Try This CHALLENGE

Yes or No? Write *yes* or *no* to answer each question.

9. Does a snowmobile go faster than a sleigh?
10. Can you go skiing in a rink?
11. Will a parka keep your head warm?
12. Does a toboggan use gasoline?

★★ Fact File

A slalom is a ski race. In the slalom, skiers race downhill through a set of marked poles with flags on them. Skiers zigzag between the poles as fast as possible.

Spelling |ĕ| and |ē|

Read and Say

Basic

READ the sentences. **SAY** each bold word.

|ĕ| |ē|
fresh   **peach**

1. peach   The **peach** fell from the tree.
2. sweet   The cake is too **sweet**.
3. feast   Our club's dinner was a **feast**.
4. cream   The milk had **cream** on the top.
5. fresh   Maria picked a **fresh** apple.
6. free   The zoo set the bird **free**.
7. reach   Can you **reach** the shelf?
8. kept   Pam **kept** the pen I gave her.
9. spent   Tim **spent** his last dime.
10. field   Corn is growing in the **field**.
11. desk   The book is on the **desk**.
12. least   The smallest cat ate the **least**.
13. east   The sun comes up in the **east**.
14. greed   She was full of fear and **greed**.
15. real   The fake flowers look **real**.
16. dream   Do you **dream** when you sleep?
17. west   The sun sets in the **west**.
18. speed   Race cars move at a fast **speed**.
19. cheap   This **cheap** pencil costs five cents.
20. chief   The **chief** planner leads a team.

Think and Write

Each word has the short *e* sound or the long *e* sound. The short *e* sound is usually spelled *e* followed by a consonant sound. The long *e* sound is often spelled with two vowels.

|ĕ| fr**e**sh |ē| p**ea**ch, sw**ee**t

• What is one spelling pattern for |ĕ|? What are two patterns for |ē|? What pattern spells |ē| in the Elephant Words?

Now write each Basic Word under its vowel sound.

|ĕ| Sound	|ē| Sound

Review
21. need
22. three
23. left
24. seem
25. speak

Challenge
26. chef
27. yeast
28. menu
29. restaurant
30. knead

Independent Practice

Spelling Strategy Remember that the |ĕ| sound is usually spelled *e* followed by a consonant sound. When you hear the |ē| sound, think of the patterns *ea* and *ee*.

Word Analysis/Phonics Complete the exercises with Basic Words.

1–4. Write the four words that end with the cluster *st*.

5–8. Write the four words that begin or end with *ch*.

Vocabulary: Analogies An **analogy** compares word pairs that are related in the same way. Write a Basic Word to complete each analogy.

Example: Big is to **small** as **loud** is to **quiet**.

9. *Lemon* is to *sour* as *honey* is to _____.

10. *Came* is to *went* as *saved* is to _____.

11. *Kitchen* is to *table* as *classroom* is to _____.

12. *Hockey* is to *rink* as *football* is to _____.

13. *Sweep* is to *swept* as *keep* is to _____.

Challenge Words Write the Challenge Word that fits each meaning. Use your Spelling Dictionary.

14. a list of foods
15. to mix, roll, or press
16. a cook

17. makes bread dough rise
18. a place where meals are served

Spelling-Meaning Connection

Can you see *fresh* in these words: *freshness, refresh, refreshments*?

Think of this: The *refreshments* helped us feel *fresh* again.

19–20. Write *refreshments*. Then write the Basic Word that is related to *refreshments* in spelling and meaning.

fresh
fresh**ness**
re**fresh**
re**fresh**ments

Dictionary

Alphabetical Order How would you find *peach* quickly in a dictionary? The words in a dictionary are in alphabetical order. Turn to the part of the dictionary with the words beginning with *p*.

BEGINNING	MIDDLE	END
a b c d e f g	h i j k l m n o p	q r s t u v w x y z

Suppose you see *pear*. Does *peach* come before or after it? Look at the first letters that are different to alphabetize the words: pea**c**h, pea**r**. *Peach* comes before *pear*.

Practice 1–8. Write these words in alphabetical order.

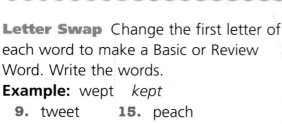

spent	speed	space	speck
spell	spare	speak	sped

Review: Spelling Spree

Letter Swap Change the first letter of each word to make a Basic or Review Word. Write the words.
Example: wept *kept*

9. tweet
10. best
11. feast
12. tree
13. fast
14. cream
15. peach
16. seed
17. deal
18. breed
19. yield
20. reach
21. thief
22. deem
23. least
24. dream

How Are You Doing?

List the spelling words that are hard for you. Practice them with a family member.

Proofreading and Writing

Proofread for Spelling Find nine misspelled Basic or Review Words in this class story. Write each one correctly.

Mr. Chang came to our class to spek about cooking. He teaches cooking at thre schools. He told us that freash vegetables and sweet fruits keep us healthy. He put some vegetables on a dask. He said they were cheep! He had speant only a few dollars for them. Mr. Chang used a special pan to cook the vegetables with spead. He made a real feast! We cept the pan when he leaft to show the other classes.

Basic

1. peach
2. sweet
3. feast
4. cream
5. fresh
6. free
7. reach
8. kept
9. spent
10. field
11. desk
12. least
13. east
14. greed
15. real
16. dream
17. west
18. speed
19. cheap
20. chief

Review

21. need
22. three
23. left
24. seem
25. speak

Challenge

26. chef
27. yeast
28. menu
29. restaurant
30. knead

Write a Review

good   very   best
        good

Write a review of your favorite place to eat. What food is served there? Is it good? Try to use five spelling words. You may want to share your review with your classmates.

Proofreading Tip

Read one line at a time. Put a strip of paper under the line to stay focused.

Proofreading Marks

¶ Indent
∧ Add
⌙ Delete
≡ Capital letter
/ Small letter

Vocabulary Enrichment

Expanding Vocabulary

festival
festoon
festive
songfest

Word Family for *feast* *Feast* comes from an old word meaning "festive, merry." A feast is a fancy meal served at a party or festive event. The word box includes other words related to festive times. Where are their spellings the same? Find these words in your Spelling Dictionary. Then read each definition. Write the letters to complete each word that fits the meaning. Write the whole word.

Meaning	Complete the word.	Write the word.
• merry, joyous	fest __ive__	festive
• to decorate with a garland hung in a loop between two points	**1.** fest ___?___	**2.** ___?___
• a casual gathering for group singing	**3.** ___?___ fest	**4.** ___?___
• a day or period of celebrating; holiday	**5.** fest ___?___	**6.** ___?___

Work Together With a partner write a sentence to answer each question about the picture. Use the word in ( ).

Foods of the World Festival

7. Why is this group gathered to celebrate? (festival)

8. How do these people feel about the event? (festive)

9. How is the room decorated? (festoon)

Fact File

The Spanish word *fiesta* and the French word *fête* are also related to *feast* and *festival. Fiesta* and *fête* both mean "festival or celebration."

Vocabulary Enrichment

Real-World Connection

Home Economics: Cooking All the words in the box relate to cooking. Look up these words in your Spelling Dictionary. Write the words to complete these cooking ideas.

Spelling Word Link

chef

sift
grate
measure
barbecue
simmer
fry
mince
poach

Ways to Cook Fish

Here are three great ways to cook fish.

- You can __(1)__ it on a grill.

- Another way is to heat water just below the boiling point and let it __(2)__. Then you can __(3)__ the fish in the water.

- You can also make a batter for the fish. Use a measuring cup to __(4)__ the flour. Then __(5)__ it to remove the lumps. Next, you can shred or __(6)__ some cheese and use a sharp knife to __(7)__ some onion. Finally, roll the fish in the batter, and __(8)__ it in a pan.

Try This CHALLENGE

Questions and Answers Write a word from the box to answer each question.

9. What can you do to flour but not to milk?
10. What can you do to water but not to bread?
11. What do you do with butter melted in a pan?
12. What do you do with a tablespoon?

Spelling |ĭ| and |ī|

Read and Say

READ the sentences. **SAY** each bold word.

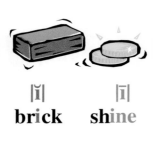

|ĭ|
brick

|ī|
shi**ne**

Basic

1.	brick	The wall is missing a **brick**.
2.	skill	That game takes **skill** to play.
3.	lift	You can **lift** the big box for me.
4.	pride	She took **pride** in her work.
5.	grind	Do we need to **grind** the corn?
6.	still	I stepped into the **still** waters.
7.	crime	Breaking the law is a **crime**.
8.	flight	I had a long airplane **flight**.
9.	live	The band will play **live** on TV.
10.	build	Did Joan **build** the red barn?
11.	blind	A **blind** bear cannot see you.
12.	sting	Do not let the bee **sting** you.
13.	fright	The lost boy shook with **fright**.
14.	wind	I can **wind** the string into a ball.
15.	hint	He had no **hint** of where to go.
16.	ripe	This green apple is not **ripe**.
17.	shine	The star will **shine** in the sky.
18.	inch	Is her toe an **inch** long?
19.	sigh	The sad news made me **sigh**.
20.	built	My father **built** a new house.

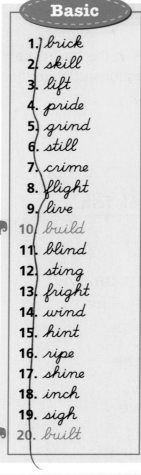

Think and Write

The short *i* sound is often spelled *i* followed by a consonant sound. The long *i* sound can be spelled *i*-consonant-*e* or with one or more letters.

|ĭ| br**i**ck |ī| pr**ide**, fl**igh**t, gr**i**nd

• What is one pattern for |ĭ|? What are three patterns for |ī|? What pattern spells |ĭ| in the Elephant Words?

Now write each Basic Word under its vowel sound. Include *live* and *wind* with |ī|.

|ĭ| Sound	|ī| Sound

Review		**Challenge**	
21. mix	23. sight	26. inspect	28. rigid
22. tight	24. mind	27. polish	29. advice
	25. smile		30. recognize

Independent Practice

Spelling Strategy Remember that the |ī| sound is often spelled *i* followed by a consonant sound. When you hear the |ī| sound, think of the patterns *i*-consonant-*e*, *igh*, and *i*.

Word Analysis/Phonics Complete the exercises with Basic Words.

1–2. Write *build*. Then write its past tense.

3–6. Write the word that begins with each consonant cluster.

    3. pr   **4.** bl   **5.** fl   **6.** fr

7–8. Write the two words that rhyme with *hill*.

Vocabulary: Classifying Write the Basic Word that belongs in each group.

  9. rain, snow, _____   **12.** foot, yard, _____

 10. board, stone, _____   **13.** whisper, shout, _____

 11. chop, slice, _____

Challenge Words Write the Challenge Word that fits each meaning. Use your Spelling Dictionary.

 14. to look at carefully   **17.** to know from the past

 15. stiff or not easily bent   **18.** a suggestion about how to solve

 16. to make shiny   a problem

Spelling-Meaning Connection

Crime and *criminal* have different vowel sounds, but they are related in spelling and meaning. **Think of this:** A *criminal* commits a *crime*.

crime
criminal

19–20. Write *criminal*. Then write the Basic Word that is related to *criminal* in spelling and meaning.

Dictionary

Guide Words To find an **entry word**, or main word, on a dictionary page, use the guide words. The **guide words** show the first and last entry words on the page. Why would *sting* be on the same page as these guide words?

sticky - stitch

stick·y |stĭk' ē| *adj.* stickier, stickiest
1. Tending to stick.

Practice 1–8. Write the eight words below that would be on a dictionary page with the guide words *sift - sky*.

silver	still	shy	six	shine	skunk
skip	silent	skill	sight	silly	slope

Review: Spelling Spree

Word Addition Write a Basic or Review Word by adding the beginning of the first word to the middle and end of the second word.
Example: mend + right   *might*

9. seven + high
10. west + find
11. blade + kind
12. hang + print
13. flood + night
14. steal + hill
15. magic + six
16. lamb + gift

17. free + might
18. rang + wipe
19. stare + king
20. lazy + give
21. cream + time
22. group + find
23. safe + light

24. brush + thick
25. tape + fight

How Are You Doing?

Write each spelling word as a partner reads it aloud. Did you misspell any words?

mend + right =
end
r might

Proofreading and Writing

Proofread for Spelling Find eight misspelled Basic or Review Words in this character sketch. Write each one correctly.

My cousin Alex likes to bild dollhouses. The furniture he makes is often less than an intch tall. He does not minde spending hours carving little brick fireplaces and trying to shin tiny brass doorknobs. In fact, Alex takes great pried in it. Once I asked him why he has not bilt any houses for people to live in. He said that he likes using his skil to make children smil.

Basic

1. brick
2. skill
3. lift
4. pride
5. grind
6. still
7. crime
8. flight
9. live
10. build
11. blind
12. sting
13. fright
14. wind
15. hint
16. ripe
17. shine
18. inch
19. sigh
20. built

Review

21. mix
22. tight
23. sight
24. mind
25. smile

Challenge

26. inspect
27. polish
28. rigid
29. advice
30. recognize

Write a Description

Describe a building in your town. How tall is it? What does it look like? Try to use five spelling words. You may also want to draw a picture of the building.

LIBRARY

Proofreading Tip

As you check each word, touch it with your finger. Then you will know that you have not missed any words.

Proofreading Marks

¶ Indent
∧ Add
⌐ Delete
≡ Capital letter
／ Small letter

Expanding Vocabulary

Homographs Homographs are words that are spelled the same but have different meanings and may be pronounced differently.

wind[1]	|wīnd|	to tighten the spring of	I'll wind the music box.
wind[2]	|wĭnd|	moving air	A kite needs wind to fly.

Here are more homographs. Use your Spelling Dictionary to write each meaning.

Homograph	Pronunciation	Meaning	
lead[1]	|lēd| rhymes with *bead*	**1.**	?
lead[2]	|lĕd| rhymes with *head*	**2.**	?
tear[1]	|târ| rhymes with bear	**3.**	?
tear[2]	|tîr| rhymes with *fear*	**4.**	?

Work Together Write a sentence for each homograph. Then trade sentences with a partner or small group. Read each sentence aloud, and pronounce the homograph correctly.

5. wind
6. lead
7. tear

Real-World Connection

Industrial Arts: Construction All the words in the box relate to construction. Look up these words in your Spelling Dictionary. Write the words to complete these instructions.

Spelling Word Link

build

plank
hammer
clamp
screwdriver
wrench
drill
pliers
handsaw

INSTRUCTIONS

To build a birdhouse, start by using a ___(1)___ to hold a long ___(2)___ of wood in place. Then cut the wood into pieces with a ___(3)___. After you nail the pieces together with a ___(4)___, use screws and a ___(5)___ to attach hinges to the top. Make a hole for the perch with a ___(6)___. Then use nuts and bolts to attach a handle. Be sure to tighten the bolts with a ___(7)___. Finally, with a pair of ___(8)___, twist some wire into a loop and hang the birdhouse up outside.

Try This CHALLENGE

Yes or No? Write *yes* if the underlined word is used correctly. Write *no* if it is not.

9. Liz used her <u>handsaw</u> to tighten the bolt.
10. A <u>clamp</u> would hold these two boards together.
11. Which <u>drill</u> did you use to make this hole?
12. The <u>wrench</u> cut completely through the wood.

★ Fact File

People often build things from available materials. The Inuit of Alaska and Canada used blocks of hard-packed snow and ice to build temporary shelters, called igloos, for hunting and fishing.

Spelling |ŏ| and |ō|

|ŏ| |ō|
block   **gold**

Basic

READ the sentences. **SAY** each bold word.

1.	globe	Is a **globe** like a map?
2.	coast	Ships sailed up the **coast**.
3.	goal	The **goal** is to get a job.
4.	spoke	My teacher **spoke** loudly.
5.	odd	Is it **odd** to fish at night?
6.	shown	He has **shown** us how to fly.
7.	gold	My ring is made of **gold**.
8.	wrote	Pete **wrote** with red ink.
9.	snow	A lot of **snow** fell last winter.
10.	block	A **block** of ice will chill the room.
11.	crow	A black **crow** hurt its wing.
12.	stock	The store has pens in **stock**.
13.	chose	Pat **chose** red instead of blue.
14.	folk	The island **folk** are farmers.
15.	coal	We use **coal** to keep warm.
16.	host	Will our **host** serve the meal?
17.	bowl	I filled the **bowl** with nuts.
18.	grown	I need a team of **grown** men.
19.	shock	The sad news was a **shock**.
20.	broke	He **broke** the stick in two.

Think and Write

Each word has the short *o* or the long *o* sound. Usually |ŏ| is spelled *o* followed by a consonant sound. Often |ō| is spelled *o*-consonant-*e* or with patterns of one or more letters.

> |ŏ| bl**o**ck |ō| gl**o**b**e**, g**oa**l, sh**ow**n, g**o**ld

• What is one spelling pattern for |ŏ|? What are four patterns for |ō|?

Now write each Basic Word under its vowel sound.

|ŏ| Sound	|ō| Sound

Review	23. smoke	**Challenge**	28. approach
21. know	24. drop	26. continent	29. motion
22. most	25. soap	27. longitude	30. accomplish

Independent Practice

Spelling Strategy
Remember that the |ŏ| sound is usually spelled *o* followed by a consonant sound. When you hear the |ō| sound, think of the patterns *o*-consonant-*e*, *oa*, *ow*, and *o*.

Word Analysis/Phonics Complete the exercises with Basic Words.

1. Write the word that has a double consonant.

2–5. Write the past tense of each word below.

    2. break   **3.** speak   **4.** write   **5.** choose

Vocabulary: Making Inferences Write the Basic Word that fits each clue.

6. Soup is served in it.
7. It's burned for heat.
8. Jewelry is made from it.
9. It falls in winter.
10. A scarecrow will scare it.
11. Electricity can give you one.
12. It can be a cube with letters.
13. It is shaped like a ball.

Challenge Words Write the Challenge Word that fits each meaning. Use your Spelling Dictionary.

14. to carry out or achieve
15. a main land mass
16. movement
17. to come near
18. distance measured in degrees east or west of the meridian at Greenwich, England

Spelling-Meaning Connection

Can you see *coast* in these words: *coastal, seacoast, coastline*? These words are related in spelling and meaning. **Think of this:** The *Coast* Guard sailed along the *coastline*.

19–20. Write *coastal*. Then write the Basic Word that you see in *coastal*.

coast
coastal
coastline
seacoast

Review: Spelling Spree

Finding Words Write the Basic or Review Word in each word below.

1. unblock
2. oddness
3. spoken
4. bowls
5. chosen
6. restock
7. broken
8. knowing
9. rewrote
10. soapy
11. crowed
12. coastal
13. golden

Puzzle Play Write a Basic or Review Word to fit each clue.
Circle the letter that would appear in the box.
Example: a round dish _ _ _ □ *bowl*

14. one who has guests _ _ _ □
15. a bad surprise _ □ _ _ _
16. comes from fires _ _ _ _ □
17. white ice crystals _ □ _ _
18. black lumps that burn _ □ _ _
19. form of *grow* _ □ _ _ _
20. greatest number _ _ _ □
21. form of *show* _ □ _ _ _
22. to let fall _ _ _ □
23. people _ □ _ _
24. purpose or aim _ _ _ □
25. earth _ _ _ _ □

Now write the circled letters in order. They spell three mystery words that name a place.

Mystery Words: __ ? __
__ __ ? __ __   __ ? __ __

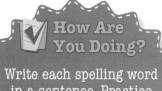

How Are You Doing?

Write each spelling word in a sentence. Practice any misspelled spelling words with a partner.

32

Proofreading and Writing

Proofread: Spelling and Proper Nouns A **proper noun** names a particular person, place, or thing. Capitalize proper nouns.

Aunt Mary   Chicago   Fourth of July

Find four misspelled Basic or Review Words and three missing capital letters in this part of a post card. Write the post card correctly.

Dear Kate,

Did you no that I am in south america with Dad? We are exploring the cost. He has shown me many odd sights. What a shok it was to see sno here when it is summer at home!

maria

Basic
1. globe
2. coast
3. goal
4. spoke
5. odd
6. shown
7. gold
8. wrote
9. snow
10. block
11. crow
12. stock
13. chose
14. folk
15. coal
16. host
17. bowl
18. grown
19. shock
20. broke

Review
21. know
22. most
23. smoke
24. drop
25. soap

Challenge
26. continent
27. longitude
28. approach
29. motion
30. accomplish

Write an Essay

Write a paragraph about a place you would like to explore. What makes it special? Why would you go there? What might you expect to see? Try to use five spelling words and at least one proper noun.

Proofreading Tip **Check that the first letter in each word of a proper noun is capitalized.**

WORLD MAP

Proofreading Marks

¶ Indent
∧ Add
⌐ Delete
≡ Capital letter
/ Small letter

Expanding Vocabulary

Thesaurus: Exact Words for *show* The spelling word *shown* is a form of *show*. First, find *show* in your Thesaurus. Then look at the photo below. Why is *demonstrate* a more exact word for *show*?

May I **show** the class how my camera works?

Sure, you can **demonstrate** it now.

Read the sentence in each box. Write the word that best replaces *show*. Use your Thesaurus.

Sentences

Words for *show*

Sentences		Words for *show*
We <u>show</u> our flag on the Fourth of July.	→	1. ?
Ms. Ide will <u>show</u> the hikers through the woods.	→	2. ?
Don't <u>show</u> where the gifts are hidden!	→	3. ?
Will you <u>show</u> the experiment to the class?	→	4. ?

Work Together With a partner write a sentence for each word you wrote.

Real-World Connection

Social Studies: Exploration All the words in the box relate to exploration. Look up these words in your Spelling Dictionary. Then write the words to complete this social studies journal entry.

I would love to __(1)__ a dark cave or __(2)__. I wonder how the early explorers knew which __(3)__ or path to follow. They did not have a written __(4)__ that told which way to go. In Africa how did David Livingstone get through the steamy, overgrown __(5)__ near the __(6)__ ? How did Heinrich Barth cross the hot, dry __(7)__ ? A simple tool called the __(8)__ helped explorers tell direction long ago. We use that same tool today.

Spelling Word Link

globe

explore
cavern
jungle
equator
desert
route
map
compass

Try This CHALLENGE

Write a Message You are stranded in a very strange, faraway place. Write the message you would use to ask for help. Try to use words in the box.

Fact File

In 1513 Juan Ponce de León, a Spanish explorer, searched for a fountain of youth. In his search, he discovered land. He named it Florida, or "full of flowers."

35

Homophones

ring

wring

Basic

READ the sentences. **SAY** each bold word.

1. *steel*	The wall is made of **steel**.
2. *steal*	Did he **steal** a key from me?
3. *lead*	Use this **lead** pencil.
4. *led*	He **led** the cow to the barn.
5. *wait*	Please **wait** for the bus.
6. *weight*	I can lift that **weight**.
7. *wear*	She likes to **wear** a hat.
8. *ware*	We sell heavy cooking **ware**.
9. *creak*	Rusty old doors **creak**.
10. *creek*	Fish swim in the **creek**.
11. *beet*	I ate a **beet** from the garden.
12. *beat*	Jim **beat** me in the race.
13. *meet*	Will I **meet** my new teacher?
14. *meat*	I like fish better than **meat**.
15. *peek*	Did you **peek** in the window?
16. *peak*	The hikers reached the **peak**.
17. *deer*	A **deer** leaped across the road.
18. *dear*	Jill is my very **dear** aunt.
19. *ring*	The **ring** on her finger is gold.
20. *wring*	Please **wring** the wet towels.

Think and Write

Homophones are words that sound alike but have different meanings and spellings.

|stēl| **steel**   a metal made from iron and carbon
|stēl| **steal**   to take without being allowed

• How do the spellings differ in each pair of homophones? What does each word mean?

Now write the Basic Words under the matching sounds.

|ē|	|ĕ|	|ā|	**Rhymes with *sing***	**Vowel Sound + *r***

Review	23. there	**Challenge**	28. vain
21. its	24. their	26. ore	29. vein
22. it's	25. they're	27. oar	30. vane

Independent Practice

Spelling Strategy

Homophones are words that sound alike but have different meanings and spellings. When you write a homophone, be sure to spell the word that has the meaning you want.

Context Sentences Write Basic Words to complete the sentences.

1–2. We climbed to the __(1)__ to __(2)__ at the eagle's nest.

3–4. I can __(3)__ you at the __(4)__ counter in the market.

5–6. Sal was as red as a __(5)__ after he __(6)__ David at tennis.

7–8. Please __(7)__ in line for the nurse to check your __(8)__.

9–10. Niki __(9)__ me to the pencil sharpener so that I could sharpen my __(10)__ pencil.

11–12. I had to __(11)__ out my clothes after I jumped in the pool to find my __(12)__.

Challenge Words Write the Challenge Word that fits each meaning. Use your Spelling Dictionary.

13. a mineral from which a metal, such as gold, can be mined

14. a long, narrow deposit of a mineral in rock

15. having no success

16. used to row a boat

17. a piece of wood or metal that shows wind direction

Spelling-Meaning Connection

Can you see *creak* in these words: *creaky, creaking, creakiness*? **Think of this:** I heard a *creak* in the *creaky* old house.

18–19. Write *creaky*. Then write the Basic Word that is related to *creaky* and means "a squeaking sound."

20. Write the Basic Word that is a homophone for *creak* and means "a small stream."

creak
creaky
creaking
creakiness

Dictionary

Homophones A dictionary entry shows homophones.

> **peak** |pēk| *n., pl.* **peaks** The top of a mountain.
> • *These sound alike* **peak**, **peek**.

Practice Write the answers to these questions.
Use your Spelling Dictionary.

1. Look up *hall*. What word is a homophone
   for *hall*?
2. Which spelling of |hôl| means "a large room"?
3. Which spelling of |hôl| means "to pull or carry"?
4. Which spelling of |hôl| means "a passageway"?

Write the spelling for |hôl| that fits each sentence.

5. Mrs. Wong does not allow us to run down
   the _____.
6. We need to _____ this heavy trash to the dump.
7. Our meeting took place in the _____ on the first floor.
8. It takes two people to _____ our tent to the campgrounds.

Review: Spelling Spree

Homophone Riddles Write a pair of Basic Words to answer each
silly riddle.

Example: What do thieves do when they take a piece of metal?
steal steel

9–10. What do you call a squeaky sound made by a stream?

11–12. What did the parade leader do to a float made of pencils?

13–14. What is a drum noise made by a purplish-red vegetable?

15–16. What do you call clothes for sale?

17–18. What is a circle of people twisting
their clothes dry?

19–20. How did the fork introduce the
peas to the steak?

21–22. What is a quick look at
a mountain from behind a tree?

23–24. What do you call a lovable fawn?

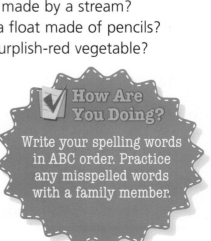

**How Are
You Doing?**

Write your spelling words
in ABC order. Practice
any misspelled words
with a family member.

Proofreading and Writing

Proofread for Spelling Find nine Basic or Review Words that are misused in this script for a factory tour. Write each one correctly.

The Steel Factory   1801 Ore Road, Erie, PA 16510

Hello and welcome to your tour. Before you go in,

you must weight here, but you may steel a peek

through the window.

First, you may wonder why you see workers

wearing masks. We have to heat steal to work

with it. The masks there wearing protect they're faces.

Now look at that huge machine in their. Can you

guess it's wait? Well, its over two thousand pounds.

WELCOME

Basic

1. steel
2. steal
3. lead
4. led
5. wait
6. weight
7. wear
8. ware
9. creak
10. creek
11. beet
12. beat
13. meet
14. meat
15. peek
16. peak
17. deer
18. dear
19. ring
20. wring

Review

21. its
22. it's
23. there
24. their
25. they're

Challenge

26. ore
27. oar
28. vain
29. vein
30. vane

Write Instructions

You have been chosen to lead some visitors on a tour of your town or school. Write instructions to tell them what to wear, where to meet you, and where you will lead them. Try to use five spelling words.

*Monday:
School Tour
at
3:00 p.m.*

Proofreading Tip

If you use a computer to check spelling, it will not tell you if you used the wrong homophone.

Proofreading Marks

¶   Indent
∧   Add
⌐   Delete
≡   Capital letter
/   Small letter

Expanding Vocabulary

Spelling
Word Link

ware

soft
foot
hard
glass
sleep
head
silver
swim

Building Words with Homophones Homophones are sometimes joined with other words to make new words. Then the meaning of the homophone becomes part of the meaning of the new word.

meat flesh of an animal eaten as food
meatball a small ball of ground meat

Draw the web. Use the words in the box to create longer words with *ware* and *wear* in each web. Use your Spelling Dictionary.

1. ?
2. ?
4. ?

ware

3. ?

5. ?
6. ?

wear

8. ?
7. ?

Show You Know! Select two words from each web. Write a sentence of your own for each one.

Real-World Connection

Science: Metals All the words in the box are related to metals. Look up these words in your Spelling Dictionary. Then write the words to complete this science book page.

Spelling Word Link

steel

iron
copper
zinc
mercury
tin
bronze
calcium
aluminum

METALS   **Chapter 11**

Metals have many forms and uses. The liquid in a thermometer is the metal __(1)__. Your teeth and bones are made of __(2)__. A reddish-brown metal that conducts heat is __(3)__. A blue-white metal used in batteries is __(4)__. Steel is made from a mixture of __(5)__ and carbon. Another combination, copper and tin, creates the metal — and color — __(6)__. Pots and pans are often made of __(7)__, while cans made of __(8)__ won't rust.

Try This CHALLENGE

Write a Product Chart Create a product chart on metals. Choose some metals. Include on your chart the name of each metal, a product made from that metal, a picture of the product, and a sentence to tell how each metal is used. Use your Spelling Dictionary.

METALS
Zinc
electric battery
We use zinc to make electric batteries and as a coating for iron.

★★ **Fact File**

When two or more metals are melted and mixed together, they form a stronger metal called an alloy. Bronze is an alloy made by mixing together copper and tin.

6 Review: Units 1–5

|ă|
plant

|ā|
skate

Unit 1 Spelling |ă| and |ā| pages 12–17

skate	aid	gray	past	break
pain	hang	shape	pray	steak

Spelling Strategy Remember that the |ă| sound is usually spelled **a** followed by a consonant sound. When you hear the |ā| sound, think of the patterns **a-consonant-e**, **ai**, and **ay**.

Write the word that fits each clue.

1. help
2. rhymes with *rain*
3. something to eat
4. a time before the present

Write six words by adding the missing letters. Circle the word with the |ă| sound.

5. br __ __ k
6. pr __ __
7. gr __ __
8. sk __ __ __
9. h __ __ __
10. sh __ __ __

|ĕ| |ē|
fresh   **peach**

Unit 2 Spelling |ĕ| and |ē| pages 18–23

kept	reach	spent	sweet	field
least	cheap	greed	west	chief

Spelling Strategy Remember that the |ĕ| sound is usually spelled **e** followed by a consonant sound. When you hear the |ē| sound, think of the patterns **ea** and **ee**.

Write the word that rhymes with each word below.

11. speed
12. teach
13. yield
14. leap

Write the word that means the opposite of each word or phrase below. Circle the words with the |ē| sound.

15. east
16. most
17. saved
18. sour
19. given away
20. lowest in rank

Unit 3	Spelling |ĭ| and |ī|	pages 24–29

live	grind	flight	still	build
hint	fright	shine	blind	built

|ĭ| |ī|
brick   shine

Spelling Strategy
Remember that the |ĭ| sound is often spelled **i** followed by a consonant sound. When you hear the |ī| sound, think of the patterns **i**-consonant-**e**, **igh**, and **i**.

Write the word that fits each meaning.

21. not able to see
22. to give off light
23. a useful clue
24. calm

25. to crush or pound
26. act of flying
27. to be alive
28. strong fear

Write an Elephant Word to complete each sentence.

29. Did you _____ the new clubhouse?
30. Was the clubhouse _____ quickly?

Unit 4	Spelling |ŏ| and |ō|	pages 30–35

block	shown	wrote	coast	gold
grown	stock	crow	broke	coal

|ŏ| |ō|
block   gold

Spelling Strategy
Remember that the |ŏ| sound is usually spelled **o** followed by a consonant sound. When you hear the |ō| sound, think of the patterns **o**-consonant-**e**, **oa**, **ow**, and **o**.

**Change a vowel in each word below to write a spelling word.
Circle the words with the |ō| sound.**

31. gild
32. cool

33. crew
34. stick

35. black
36. write

Write the word that fits each clue.

37. shattered into pieces
38. not hidden

39. a form of *grow*
40. near the sea

ring

wring

wait	wear	steel	meet	ring
weight	ware	steal	meat	wring

Spelling Strategy   **Homophones** are words that sound alike but have different meanings and spellings. When you write a homophone, be sure to spell the word that has the meaning you want.

Write the word that completes each analogy.

41. *Drink* is to *water* as *chew* is to _____.

42. *Good-bye* is to *leave* as *hello* is to _____.

43. *House* is to *wood* as *bridge* is to _____.

44. *Give* is to *provide* as *rob* is to _____.

Write the word that fits each clue.

45. to put on   **48.** heaviness

46. goods for sale   **49.** a bell's sound

47. stop for a time   **50.** to twist

Challenge Words   Units 1–5   pages 12–41

knead	ore	continent	polish	approach
chef	oar	graceful	inspect	athletic

Write the word that completes each analogy.

51. *Artist* is to *artistic* as *athlete* is to _____.

52. *Wood* is to *carpenter* as *food* is to _____.

53. *Soup* is to *stir* as *dough* is to _____.

54. *Boring* is to *interesting* as *clumsy* is to _____.

55. *Car* is to *wax* as *shoe* is to _____.

56. *Water* is to *ocean* as *land* is to _____.

Write the word that fits each clue.

57. to come toward   **59.** a paddle

58. to examine   **60.** a mineral containing metal

Spelling-Meaning Strategy

Vowel Changes: Long to Short Vowel Sound

You know that words, like people, can be related to each other. Look at the related words *steal* and *stealth*.

If you leave money lying around, someone might **steal** it. A thief can move with such **stealth** that your money will be gone without your knowing it.

steal
stealth

Think

- How are *steal* and *stealth* related in meaning?
- What vowel sound do you hear in each word? How is each vowel sound spelled?

Here are more related words with the *ea* spelling pattern and the same change from the |ē| sound to the |ĕ| sound.

h**ea**l	pl**ea**se	br**ea**the
h**ea**lth	pl**ea**sant	br**ea**th

Apply and Extend

Complete these activities on a separate sheet of paper.

1. Use your Spelling Dictionary to look up the words in the box above. Write their meanings. Then write a short paragraph, using one pair of words.

2. With a partner, list as many words as you can that are related to *steal*, *heal*, *please*, and *breathe*. Then look at the section "Vowel Changes: Long to Short Vowel Sound" beginning on page 273 of your Spelling-Meaning Index. Add to your list any other words that you find in these families.

Summing Up

Words that are related in meaning are often related in spelling, even though one word has a long vowel sound and the other word has a short vowel sound.

Personal Narrative

from

Hurdles

by Mary Blocksma with Esther Romero

Who is telling this story about a class race?

The whistle shrieked and I lunged forward. I made those little wheels whine so fast my ears hurt. I glanced back and saw with joy that I was ahead of everyone, even Ramos! I could hear the roar of the roller skates behind me, thundering toward the turn at the path—

The sharp turn! I had misjudged the sharp turn! I came up on it too fast to slow down. I tried crossing my right foot over my left foot for one of those smooth turns, but my legs twisted like pretzels. Still in full view of the crowd, I bounced off a tree and into the bushes.

I heard the skates spin by me, but I couldn't move. I couldn't face it. I was going to stay there forever when I felt a tug on my skates. "Come on, Vicente!"

It was Ramos. Painfully I got up.

"Move!" shouted Ramos.

"I'll be last!" I could barely whisper.

"Try!" begged Ramos. "Please!" Then he was gone.

Trying to feel grateful, I wobbled off behind him.

Think and Discuss

1 Through whose eyes, or **point of view**, is this story told?

2 How do you know who is telling the story?

3 What **details** let you see and hear the race?

The Writing Process
Personal Narrative

What interesting times have you had? Write a story about one of them. Follow the guidelines, and use the Writing Process.

1 Prewriting
- Find a partner. Interview each other about your topics. Ask for details.

2 Draft
- Write two or three beginnings. Which one is most interesting?

3 Revise
- Add details and dialogue.
- Use your Thesaurus to find exact words.
- Have a writing conference.

4 Proofread
- Did you spell each word correctly?
- Did you use correct end marks?
- Did you capitalize proper nouns?

5 Publish
- Make a neat final copy, and add a good title.
- Read your story aloud to a friend.

Guidelines for Writing a Personal Narrative

✓ Tell the story from your point of view. Use the pronoun *I*.

✓ The story should have a beginning, a middle, and an end.

✓ Write an interesting beginning.

✓ Use details and dialogue to bring the story to life.

Composition Words

skate
tease
spent
dream
hint
sigh
peek
goal

How We Won the Championship

Spelling |ŭ|, |yōō|, and |ōō|

Read and Say

|ōō| |ŭ|
tube **brush**

Basic

READ the sentences. **SAY** each bold word.

1.	brush	Fix your hair with a **brush**.
2.	juice	I drink apple **juice**.
3.	fruit	Grapes are another **fruit**.
4.	tube	Is paint sold in a **tube**?
5.	lunch	Let's eat **lunch** at noon.
6.	crumb	The birds ate every **crumb** of bread.
7.	few	My coin jar has a **few** dimes in it.
8.	true	The newspaper gave a **true** report.
9.	truth	Tell the **truth** and do not lie.
10.	done	I have **done** all my work.
11.	suit	I wore a **suit** to the meeting.
12.	pump	Use a **pump** to fill the tire.
13.	due	The money is **due** today.
14.	dull	The story was **dull** and long.
15.	tune	I played a **tune** on my flute.
16.	blew	The wind **blew** a chair over.
17.	trunk	Pack my bag in the car **trunk**.
18.	sum	What is the **sum** of ten and ten?
19.	glue	I can **glue** the broken vase.
20.	threw	She **threw** the ball too hard.

Think and Write

The |ŭ| sound is usually spelled *u* followed by a consonant sound. The |yōō| and the |ōō| sounds can be spelled *u-consonant-e* or with two letters. The pattern *ui* is usually followed by a consonant sound.

|ŭ| br**u**sh |yōō| and |ōō| t**u**be, f**ew**, tr**ue**, j**ui**ce

- What is one spelling pattern for the |ŭ| sound? What are four spelling patterns for |yōō| and |ōō|? How are the Elephant Words different?

Now write each Basic Word under its vowel sound.

|ŭ| Sound	|yōō| or |ōō| Sound

Review   23. rub
21. chew   24. shut
22. blue   25. June

Challenge   28. tissue
26. newscast   29. attitude
27. commute   30. slumber

Independent Practice

Spelling Strategy

Remember that the |ŭ| sound is usually spelled *u* followed by a consonant sound. When you hear the |yōō| or the |ōō| sound, think of the patterns *u*-consonant-*e*, *ew*, *ue*, and *ui*.

Word Analysis/Phonics Complete the exercises with Basic Words.

1. Write the word that has the |s| sound spelled *ce*.
2–3. Write *tune*. Then change one letter and write another word.
4–5. Write the two words that are homophones for these words.
    4. dew   5. through

Vocabulary: Word Clues Write the Basic Word that fits each clue.

6. opposite of *false*
7. the whole amount
8. not a lie
9. form of *do*
10. means the same as *boring*
11. opposite of *many*
12. form of *blow*
13. a set of clothes

Challenge Words Write the Challenge Word that fits each meaning. Use your Spelling Dictionary.

14. sleep
15. state of mind
16. to travel to work
17. soft paper
18. a broadcast of information about recent events

Spelling-Meaning Connection

How can you remember that *crumb* ends with a *b*? Think of the related word *crumble*, in which the *b* is pronounced.

19–20. Write *crumb* and *crumble*. Underline the letter that is silent in one word and pronounced in the other.

Dictionary

Spelling Table How can you look up *juice* in a dictionary if you do not know how to spell the |s| sound? Turn to page 277 to find the **Spelling Table**, which lists the different ways a sound can be spelled. Begin with the first spelling for the |s| sound, and look up *juic*. Check each spelling until you find *juice*.

SOUND	SPELLINGS	SAMPLE WORDS
|s|	**c, ce, ps, s, sc, ss**	**c**ity, fen**ce**, **ps**ychology, **s**ame, **sc**ent, le**ss**on

Practice Write the correct spelling for each of these words with the |ē| sound. Use the Spelling Table and your Spelling Dictionary.

1. |fēld| **2.** |rēf| **3.** |skē| **4.** |spēk| **5.** |ēl| **6.** |yēst|

Review: Spelling Spree

Hink Pinks Write a Basic or Review Word that answers the question and rhymes with the given word.

Example: What makes the best fires? good _____ *wood*

  7. What is a boring sea bird called? _____ gull
  8. What do you call a nice set of clothes? cute _____
  9. What is a sad math problem called? glum _____
 10. What is a true statement for a child? youth _____
 11. What is a stupid piece of bread called? dumb _____
 12. What is a container for a square object? cube _____
 13. What is a group that eats at noon? _____ bunch
 14. What do you call a fresh bite? new _____
 15. What do you call a round water faucet? plump _____
 16. What is a song that is sung at lunchtime? noon _____
 17. What do you call a shriveled tree part? shrunk _____
 18. What did the wind do to the window? _____ through
 19. What is cutting bushes in late spring called? _____ prune
 20. What is a hint about something sticky called? _____ clue

How Are You Doing?

List the spelling words that are hard for you. Practice them with a family member.

Proofreading and Writing

Proofread for Spelling Find eleven misspelled Basic or Review Words in this story. Write each one correctly.

Alex shot his eyes and gave them a rob. Was it really troo? His report was dew today on June 1! Alex through on his blew gym suit and ran to bruch his teeth. He took a fue gulps of frute juise and ran to the library. How would he get the report dun on time?

NEW!
Lou's Morning Dew
Toothpaste

Basic

1. brush
2. juice
3. fruit
4. tube
5. lunch
6. crumb
7. few
8. true
9. truth
10. done
11. suit
12. pump
13. due
14. dull
15. tune
16. blew
17. trunk
18. sum
19. glue
20. threw

Review

21. chew
22. blue
23. rub
24. shut
25. June

Challenge

26. newscast
27. commute
28. tissue
29. attitude
30. slumber

Write a Personal Story

Have you had a morning when things went wrong? Write a paragraph about it. Try to use five spelling words.

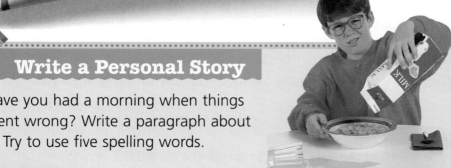

Proofreading Tip

Put a check mark on each word to show that you looked at it.

Proofreading Marks

¶ Indent
∧ Add
✐ Delete
≡ Capital letter
/ Small letter

Vocabulary Enrichment

Expanding Vocabulary

Thesaurus: Exact Words for *throw* Which sentence better describes how a basketball player throws the ball through a hoop?

Willy **throws** the basketball.   Willy **shoots** the basketball.

Shoots describes a throwing action aimed at a target. It is more exact than *throws.*

Find *throw* in your Thesaurus. Write a subentry to match each meaning in the web.

1. to **throw** a baseball or horseshoe
?

5. to **throw** with great force
?

throw

2. to **throw** quickly and easily
?

4. to hand or **throw** to someone
?

3. to **throw** or fling
?

Work Together With a partner write a more exact word to replace *throw* in this paragraph. Write the paragraph.

Our field day was so much fun! Joe was able to <u>throw</u> strikes to six batters. We saw Rosa <u>throw</u> the football gracefully to her halfback. To break a tie, Sue had to <u>throw</u> the basketball into the hoop. We all tried to <u>throw</u> ourselves over the high jump! Afterward our Clean Team worked to <u>throw</u> all the trash into the recycle bin.

Vocabulary Enrichment

Real-World Connection

Health: Morning Activities All the words in the box relate to morning activities. Look up these words in your Spelling Dictionary. Then write the words to complete this schedule.

Spelling Word Link

brush

radio
awake
mirror
cereal
muffin
cupboard
routine
comb

To get ready for school, follow this morning __(1)__.

6:20	Wake up to music on the __(2)__. Listen for thirty minutes.
6:50	Now you must be really __(3)__! Get out of bed.
7:05	Stand in front of the __(4)__ and __(5)__ your hair.
7:10	In the kitchen, open the food __(6)__ and take out your usual box of __(7)__.
7:20	Eat a corn __(8)__. Drink some juice.
7:30	Walk out the door!

Try This CHALLENGE

Write a Cereal Ad Write an ad for a new breakfast cereal. Why is it good? Why should people buy it? End your ad with a clever slogan to help people remember the cereal. Try to use words in the box.

Fact File

Do you know why we say a grouchy person "got up on the wrong side of the bed"? Long ago people thought that the left side brought bad luck. They always tried to get up on the right side.

Spelling |ōō| and |ŏŏ|

Read and Say

|ŏŏ| |ōō|
wood stool

Basic

READ the sentences. **SAY** each bold word.

1.	wood	Jan cut the **wood** with a saw.
2.	brook	We swam in the cool **brook**.
3.	tool	A hammer is a simple **tool**.
4.	put	Did you **put** the key down?
5.	wool	She bought a warm **wool** coat.
6.	push	Help me **push** my bike up the hill.
7.	full	The room is **full** of people.
8.	roof	We put a new **roof** on our house.
9.	group	The **group** became a team.
10.	prove	I will **prove** that I am right.
11.	stood	The girl **stood** on the hill.
12.	stool	A **stool** is a seat with no arms.
13.	hook	Hang your coat on the **hook**.
14.	smooth	The skin of a baby is **smooth**.
15.	shoot	Can I **shoot** the ball in the hoop?
16.	bush	He will hide behind the **bush**.
17.	fool	Only a **fool** would take that risk.
18.	pull	Try to **pull** the kite from the tree.
19.	soup	This **soup** tastes good on a cold day.
20.	move	Please **move** your car to the lot.

Think and Write

The |ōō| sound is often spelled *oo*. The |ŏŏ| sound is often spelled *oo* or *u* followed by a consonant sound.

|ōō| t**oo**l |ŏŏ| w**oo**d, p**u**t

• What is one spelling pattern for |ōō|? How is |ōō| spelled in the Elephant Words? What are two spelling patterns for |ŏŏ|?

Now write each Basic Word under its vowel sound. Include *roof* with the |ōō| sound.

|ōō| Sound	|ŏŏ| Sound

Review	23. shook
21. cook	**24.** school
22. spoon	**25.** tooth

Challenge	28. bulletin
26. soot	**29.** cocoon
27. marooned	**30.** superb

Independent Practice

 Spelling Strategy When you hear the |ōō| sound, think of the pattern *oo*. Remember that the |ŏŏ| sound is often spelled *oo* or *u* followed by a consonant or a cluster.

Word Analysis/Phonics Complete the exercises with Basic Words.

1–2. Write *full*. Change one letter, and write another word.

3–5. Write three words by adding the missing letters.

    3. pr _ _ _   **5.** gr _ _ p

    4. m _ _ _

6–8. Write the three words that begin or end with *sh*.

Vocabulary: Making Inferences Write a Basic Word to fit each clue.

  9. It often flows in the woods.

10. It is often found on the end of a fishing pole.

11. It is often found in a pot, and it is good to eat.

12. It is often found in a fireplace.

13. It is often used as a chair or a footrest.

Challenge Words Write the Challenge Word that fits each meaning. Use your Spelling Dictionary.

14. short announcement

15. excellent

16. caterpillar's covering

17. abandoned on an island

18. fine, black powder produced by burning wood or coal

Spelling-Meaning Connection

Can you see *wool* in *woolly* and *woolen*? These words are all related in spelling and meaning. **Think of this:** My *woolen* jacket is made of lamb's *wool*.

19–20. Write *woolen* and the Basic Word that you see in *woolen*.

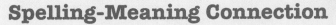

Review: Spelling Spree

Phrases Write Basic or Review Words to finish the phrases.

1. lamb's _____
2. _____ and pull
3. fork and _____
4. a loose front _____
5. a yellow _____ bus
6. chicken noodle _____

7. a _____ of people
8. to sit on a three-legged _____
9. trembled and _____ like a leaf
10. to _____ a hot meal
11. carved out of _____
12. the _____ of a house

Word Search Write the Basic Word that is hidden in each sentence.

Example: The kanga<u>roo</u> followed us home.   *roof*

13. The bus had a flat tire.
14. The farmer tried to shoo the cows out of the corn.
15. Did you hear the cows moo this morning?
16. This shirt is too dirty to wear.
17. The puppies were too little to be taken from their mother.
18. Amy is putting another log on the fire.
19. We saw some brookweed on our walk.
20. The worker used a rope and pulley to raise the box.
21. Don't be foolish. Study for the test.
22. I am overjoyed at the news.
23. Timmy tied the fishhook onto the fishing line.
24. The helpful lady gave us directions.
25. The teacher approved the students' plans.

How Are You Doing?

Write your spelling words in ABC order. Practice any misspelled words with a family member.

Proofreading and Writing

Basic

1. wood
2. brook
3. tool
4. put
5. wool
6. push
7. full
8. roof
9. group
10. prove
11. stood
12. stool
13. hook
14. smooth
15. shoot
16. bush
17. fool
18. pull
19. soup
20. move

Review

21. cook
22. spoon
23. shook
24. school
25. tooth

Challenge

26. soot
27. marooned
28. bulletin
29. cocoon
30. superb

Proofread: Spelling and Singular Possessives To make a singular noun show ownership, add an apostrophe and *s ('s)*.

the teacher**'s** note   Gus**'s** lunch

Find four misspelled Basic or Review Words and two incorrect possessive nouns in this teacher's note. Write the note correctly.

Dear Parents,

On the last day of scool, our

class will go to Pride Park in the

principals van. Marys father will kook

lunch for the groupe over a wod fire.

The day should be full of fun!

Sincerely,

A. Tilden

Mr. Tilden

Write a Letter

Write a letter to someone you know well, telling him or her about a field trip you have taken or would like to take. Try to use five spelling words and at least one singular possessive noun.

Proofreading Tip

Check that you used apostrophes correctly with singular possessive nouns.

Jamie Flynn
10 White Street
Durham, NH 03824

Sarah Varela
544 Hill Road
Woburn, MA 01890

Proofreading Marks

¶ Indent
∧ Add
⌐ Delete
≡ Capital letter
/ Small letter

Expanding Vocabulary

Building Words with -y A **suffix** is a word part added to the end of a base word. A suffix can add meaning to the word. The suffix -*y* can mean "like a" or "full of." Notice that words ending with *e* drop the *e* when -*y* is added.

MEANING	BASE WORD	SUFFIX	NEW WORD
like wood	wood	+ **y**	= wood**y**
full of bones	bone	+ **y**	= bon**y**

Nick Negative hates camp and always complains. Read each caption. Then, with a partner, replace the words in dark print with a word that ends with the suffix -*y*. Write the words. Use your Spelling Dictionary.

Example: My bunk bed is **full of squeaks**. *squeaky*

1–2. How can I use a pillow this **full of lumps**? That other pillow feels **like a sponge** to me.

3–4. This path is too **full of stones**. It will hurt my feet. The other is **full of bushes**.

5–6. Our campfire is so **full of smoke** that I cannot breathe, and all my clothes are **full of the smell**.

7–8. This soup is too **full of salt**, and I hate how that one is so **full of spice**.

Work Together Write a sentence for each word you wrote.

Real-World Connection

Recreation: Camping All the words in the box relate to camping. Look up these words in your Spelling Dictionary. Write the words to complete this part of a post card.

Hi, Grandma,

I'll never forget this camping trip! After we hiked to our __(1)__ and I took off my heavy __(2)__ that held my gear, it began to rain. My father and I lit a __(3)__ and went off to search for __(4)__ for a fire and for water to fill our __(5)__. We came back to pitch the __(6)__ and discovered we had forgotten it! Dad took off his long __(7)__ and tied it to some branches to make a shelter. Because it was __(8)__, we stayed dry all night.

Love,
Ivette

Spelling Word Link

brook

lantern
kindling
canteen
backpack
tent
campsite
waterproof
poncho

Try This CHALLENGE

Questions and Answers Write the word in the box that answers each question.

9. Which is used to carry food: a canteen or a backpack?
10. Which keeps you drier: a backpack or a poncho?
11. Which helps you see: a canteen or a lantern?
12. Which needs a match: a campsite or kindling?

Fact File

The Great Smoky Mountains National Park was once wilderness that was settled by Cherokee Indians and pioneers. It lies on the border of North Carolina and Tennessee.

Spelling |ou| and |ô|

Read and Say

|ou|
pound
howl

Basic

READ the sentences. **SAY** each bold word.

1. pound	My dog came from the **pound**.
2. howl	The dogs **howl** all night.
3. jaw	The shark opened its **jaw** wide.
4. bounce	How high will the ball **bounce**?
5. cause	A deep cut can **cause** pain.
6. always	I **always** brush my teeth.
7. shout	Children **shout** when they play.
8. aloud	She read a letter **aloud** in class.
9. south	Do birds fly **south** for the winter?
10. couple	I can carry only a **couple** of logs.
11. drawn	He has **drawn** an outline of a dog.
12. scout	I can **scout** for details in this book.
13. false	A true story cannot be **false**.
14. proud	Dad feels **proud** of my good work.
15. frown	The sad boy has a **frown** on his face.
16. sauce	She put **sauce** on the fish dinner.
17. gown	The bride wore a white **gown**.
18. couch	He likes to sleep on the **couch**.
19. dawn	My cat wakes me up at **dawn**.
20. mount	The campers **mount** the steep hill.

Think and Write

The |ou| and the |ô| sounds are usually spelled with two letters. The patterns *ou* and *au* are usually followed by a consonant sound.

|ou| h**ow**l, p**ou**nd |ô| j**aw**, c**au**se, **a**lways

• What are two spelling patterns for |ou|? What are three patterns for |ô|? What consonant follows *a* when it spells |ô|? How is the Elephant Word different?

Now write each Basic Word under its vowel sound.

|ou|	|ô|	Another Vowel Sound

Review	23. loud	**Challenge**	28. pounce
21. walk	**24.** sound	**26.** gnaw	**29.** doubt
22. lawn	**25.** clown	**27.** prowl	**30.** scrawny

Independent Practice

Spelling Strategy

When you hear the |ou| or the |ô| sound, think of these patterns:

|ou| *ou* or *ow* |ô| *aw, au,* or *a* before *l*

Remember that a consonant sound usually follows the *ou* or the *au* pattern.

Word Analysis/Phonics Complete the exercises with Basic Words.

1–2. Write the two words that have the |s| sound spelled *ce*.

3–4. Write the two words that have the |z| sound.

5. Write the word that rhymes with *paw*.

Vocabulary: Word Clues Write the Basic Word that fits each clue.

6. means the same as *sunrise*

7. often found in a living room

8. a good place to find a dog

9. two people

10. worn at a ball or a party

11. sound made by a wolf

12. an unhappy look

13. a loud cry

Challenge Words Write the Challenge Words to complete the paragraph. Use your Spelling Dictionary.

Stray dogs and cats __(14)__ through streets at night. Cats __(15)__ on mice and catch them. Today a hungry, __(16)__ dog followed me home from school. I gave him a bone to __(17)__ on. I want to keep him, but I __(18)__ that my parents will let me.

Spelling-Meaning Connection

Can you see *south* in the word *southern*? These words are related in spelling and meaning, even though they have different vowel sounds.

19–20. Write *south* and *southern*. Then, in each word, underline the two letters that spell different vowel sounds.

Dictionary

Entry Words and Their Meanings A dictionary may list several meanings for an entry word. A **sample sentence** or **phrase** may be given to help make a meaning clear.

sample phrase

false |fôls| *adj.* **falser, falsest** **1.** Not true, real, honest, or correct: *a false statement.* **2.** Lacking loyalty: *They turned out to be false friends.*

sample sentence

Practice Look up *always* in your Spelling Dictionary. Write the sample sentence given for each meaning below.

1. at all times

2. for as long as one can imagine

Review: Spelling Spree

Code Breaker Some Basic and Review Words have been written in the code below. Use the code to figure out each word. Write the words correctly.

CODE:	z	y	x	w	v	u	t	s	q	o	n	m	l	k	i	h	g	f	d	b
LETTER:	a	b	c	d	e	f	g	h	j	l	m	n	o	p	r	s	t	u	w	y

Example: hlfgs *south*

3. xoldm	**7.** zolfw	**11.** nlfmg	**15.** wizdm	**19.** klfmw
4. uzohv	**8.** hlfmw	**12.** qzd	**16.** xlfkov	**20.** ylfmxv
5. xlfxs	**9.** hzfxv	**13.** wzdm	**17.** sldo	
6. uildm	**10.** hxlfg	**14.** tldm	**18.** xzfhv	

How Are You Doing?
Write each spelling word in a sentence. Practice any misspelled spelling words with a partner.

Proofreading and Writing

Proofread for Spelling Find ten misspelled Basic or Review Words in this story summary. Write each one correctly.

Alex had allways wanted to enter his dog Rags in the Dog Show. Every day he and Rags were up at dawn to practice. Now the prowd moment had come. Alex and Rags began to wok past the judges. Then Rags let out a lowd howl. With one big bonce, Rags jumped over the judges' table and raced across the soth lown. People began to showt. A tiny chipmunk weighing little more than a pond was the couse of poor Rags's downfall.

Basic

Basic
1. pound
2. howl
3. jaw
4. bounce
5. cause
6. always
7. shout
8. aloud
9. south
10. couple
11. drawn
12. scout
13. false
14. proud
15. frown
16. sauce
17. gown
18. couch
19. dawn
20. mount

Review
21. walk
22. lawn
23. loud
24. sound
25. clown

Challenge
26. gnaw
27. prowl
28. pounce
29. doubt
30. scrawny

Write Funny Dog Rules

Write a list of rules that dogs should follow if they could read. Make your rules funny. Try to use five spelling words. You may also want to share your list. **Example:** To scare a cat, make no **sound** at all. Then bark your head off!

Proofreading Tip **Read your paper from right to left so that you focus on each word by itself.**

Proofreading Marks

¶ Indent
∧ Add
⤷ Delete
≡ Capital letter
/ Small letter

Expanding Vocabulary

Spelling Word Link

howl
shout

bellow
cheer
scream
yell

Thesaurus: Exact Words for *shout* *Howl* and *shout* both describe loud cries, but *howl* is more exact. It often means "a long wail."

> Marcy let out a **shout** when I stepped on her foot.
> Marcy let out a **howl** when I stepped on her foot.

Find *shout* in your Thesaurus. Read the meaning for each subentry. Then write the best word from the box to replace *shout* in each sentence.

1. The children on the roller coaster <u>shout</u> with fright.
2. The coaches <u>shout</u> instructions in deep voices.
3. The fans <u>shout</u> each time their team scores.
4. Never <u>shout</u> "fire" unless there really is a fire.

Show You Know! Write a caption for each picture. Use a different word for *shout* in each one.

5.

6.

Real-World Connection

Science: Dogs All the words in the box relate to dogs. Look up these words in your Spelling Dictionary. Then write the words to complete this field guide to dogs.

Spelling Word Link

pound

spaniel
collie
greyhound
Saint Bernard
terrier
husky
poodle
basset hound

All About Dogs

There are many kinds of dogs. The long-haired __(1)__ is often used to herd sheep. In the far north, a __(2)__ pulls sleds. In Switzerland the __(3)__ was used to rescue people in the mountains. Two hunting dogs are the small, short-haired __(4)__ and the __(5)__, which has a long body, short legs, and long, drooping ears. Two show dogs are the curly-haired __(6)__ and the __(7)__, which has long ears and a silky coat. The __(8)__ is a fast runner.

Try This CHALLENGE

Right or Wrong? Write *T* if the sentence is true. Write *F* if it is false.

9. The collie has a curly coat.
10. The greyhound has short legs.
11. The Saint Bernard is bigger than the terrier.
12. The basset hound is shorter than the greyhound.

★★ Fact File

The saying "His bark is worse than his bite" comes from a thirteenth-century proverb. It describes a person who may frighten you with loud talk but never really hurt you.

Spelling |îr|, |är|, and |âr|

Read and Say

|îr|	|âr|
gear	**stare**

Basic

READ the sentences. **SAY** each bold word.

1.	gear	Shift the car into **gear**.
2.	spear	Each hunter carried a **spear**.
3.	sharp	The tip of the pencil is **sharp**.
4.	stare	Can he **stare** without blinking?
5.	alarm	Set the **alarm** on the clock.
6.	cheer	The fans gave a loud **cheer**.
7.	square	A **square** has four sides.
8.	hairy	Cats are **hairy** animals.
9.	heart	My **heart** is beating fast.
10.	weird	Our bird makes **weird** noises.
11.	starve	Plants **starve** without water.
12.	charm	Flowers add **charm** to a room.
13.	beard	A **beard** covered his small face.
14.	scarf	Tie a **scarf** around your neck.
15.	spare	Inside the trunk is a **spare** tire.
16.	stairs	Walk slowly up the **stairs**.
17.	year	Our baby is one **year** old.
18.	charge	Is this gift free of **charge**?
19.	dairy	We buy milk at a **dairy**.
20.	scarce	Water is **scarce** in the summer.

Think and Write

Each word has a vowel sound + *r*. The |îr| sounds are close to the |ē| sound. The |är| sounds are close to |ă|. The |âr| sounds are close to |ā|.

|îr| g**ear**, ch**eer** |är| sh**ar**p |âr| st**are**, h**air**y

• What are two patterns for |îr|? What is one pattern for |är|? What are two patterns for |âr|? How are the Elephant Words different?

Now write each Basic Word under its vowel + |r| sounds.

|îr| Sounds	|är| Sounds	|âr| Sounds

Review			**Challenge**	
21. air	23. large		26. barnacle	28. startle
22. near	24. scare		27. awareness	29. marvel
	25. chair			30. weary

Independent Practice

Spelling Strategy

When you hear the |îr|, |är|, or |âr| sounds, think of these patterns:

|îr| *ear, eer* |är| *ar* |âr| *are, air*

Word Analysis/Phonics Complete the exercises with Basic Words.

1–3. Write the three words that have the consonant cluster *st*.

4–5. Write the two words that end with the |ē| sound.

6–7. Write two words by adding the missing letters.

  6. w __ __ __ d   **7.** sc __ __ ce

Vocabulary: Classifying Write the Basic Word that fits with each group of words.

  8. brain, lung, _____   **11.** week, month, _____

  9. hat, mittens, _____   **12.** arrow, harpoon, _____

  10. siren, bell, _____   **13.** circle, triangle, _____

Challenge Words Write the Challenge Word that completes each sentence. Use your Spelling Dictionary.

14. Scuba diving can give you a new _____ of sea life.

15. You should rest for a while if you become _____.

16. The fish often dart away when you _____ them.

17. Have you ever seen a _____ attached to a rock?

18. Most people _____ at the beauty of the underwater world.

Spelling-Meaning Connection

Can you see *cheer* in these words: *cheerful, cheerless, cheery*? **Think of this:** A *cheerful* smile makes you feel *cheery*.

19–20. Write *cheerful*. Then write the Basic Word that is related to *cheerful* in spelling and meaning.

cheer
cheerful
cheerless
cheery

Review: Spelling Spree

Word Addition Write a Basic or Review Word by adding the beginning of the first word to the end of the second word.

Example: chill + start   *chart*

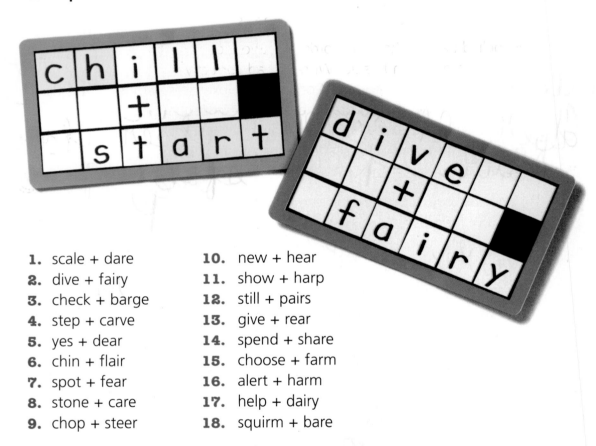

1. scale + dare
2. dive + fairy
3. check + barge
4. step + carve
5. yes + dear
6. chin + flair
7. spot + fear
8. stone + care
9. chop + steer
10. new + hear
11. show + harp
12. still + pairs
13. give + rear
14. spend + share
15. choose + farm
16. alert + harm
17. help + dairy
18. squirm + bare

Questions   Write a Basic or Review Word to answer each question.

19. What keeps your neck warm in winter?
20. What can we breathe but not see?
21. If an ant is small, what is an elephant?
22. What is a valentine often shaped like?
23. What might grow on a man's face?
24. If you saw something strange, what would you call it?
25. What adjective describes water in the desert?

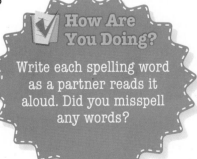

How Are You Doing?

Write each spelling word as a partner reads it aloud. Did you misspell any words?

Proofreading and Writing

Basic

Proofread: Spelling and Plural Possessives To form the possessive of a plural noun that ends with *s*, add an apostrophe. If the word does not end with *s*, add an apostrophe and *s*.

spears' points   men**'s** classes

Find four misspelled Basic or Review Words and two incorrect plural possessive nouns in this ad. Write the ad correctly.

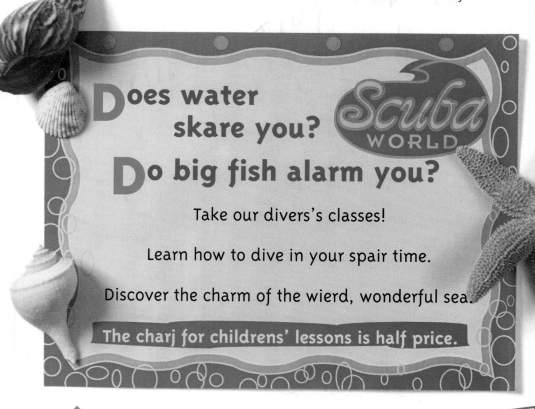

Does water
skare you?

Do big fish alarm you?

Scuba WORLD

Take our divers's classes!

Learn how to dive in your spair time.

Discover the charm of the wierd, wonderful sea.

The charj for childrens' lessons is half price.

Basic

1. gear
2. spear
3. sharp
4. stare
5. alarm
6. cheer
7. square
8. hairy
9. heart
10. weird
11. starve
12. charm
13. beard
14. scarf
15. spare
16. stairs
17. year
18. charge
19. dairy
20. scarce

Review

21. air
22. near
23. large
24. scare
25. chair

Challenge

26. barnacle
27. awareness
28. startle
29. marvel
30. weary

Write a Paragraph

The Octoplant

Describe an imaginary underwater creature that is half plant and half animal. What does it eat? Can it move? Try to use five spelling words and at least one plural possessive noun. You may want to draw a picture of your creature.

Proofreading Tip   **Check that you used apostrophes correctly with plural possessive nouns.**

Proofreading Marks

¶ Indent
∧ Add
⌒ Delete
≡ Capital letter
/ Small letter

Expanding Vocabulary

Idioms Look at the picture, and read the caption.

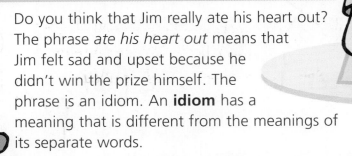

Jim ate his heart out as Kate collected her prize.

Do you think that Jim really ate his heart out? The phrase *ate his heart out* means that Jim felt sad and upset because he didn't win the prize himself. The phrase is an idiom. An **idiom** has a meaning that is different from the meanings of its separate words.

Write the meaning of each underlined idiom.

1. Todd cares so much for Jill that he <u>wears his heart on his sleeve</u>.
2. Mom and I had a <u>heart-to-heart</u> talk about the problem.
3. They must <u>have hearts of stone</u> to say no to the kitten's cries.
4. When you try and fail, it is easy <u>to lose heart</u>.
5. Good actors know their lines <u>by heart</u>.

Work Together With a partner rewrite the five sentences from this page without using idioms.

Meanings
- to be cruel, unfeeling
- to display one's feelings for all to see
- from memory
- to feel a lack of hope
- honest, personal, and deep

★★ **Fact File**

Every language has idioms. In Spanish *no tener pelos en la lengua* means "to express oneself clearly." However, if you read each word separately, it says "not to have hair on one's tongue."

Real-World Connection

Recreation: Scuba Diving All the words in the box relate to scuba diving. Look up these words in your Spelling Dictionary. Then write the words to complete this story beginning.

Spelling
Word Link

gear

scuba diver
tank
mask
flippers
shipwreck
island
lagoon
reef

From the boat Alice could see a tree-covered __(1)__ . She knew that just beyond it was a shallow, sandy __(2)__ where the __(3)__ of the *Maria* lay. Many years ago the ship had run aground on a coral __(4)__ and sunk. Now the spot was Alice's favorite place to dive. Alice was a skilled __(5)__ . Carefully she checked her air __(6)__ , the face of her __(7)__ , and the heel straps of her __(8)__ . With a splash, she was off!

Try This CHALLENGE

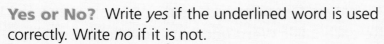

Yes or No? Write *yes* if the underlined word is used correctly. Write *no* if it is not.

9. The <u>flippers</u> kept my hands dry.
10. The <u>mask</u> will protect your feet from the sharp coral.
11. The <u>reef</u> scratched the bottom of the boat.
12. We could reach the <u>island</u> only by boat.

Spelling |ôr|, |ûr|, and |yŏŏr|

Read and Say

|ôr| |ûr|
worn   **shirt**

Basic

READ the sentences. **SAY** each bold word.

1.	horse	A **horse** is a smart animal.
2.	chore	Feeding the cat is my **chore**.
3.	firm	The wooden chair is **firm**.
4.	learn	He will **learn** how to cook.
5.	dirty	The **dirty** room is full of mud.
6.	curve	He turned the car to follow the **curve**.
7.	world	How many cities are in the **world**?
8.	pure	This water is clean and **pure**.
9.	board	One **board** in the door is new.
10.	course	I am taking a math **course**.
11.	earn	Joe will **earn** one dollar.
12.	burn	The sun will **burn** my skin.
13.	cure	Who can **cure** the sick boy?
14.	score	Five is a lower **score** than six.
15.	worm	The baby bird ate a **worm**.
16.	thirteen	Ten is less than **thirteen**.
17.	worn	I have not **worn** my new hat.
18.	curl	Can you make your hair **curl**?
19.	shirt	Each player wears a red **shirt**.
20.	search	Help us **search** for the lost book.

Think and Write

Each word has a vowel sound + *r*. The |ôr| sounds are close to the |ō| sound. The |ûr| sounds have a weak vowel sound. The |yŏŏr| sounds are close to the |yŏŏ| sound.

|ôr| h**or**se, ch**ore** |ûr| f**ir**m, c**ur**ve, l**ear**n, w**or**m |yŏŏr| p**ure**

• What are two patterns for |ôr|? How are the Elephant Words different? What are four patterns for |ûr|? What is a pattern for |yŏŏr|?
Now write each Basic Word under its vowel + |r| sounds.

|ôr| Sounds	|ûr| Sounds	|yŏŏr| Sounds

Review	23. work
21. first	24. third
22. hurt	25. storm

Challenge	28. hurdle
26. thoroughbred	29. foreign
27. enormous	30. earnest

Independent Practice

Spelling Strategy Remember these spelling patterns for the vowel + |r| sounds:

|ôr| *or, ore* |ûr| *ur, ear, ir, or* |yŏŏr| *ure*

Word Analysis/Phonics Complete the exercises with Basic Words.

1. Write the word that begins with the |th| sound.

2–3. Write the two words that rhyme with *tore*.

4–7. Write a homophone for each word below.

   4. hoarse   6. bored
   5. coarse   7. urn

Vocabulary: Synonyms

A **synonym** is a word that means the same or nearly the same as another word. Write the Basic Word that is a synonym for each word below.

   8. scorch   11. unclean
   9. seek   12. heal
   10. hard   13. earth

Excuse my voice. I'm a little hoarse.

Challenge Words Write the Challenge Word that fits each meaning. Use your Spelling Dictionary.

14. from another country   17. a barrier to jump over
15. huge   18. sincere
16. an animal of pure stock

Spelling-Meaning Connection

Can you see *learn* in these words: *learner, learned, unlearn*? These words are all related in spelling and meaning. **Think of this:** If you *learn* a bad habit, you can *unlearn* it.

learn
learner
learned
unlearn

19–20. Write *learner* and the Basic Word that you see in *learner*.

Dictionary

Pronunciation Key A **pronunciation key** helps you understand the symbols in the pronunciation given after an entry word. Look at the pronunciation for *search*. How do you pronounce the |û| sound? The pronunciation key shows that the *u* in *fur* has the |û| sound. Say *fur*. Listen for |û|.

pronunciation   part of a pronunciation key

search |sûrch|

ā pay	ē be	ŏ pot	ô paw, for
â care	î near	ō go	û fur

Practice Write the word from the word box below that matches each pronunciation. Use the pronunciation key above. Check your answers in your Spelling Dictionary.

chore	chair	cheer	score	scare

1. |chîr| **2.** |skôr| **3.** |chôr| **4.** |skâr| **5.** |châr|

Review: Spelling Spree

Letter Math Write a Basic or Review Word by solving each word problem.
Example: first – st + m = *firm*

6. s + tore – e + m =
7. worry – ry + k =
8. c + sure – s =
9. curb – b + l =
10. third – d + teen =
11. p + sure – s =
12. l + earth – th + n =
13. horn – n + se =
14. sh + dirt – d =
15. thirst – st + d =
16. s + earn – n + ch =

17. b + turn – t =
18. world – ld + m =
19. sc + store – st =
20. curl – l + ve =
21. ch + shore – sh =
22. b + soar – s + d =

How Are You Doing?
List the spelling words that are hard for you. Practice them with a family member.

– ld + m =

Proofreading and Writing

Proofread for Spelling Find eight misspelled Basic or Review Words in this journal entry. Write each one correctly.

Saturday, May 12

    Today I went to Cobb Stables. Mrs. Cobb is helping me *ern* money by letting me do a chore or two. The work is hard and *durty*, but it is worth it. Someday I will be allowed to take a horse around the *coarce*. However, *frist* I must learn to be a *ferm* and skillful rider. Right now I feel *warn* out and my muscles *hirt*, but I wouldn't trade this job for the *wold*!

Basic

1. horse
2. chore
3. firm
4. learn
5. dirty
6. curve
7. world
8. pure
9. board
10. course
11. earn
12. burn
13. cure
14. score
15. worm
16. thirteen
17. worn
18. curl
19. shirt
20. search

Review
21. first
22. hurt
23. work
24. third
25. storm

Challenge
26. thoroughbred
27. enormous
28. hurdle
29. foreign
30. earnest

Write to Compare and Contrast

Do you love to feed the dog but hate to clean your room? Write a paragraph about one chore you like and another you hate. Describe how they are alike and different. Try to use five spelling words.

Proofreading Tip

If you use a computer to check spelling, remember that it will not find a word that is misspelled as another word.

Proofreading Marks

¶ Indent
∧ Add
⌐ Delete
≡ Capital letter
/ Small letter

Expanding Vocabulary

Spelling Word Link

dirty
firm

firm
false
tiny
fancy
beautiful
forget

Antonyms Would you be dirty or clean after working all day in a garden? *Dirty* and *clean* are **antonyms**, or words with opposite meanings. Write an antonym from the box for each word below. Use your Spelling Dictionary.

Word	Antonym
soft	1. ?
remember	2. ?
simple	3. ?
huge	4. ?
true	5. ?
ugly	6. ?

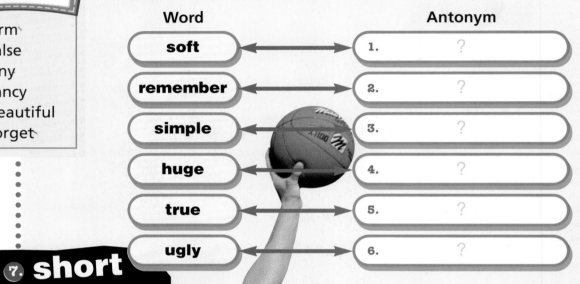

Show You Know! Each picture is labeled with the wrong word. Write an antonym for the word. Then write a sentence, describing each picture and using the antonym.

7. **short**

8. **day**

Real-World Connection

Science: Horses All the words in the box relate to horses. Look up these words in your Spelling Dictionary. Then write the words to complete this horse guidebook.

Spelling Word Link

horse

colt
mustang
filly
saddle
reins
bridle
stirrups
mare

Horse Terms

- A __(1)__ is a small horse that runs wild in the western part of North America.
- A __(2)__ is an adult female horse.
- A __(3)__ is a young male horse.
- A __(4)__ is a young female horse.

Equipment for Horses

- The __(5)__ is the rider's seat strapped to a horse's back.
- The __(6)__ are loops for the rider's feet.
- The __(7)__ fits over the horse's head and controls movement.
- The __(8)__ are long, thin leather straps that the rider holds loosely to guide the horse.

Try This CHALLENGE

Yes or No? Write *yes* or *no* to answer each question.

9. Do you need a saddle to have stirrups on a horse?
10. Do you need a bridle to have reins on a horse?
11. Can a colt give birth to a filly?
12. Can a horse be both a mare and a mustang?

Fact File

In 1860 and 1861, the pony express brought mail from Missouri to California. Riders carried the mail on horseback, stopping only to change horses at stations along the way.

12 Review: Units 7–11

|ōo| |ŭ|
tube **brush**

Unit 7   Spelling |ŭ|, |yōo|, and |ōo| pages 48–53

tube	lunch	fruit	truth	done
suit	threw	trunk	tune	glue

Spelling Strategy

|ŭ| → **u** followed by a consonant sound

|yōo| or |ōo| → **u**-consonant-**e, ew, ue, ui**

Write the word that belongs in each group.

1. song, melody, _____
2. dress, slacks, _____
3. paste, tape, _____
4. breakfast, dinner, _____
5. vegetables, bread, _____

Write the word that fits each clue.

6. past tense of *throw*
7. opposite of *not finished*
8. Toothpaste comes in one.
9. storage space in a car
10. something that is true

|ŏo| |ōo|
wood **stool**

Unit 8   Spelling |ōo| and |ŏo| pages 54–59

tool	push	wood	group	prove
pull	hook	stool	soup	move

Spelling Strategy

|ōo| → **oo** |ŏo| → **oo** or **u** followed by a consonant sound

Write a spelling word by changing one letter in each word below.

11. stoop 12. bush 13. fool 14. look 15. good 16. bull

Write the Elephant Words that complete these sentences.

17. Can you _____ that your statement is true?
18. We will _____ into another house next summer.
19. Please have another bowl of hot _____.
20. The play was put on by a small _____ of students.

Unit 9   Spelling |ou| and |ô| pages 60–65

howl	cause	always	pound	couple
dawn	couch	sauce	false	frown

|ou|
pound
howl

Spelling Strategy

|ou| → **ou, ow**
|ô| → **aw, au, a** before **l**

Write the word that rhymes with each word below.

21. gown   **24.** lawn
22. pause   **25.** sound
23. growl   **26.** pouch

Write the words that complete these sentences.

27. Last night we had spaghetti with tomato _____.
28. You should _____ tell the truth.
29. Is the answer to this question true or _____?
30. I wrote a _____ of letters to two friends.

Unit 10   Spelling |îr|, |är|, and |âr| pages 66–71

cheer	alarm	square	heart	weird
charm	beard	dairy	spare	scarce

|îr| |âr|
gear   stare

Spelling Strategy

|îr| → **ear, eer** |är| → **ar** |âr| → **are, air**

Write the word that completes each analogy.

31. *Air* is to *lungs* as *blood* is to _____.
32. *Head* is to *hair* as *chin* is to _____.
33. *Ball* is to *circle* as *cube* is to _____.
34. *Wheat* is to *mill* as *milk* is to _____.

Write the word that fits each meaning.

35. strange   **37.** rare   **39.** to shout
36. warning   **38.** to delight   **40.** extra

|ôr| |ûr|
worn   shirt

Unit 11   Spelling |ôr|, |ûr|, and |yo͝or| pages 72–77

horse	curve	learn	board	course
cure	worm	score	search	thirteen

Spelling Strategy

|ôr| → **or, ore** |ûr| → **ur, ear, ir, or** |yo͝or| → **ure**

Write six words. Add letters that spell the vowel + |r| sounds.

41. c _ _ ve   **44.** s _ _ _ ch
42. h _ _ se   **45.** b _ _ _ d
43. c _ _ _   **46.** w _ _ m

Write the words that complete these sentences.

47. Did you _____ about fractions in your math lesson today?
48. Did you have a high or a low _____ on your math test?
49. I answered _____ out of fifteen questions correctly.
50. I am going to take a special math _____ next year.

Challenge Words   Units 7–11   pages 48–77

commute	scrawny	marooned	bulletin	thoroughbred
pounce	barnacle	newscast	enormous	awareness

Write the word that belongs in each group.

51. giant, huge, _____   **54.** stranded, deserted, _____
52. clam, snail, _____   **55.** knowledge, understanding, _____
53. memo, notice, _____

Write the word that fits each clue.

56. It describes a chicken without much meat on it.
57. Many working people do this Monday through Friday.
58. It describes an animal from good stock.
59. Kittens do this when they play with a ball of yarn.
60. You watch this to find out about world events.

Spelling-Meaning Strategy

Consonant Changes: Silent to Sounded

crumb
crumble

Sometimes you can remember how to spell a word by thinking of a word that is related in spelling and meaning. Read this paragraph.

> These cookies are messy to eat because they **crumble** easily. Fortunately, the pigeons are happy to eat every **crumb** that we drop.

Think

• How are *crumb* and *crumble* related in meaning?
• Which letter is silent in *crumb* but pronounced in *crumble*?

Here are more related words in which a consonant is silent in one word and pronounced in the other.

sof**t**en	fas**t**en	has**t**en
sof**t**	fas**t**	has**t**e

Apply and Extend

Complete these activities on a separate sheet of paper.

1. Use your Spelling Dictionary to look up the words in the box above. Write a sentence for each word. Can you make the words' meanings clear?

2. With a partner, list as many words as you can that are related to *crumb, soften, fasten,* and *hasten.* Then look at the section "Consonant Changes: Silent to Sounded" beginning on page 272 of your Spelling-Meaning Index. Add to your list any other words that you find in these families.

Summing Up

Sometimes you can remember how to spell a word with a silent consonant by thinking of a related word in which the letter is pronounced.

from Seven True Elephant Stories

by Barbara Williams

If you think that there is only one kind of elephant, this article will surprise you. How many kinds of elephants does it compare and contrast?

There are two kinds of elephants. One kind comes from Asia; the other comes from Africa.

It is not hard to tell the difference between Asian and African elephants. African elephants have big ears that look like the two sides of a giant valentine heart. Asian elephants' ears are smaller and shaped more like a triangle. African elephants have sloping foreheads and sway backs. Asian elephants have foreheads that go straight up and down. Their backs are rounded at the top.

Among both Asian and African elephants, males are called bulls. Females are called cows. Babies are called calves. In Asia, only bulls grow tusks. In Africa, both bulls and cows grow tusks. African elephants have rings around their trunks and two "fingers" at the tips. Asian elephants have smoother trunks and one "finger" at the tips.

Think and Discuss

1 What are the two kinds of elephants?

2 What is the topic sentence of the second paragraph?

3 What supporting details in the second paragraph tell how Asian and African elephants are different?

4 How are Asian and African elephants alike?

The Writing Process
Comparison and Contrast

Compare and contrast two similar things, such as a hairbrush and a toothbrush or two kinds of cereal. Follow the guidelines and the Writing Process.

1 Prewriting
- Draw pictures of your two subjects.
- Make two lists, telling how your subjects are alike and different.

2 Draft
- Write about how your subjects are alike in one paragraph. Write about how they are different in another.

3 Revise
- Be sure each paragraph has a topic sentence.
- Use your Thesaurus to find exact words.
- Have a writing conference.

4 Proofread
- Did you spell each word correctly?
- Did you write possessive nouns correctly?

5 Publish
- Make a neat final copy, and add a good title.
- Make a colorful poster to display your paper.

Guidelines for Comparing and Contrasting

✓ Begin each paragraph with a topic sentence that tells the main idea.
✓ Include supporting details that tell how your two subjects are alike and different.

Composition Words

few
dull
smooth
prove
always
weird
sharp
firm

Compound Words

Read and Say

railroad

Basic

READ the sentences.
SAY each bold word.

1. railroad — The **railroad** has miles of train tracks.
2. airport — His plane left the **airport** at noon.
3. seat belt — Everyone in our car wears a **seat belt**.
4. everywhere — It was cold **everywhere** we went.
5. homesick — I felt **homesick** on my trip.
6. understand — Did you **understand** the lesson?
7. background — Trees fill the **background** in this picture.
8. anything — Can I have **anything** I want?
9. ninety-nine — She can count to **ninety-nine**.
10. already — Is it **already** time to leave?
11. fireplace — The **fireplace** kept the room warm.
12. ourselves — We taught **ourselves** the game.
13. all right — Was the boat **all right** after the storm?
14. forever — Pat and I will be friends **forever**.
15. breakfast — He ate two eggs for **breakfast**.
16. whenever — The cat comes **whenever** I call her.
17. everything — I liked **everything** I bought.
18. meanwhile — The children hid behind the hedge **meanwhile**.
19. afternoon — The best time at the beach is the **afternoon**.
20. make-believe — The child has a **make-believe** friend.

Think and Write

A **compound word** is made up of two or more smaller words.

rail + **road** = railroad   **seat** + **belt** = seat belt
ninety + **nine** = ninety-nine

• What three ways can a compound word be written? What words make up each compound word? How is the Elephant Word different?

Now write each Basic Word under the heading that tells how the word is written.

One Word	With a Hyphen	Two Words

Review
21. inside
22. outside
23. birthday
24. baseball
25. sometimes

Challenge
26. landmark
27. nationwide
28. postscript
29. motorcycle
30. handkerchief

Independent Practice

Spelling Strategy

A **compound word** is made up of two or more smaller words. To spell a compound word correctly, you must know if it is written as one word, as two words joined by a hyphen, or as two separate words.

Word Analysis/Phonics Complete the exercise with Basic Words.

1–8. Write the word that contains each word below.

1. place	**3.** nine	**5.** where	**7.** our
2. after	**4.** ready	**6.** believe	**8.** mean

Vocabulary: Context Sentences Write the Basic Word that completes each sentence.

9. We waved good-bye as the train left the _____ station.

10. In the dining car, we ate juice and cereal for _____.

11. Traveling was fun, but I felt a little _____ at first.

12. We went to the _____ to get on a plane to fly home.

13. Before takeoff, I fastened my _____.

Challenge Words Write the Challenge Word that fits each meaning. Use your Spelling Dictionary.

14. small square of cloth

15. throughout the country

16. a two-wheeled vehicle that is driven by an engine

17. familiar object or building

18. message added at the end of a letter

Spelling-Meaning Connection

Any means "one or some, no matter which kind." Can you see how the meaning of *any* is included in *anything, anyplace,* and *anybody?*

| any |
| anything |
| anyplace |
| anybody ✓ |

19–20. Write *anybody.* Then write the Basic Word that contains one of the words that make up *anybody.*

Dictionary

Dividing Words into Syllables A **syllable** is a word part that has one vowel sound. Some entry words have more than one syllable. In your Spelling Dictionary, the syllables in a word are divided by dots.

un·der·stand |ŭn′ dər stănd′| *v.* **understood, understanding 1.** To get the meaning of: *Do you understand my question?* **2.** To be familiar with; know well: *I wish I could understand Spanish.*

Between which letters can you divide the word *understand*?

Practice Look up these words in your Spelling Dictionary. Write the word, and draw a line between the syllables.

1. always
2. dairy
3. couple
4. already
5. anything
6. thirteen
7. homesick
8. afternoon

Review: Spelling Spree

Silly Rhymes Write the Basic or Review Word that rhymes with each pair of words.

Example: rafter spoon *afternoon*

9. then never
10. clean smile
11. wire space
12. thunder grand
13. heat melt
14. chase call
15. or never
16. many sing
17. shout hide
18. hair sort
19. thin slide
20. tall sight
21. crack sound
22. dome pick
23. pail load
24. come dimes

How Are You Doing?

Write each spelling word in a sentence. Practice any misspelled spelling words with a partner.

Proofreading and Writing

Proofread for Spelling Find nine misspelled Basic or Review Words in this personal story. Write each one correctly.

My grandmother turned nintynine yesterday. For her brithday she wanted to take a make believe trip. Whenever Grandma and I play pretend, she takes care of everthing. After brekfast she had all ready set up our pretend railroad car. Maps were everwhere. We sat down to enjoy ourselfs. Grandma told me about places she had been. In the afternon we took our pretend train home.

Basic

1. railroad
2. airport
3. seat belt
4. everywhere
5. homesick
6. understand
7. background
8. anything
9. ninety-nine
10. already
11. fireplace
12. ourselves
13. all right
14. forever
15. breakfast
16. whenever
17. everything
18. meanwhile
19. afternoon
20. make-believe

Review

21. inside
22. outside
23. birthday
24. baseball
25. sometimes

Challenge

26. landmark
27. nationwide
28. postscript
29. motorcycle
30. handkerchief

Write a List of Tips

What does a good host or overnight guest do? Write a list of tips for being either a guest or a host for overnight guests. Try to use five spelling words.

Proofreading Tip

Say each word aloud to make sure there are no missing letters.

Proofreading Marks

¶ Indent
∧ Add
ℒ Delete
≡ Capital letter
/ Small letter

Expanding Vocabulary

Spelling Word Link
breakfast
airport

Blending Word Parts What would you call a meal that is part breakfast and part lunch?

br**eak**fast + **l**unch = brunch

Compound words are formed by joining two or more words. **Blended words**, such as *brunch*, are formed by blending parts of words.

Join the word parts under each picture. Write a blended word to describe the picture. Then write a sentence for each blended word.

Example: <u>sm</u>ack + cr<u>ash</u> = *smash*   *Did a car smash into the fence?*

1. <u>smo</u>ke + <u>fog</u> = ?

4. <u>heli</u>copter + ai<u>rport</u> = ?

2. <u>mo</u>torbike + <u>pedals</u> = ?

5. <u>cheese</u> + ham<u>burger</u> = ?

3. <u>mo</u>tor + ho<u>tel</u> = ?

6. <u>tw</u>ist + wh<u>irl</u> = ?

Real-World Connection

Social Studies: Travel All the words in the box relate to travel. Look up these words in your Spelling Dictionary. Then write the words to complete this part of a post card.

Spelling Word Link

seat belt

Augusta
Topeka
Austin
Olympia
Sacramento
Columbia
Trenton
Madison

Dear Sharon,

    This summer my family drove from ___(1)___, Maine, to ___(2)___, California. First, we drove through New England and New York to ___(3)___, New Jersey. We saw Civil War battlefields on our way to ___(4)___, South Carolina. We crossed the plains to ___(5)___, Kansas, and visited friends who raise cattle near ___(6)___, Texas. On our return trip, we camped in the rain forests near ___(7)___, Washington, and toured dairy farms outside of ___(8)___, Wisconsin. We had so much fun!

                Carla

Try This CHALLENGE

Questions and Answers Write a word from the box to answer each question.

9. Which city is the state capital of Washington?
10. Which city is the state capital of Texas?
11. Which city is the state capital of Maine?
12. Which city is the state capital of Wisconsin?

⭐⭐⭐ **Fact File**

Washington, D.C., is the capital of the United States. The President lives in the White House. Other sights to see are the Lincoln Memorial and the Washington Monument.

Final |ər|

Read and Say

|ər|
sailor
collar

Basic

READ the sentences. SAY each bold word.

1. sailor — The **sailor** left his ship.
2. harbor — Was the boat safe in the **harbor**?
3. enter — You can **enter** the house from the porch.
4. weather — In the summer our **weather** is hot.
5. labor — We put hours of **labor** into the garden.
6. ladder — I will hold the **ladder** as you climb up.
7. cellar — The tools are down in the **cellar**.
8. chapter — Read the first **chapter** in your book.
9. sugar — We do not want juice with **sugar**.
10. suffer — Did you **suffer** from the heat?
11. collar — The **collar** of your shirt is dirty.
12. proper — Is this the **proper** way to hit a ball?
13. motor — My new fan has a quiet **motor**.
14. favor — You did me a **favor** by carrying my bag.
15. bitter — The lemon has a **bitter** taste.
16. beggar — At dinner our dog acts like a **beggar**.
17. shower — A little **shower** will water the flowers.
18. temper — He has a bad **temper** when he gets mad.
19. feather — The **feather** floated to the ground.
20. doctor — Please call the **doctor** for the sick child.

Think and Write

Each word has two syllables. A syllable is a word or a word part that has one vowel sound. The final syllable of each word ends with a weak vowel sound + *r*. The vowel sound is called **schwa** and is shown as |ə|.

|ər| sounds   ent**er**, sail**or**, sug**ar**

• What sounds do you hear at the end of each word? What three patterns may spell the final |ər| sounds?

Now write each Basic Word under its spelling of final |ər|.

er	or	ar

Review	
21. summer	23. neighbor
22. center	24. dollar
	25. daughter

Challenge	
26. schooner	28. stellar
27. anchor	29. lunar
	30. solar

Independent Practice

Spelling Strategy When you hear the final |ər| sounds in a two-syllable word, think of the patterns *er, or,* and *ar.*

Word Analysis/Phonics Complete the exercises with Basic Words.

1–2. Write the two words that begin with the |sh| sound spelled *s* or *sh*.

3–8. Write the six words that have double consonants.

Vocabulary: Making Inferences Write the Basic Word that fits each clue below.

9. It is part of a book.

10. It can be a command to "come in."

11. This person is trained to work on a boat.

12. Without this, a boat has no power.

13. This person often works in a hospital.

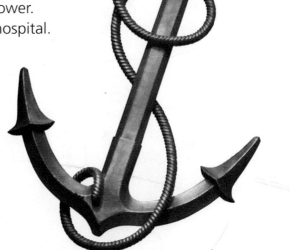

Challenge Words Write the Challenge Word that fits each clue. Use your Spelling Dictionary.

14. keeps a ship in place

15. has masts and sails

16. relating to a star

17. relating to the sun

18. having to do with the moon

Spelling-Meaning Connection

Can you see the word *labor* in *laboratory*? These two words are related in spelling and meaning. **Think of this:** Scientists *labor* in the *laboratory*.

labor
laboratory

19–20. Write *laboratory*. Then write the Basic Word that is related to *laboratory* in spelling and meaning.

Review: Spelling Spree

Jobs Match Look at the list of workers. Write a Basic or Review Word that names what each worker makes, uses, or deals with on the job.

Example: nurse *doctor*

1. baker
2. writer
3. banker
4. carpenter
5. auto mechanic
6. forecaster
7. bird watcher
8. tailor

Hidden Words Write the Basic or Review Word that you find in each row of letters. Don't let the other words fool you.

Example: m o t o r o o s t e r *motor*

9. p e n e i g h b o r e d
10. d e c e n t e r r o r
11. b e g g a r d e n
12. r a s h o w e r r o r
13. r o o f a v o r i t e
14. d o c t o r d e r
15. b u s u f f e r r y
16. e n t e r r a c e
17. e a r t h a r b o r

18. l a b o r d e r
19. l a d a u g h t e r
20. e a r s a i l o r a l
21. t e m p e r s o n
22. c r i b i t t e r
23. i m p r o p e r k
24. c e l l o c e l l a r
25. a s u m m e r c y

How Are You Doing?

Write each spelling word as a partner reads it aloud. Did you misspell any words?

Proofreading and Writing

Proofread: Spelling and Comparisons When you compare with *good* and *bad*, remember to change their forms.

	good	**bad**
COMPARING TWO:	better	worse
COMPARING THREE OR MORE:	best	worst

Find four misspelled Basic or Review Words and two incorrect forms of *good* or *bad* in this part of a book report. Write the book report correctly.

Title: <u>Trouble at Sea</u>

Author: Mary Eng

This book was best than her first book. Tina, the dauter of a sailer, is caught in a storm at sea. The wether is the worse of the year. She tries to enter a harbor, but the boat's moter stops. What will Tina do?

Basic

1. sailor
2. harbor
3. enter
4. weather
5. labor
6. ladder
7. cellar
8. chapter
9. sugar
10. suffer
11. collar
12. proper
13. motor
14. favor
15. bitter
16. beggar
17. shower
18. temper
19. feather
20. doctor

Review

21. summer
22. center
23. neighbor
24. dollar
25. daughter

Challenge

26. schooner
27. anchor
28. stellar
29. lunar
30. solar

Write a Weather Report

Think of a day that you remember well because of the weather. Write a weather report, predicting that same kind of a day. Try to use five spelling words and at least two forms of *good* or *bad*.

Proofreading Tip — **Check that you used the correct form when comparing with *good* or *bad*.**

Proofreading Marks

¶ Indent
∧ Add
⌐ Delete
≡ Capital letter
/ Small letter

Vocabulary Enrichment

Expanding Vocabulary

Spelling Word Link

sailor

Building Nouns with -or and -er A *sailor* is someone who *sails*. An *eraser* is something that *erases*. The suffixes *-or* and *-er* can be added to the end of some verbs to form nouns. These suffixes mean "something or someone who does" whatever the verb says. Notice the word *erase* in the chart below. What happens to a final *e* when the suffix is added?

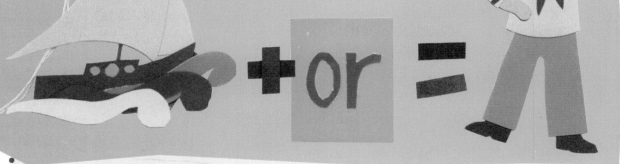

Add *-or* or *-er* to each verb to write a noun. Then write the meaning of the new word.

VERB	SUFFIX		NOUN	MEANING
sail	or	=	sailor	someone who sails
erase	er	=	eraser	something that erases
act	or	=	1. ?	2. ?
bake	er	=	3. ?	4. ?
dance	er	=	5. ?	6. ?
direct	or	=	7. ?	8. ?
broil	er	=	9. ?	10. ?
grind	er	=	11. ?	12. ?

Show You Know! Choose four words you built in the chart. Write a sentence for each one.

Real-World Connection

Recreation: Sailing All the words in the box relate to sailing. Look up these words in your Spelling Dictionary. Then write the words to complete this part of a story.

Spelling Word Link

sailor

mast
galley
stern
hull
deck
port
captain
rigging

Sid, a new sailor, had just eaten his first meal in the __(1)__. His job was interesting. The ship's __(2)__ had taught Sid how to repair the outer frame, or __(3)__, of the ship. Now Sid looked at the sea as he walked on the top __(4)__ toward the rear part, or __(5)__, of the ship. Sid gazed up at the tall, thin __(6)__ looming overhead and the mass of ropes that made up the __(7)__. If only they would leave this sheltered __(8)__ and sail out to sea!

Try This CHALLENGE

Write a Paragraph Write another paragraph to continue the story of Sid. Try to use words from the box.

Fact File

Vikings lived long ago in northern Europe. In their ships with one square sail and a row of oars on each side, they sailed to North America before Columbus did.

Read and Say

|l| |əl|
medal **eagle**

Basic

> **READ** the sentences. **SAY** each bold word.

1. nickel — Five pennies equals a **nickel**.
2. metal — The hammer hit the **metal** nail.
3. total — He counted a **total** of four dimes.
4. eagle — The **eagle** has large wings.
5. middle — We are in the **middle** of the story.
6. special — I have two pencils and a **special** pen.
7. final — The **final** game ends our baseball season.
8. model — I built a **model** airplane.
9. bottle — Did you drink your **bottle** of water?
10. double — One of the **double** doors is stuck.
11. towel — I dried my hands on the **towel**.
12. medal — The best runner won a **medal**.
13. battle — Two armies fought in a **battle**.
14. candle — The wind blew out the **candle**.
15. trouble — That loud noise could mean car **trouble**.
16. handle — Can you hold the **handle** firmly?
17. simple — I can finish this **simple** chore quickly.
18. uncle — My dad's brother is my **uncle**.
19. title — The **title** of the book is on the cover.
20. cattle — Were the **cattle** eating grass in the field?

Think and Write

Each two-syllable word has the final |l| or |əl| sounds.

|l| or |əl| nick**el**, fin**al**, midd**le**

• What are three spelling patterns for the final |l| or |əl| sounds?

Now write each Basic Word under its spelling of the final |l| or |əl| sounds.

el	*al*	*le*

Review
21. little
22. able
23. circle
24. purple
25. apple

Challenge
26. decimal
27. financial
28. trifle
29. cancel
30. industrial

Independent Practice

Spelling Strategy When you hear the final |l| or |əl| sounds in a two-syllable word, think of the patterns *el*, *al*, and *le*.

Word Analysis/Phonics Complete the exercises with Basic Words.

1–4. Write the word that rhymes with each word below.

   1. riddle   **2.** pedal   **3.** dimple   **4.** petal

5–8. Write the four words that have a long vowel sound.

Vocabulary: Analogies Write the Basic Word that completes each analogy.

  9. *Tin* is to *can* as *glass* is to _____.

10. *Niece* is to *nephew* as *aunt* is to _____.

11. *Bulb* is to *lamp* as *wick* is to _____.

12. *Once* is to *twice* as *single* is to _____.

13. *Dollar* is to *five-dollar bill* as *penny* is to _____.

Challenge Words Write the Challenge Word that fits each meaning. Use your Spelling Dictionary.

14. something unimportant

15. having to do with industry

16. to call off

17. of or based on ten

18. having to do with the management of money

Spelling-Meaning Connection

final
finality

How can you remember how to spell the schwa sound in *final*? Think of the |ă| sound in the related word *finality*.

19–20. Write *final* and *finality*. Underline the letter that has the schwa sound in one word and the |ă| sound in the other word.

Dictionary

The Schwa Sound The **schwa** sound is the weak vowel sound you hear in the last syllable of *final*. The dictionary shows this sound as |ə|. The pronunciation key shows words with different vowel letters that spell the schwa sound.

	PART OF A PRONUNCIATION KEY
final |fī′ nəl|	|ə| **a**go, it**e**m, penc**i**l, at**o**m, circ**u**s

Practice Each word below has been divided into syllables. Compare each word with its pronunciation. Then write the word, and underline the letter that spells the |ə| sound.

1. al•bum |ăl′ bəm|
2. com•pass |kŭm′ pəs|
3. lev•el |lĕv′ əl|
4. po•lite |pə līt′|
5. nick•el |nĭk′ əl|
6. fos•sil |fŏs′ əl|

Review: Spelling Spree

Syllable Addition Combine the underlined syllables in each pair of words to write a Basic or Review Word.

Example: <u>mo</u>dern + lev<u>el</u>   *model*

7. <u>cir</u>cus + un<u>cle</u>
8. <u>lit</u>ter + rat<u>tle</u>
9. <u>bat</u>ter + tat<u>tle</u>
10. <u>sim</u>mer + rip<u>ple</u>
11. <u>can</u>dy + bun<u>dle</u>
12. <u>pur</u>pose + dim<u>ple</u>
13. <u>mid</u>day + rid<u>dle</u>
14. <u>to</u>ken + men<u>tal</u>
15. <u>a</u>cre + bub<u>ble</u>
16. <u>tow</u>er + chap<u>el</u>
17. <u>un</u>til + cir<u>cle</u>
18. <u>cat</u>bird + set<u>tle</u>
19. <u>ti</u>ger + gen<u>tle</u>
20. <u>fi</u>ber + spi<u>nal</u>
21. <u>ea</u>ger + wig<u>gle</u>
22. <u>bot</u>tom + man<u>tle</u>

How Are You Doing?

Write your spelling words in ABC order. Practice any misspelled words with a family member.

mod + el = model
ern lev

Proofreading and Writing

Proofread for Spelling Find ten misspelled Basic or Review Words in this sign. Write each one correctly.

Yard sale today!

Come and buy lots of speshel items at low prices!

It's no troble to discuss prices!

modle ship in a bottal $5.00

eagle medel . . . . 50¢

aple peelers and metel tools $2.00

duble boiler and bucket with a handel $2.50

Try some juice while you look.

It's only a nickle!

Basic

1. nickel
2. metal
3. total
4. eagle
5. middle
6. special
7. final
8. model
9. bottle
10. double
11. towel
12. medal
13. battle
14. candle
15. trouble
16. handle
17. simple
18. uncle
19. title
20. cattle

Review
21. little
22. able
23. circle
24. purple
25. apple

Challenge
26. decimal
27. financial
28. trifle
29. cancel
30. industrial

Write a List

How do you earn money? Write a list of suggestions for how to earn an allowance or extra money. Try to use five spelling words. You may also want to share your list with classmates.

Proofreading Tip   **Check for words in which the order of letters has been switched.**

Proofreading Marks

¶ Indent
∧ Add
⌐ Delete
≡ Capital letter
/ Small letter

Expanding Vocabulary

Spelling Word Link

industrial

Building Words with -al Sometimes the final letters *al* are a suffix meaning "having to do with." When this suffix is added to a noun, it forms an adjective. Notice that when a word ends with e, the e is dropped before *-al* is added.

NOUN		SUFFIX		ADJECTIVE	MEANING
coast	+	**al**	=	coast**al**	having to do with the coast
tide	+	**al**	=	tid**al**	having to do with the tide

Add *-al* to each noun to write a new adjective.

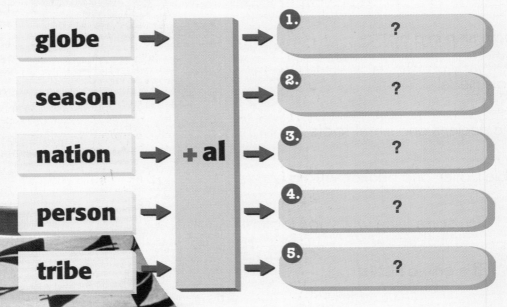

globe → + al → 1. ?

season → + al → 2. ?

nation → + al → 3. ?

person → + al → 4. ?

tribe → + al → 5. ?

Show You Know! Write a word you built with *-al* to complete each sentence.

6. "The Star-Spangled Banner" is our _____ song.
7. Many countries work together on _____ projects.
8. The flight of geese marks a _____ change.
9. These books are my _____ property.
10. Her pottery is a beautiful example of _____ art.

Real-World Connection

Math: Money All the words in the box relate to money. Look up these words in your Spelling Dictionary. Then write the words to complete this part of a letter.

Spelling Word Link

nickel

money
bank
cent
quarter
deposit
withdraw
savings
passbook

Dear Grandma,

Last Thursday I opened my first account at a __(1)__. I wanted to start a __(2)__ account in order to save for a bike. I had to __(3)__ at least ten dollars into the account. The teller said my account would earn money four times a year and would be worth the most at the end of the fourth __(4)__. The teller handed me a __(5)__ to keep track of the __(6)__ in the account. I will not __(7)__ a penny because I need every __(8)__ to buy a bike.

Write to me if you have time.

Love,

Sharon

Try This
CHALLENGE

Yes or No? Write *yes* or *no* to answer each question.
9. Is money kept in a passbook?
10. Do you take out money when you withdraw it?
11. Could you get change for a cent?
12. Do you deposit money to add it to your account?

★★★ **Fact File**

When you put your money in a bank, the bank pays you for keeping your money there. The money the bank pays you is called interest. Interest is added to your savings during the year.

Words with *-ed* and *-ing*

Read and Say

Basic

READ the sentences. **SAY** each bold word.

1. dancing — They are **dancing** slowly to the music.
2. skipped — We **skipped** with joy to the beat.
3. hiking — They are **hiking** on a mountain trail.
4. flipped — Has she **flipped** the eggs over?
5. snapping — I am **snapping** my fingers to the song.
6. raced — The runner **raced** to the finish line.
7. landed — The boats **landed** at the dock.
8. pleasing — My good report card is **pleasing** to Dad.
9. checking — The teacher is **checking** our papers.
10. dared — Who **dared** to jump so high?
11. dimmed — The lights in the room **dimmed**.
12. rubbing — I am **rubbing** butter on an ear of corn.
13. striped — The **striped** shirt is red, blue, and white.
14. wasting — Is she **wasting** time by waiting in line?
15. traced — My sister **traced** the rose with her pen.
16. stripped — He **stripped** the paper off his gift box.
17. tanning — The sun is **tanning** his skin slowly.
18. smelling — The cook is **smelling** the soup.
19. phoning — I am **phoning** Mom to ask for a ride.
20. fainted — The last runner **fainted** from the heat.

Think and Write

Each word has a base word and an ending. A **base word** is a word to which a beginning or an ending can be added.

rac**e** + **ed** = rac**ed**   land + **ed** = land**ed**   sna**p** + **ing** = sna**pping**

• Which letter was dropped when *-ed* was added to *race*? Which base word ends with one vowel followed by one consonant? How does that word change when the ending is added?

Now write each Basic Word under the heading that tells what happens to its spelling when *-ed* or *-ing* is added.

Final Consonant Doubled	Final *e* Dropped	No Change

Review
21. cared
22. joking
23. tapping
24. wrapped
25. fixing

Challenge
26. breathing
27. tiring
28. urged
29. scarred
30. striving

Independent Practice

Spelling Strategy If a word ends with *e*, drop the *e* before adding *-ed* or *-ing*. If a one-syllable word ends with one vowel followed by a single consonant, double the consonant before adding *-ed* or *-ing*.

s t r i p e e d

Word Analysis/Phonics Complete the exercises with Basic Words.
1. Write the word that has the |f| sound spelled *ph*.
2–5. Write the four words with the |ă| sound.
6–8. Write the three words that rhyme with *shipped*.

Vocabulary: Word Clues Write the Basic Word that fits each clue.
9. synonym for *sniffing*
10. People often carry a backpack when they are doing this.
11. past tense of *faint*
12. having long, narrow lines of different colors
13. copied by following lines seen through a sheet of paper

Challenge Words Write the Challenge Word that fits each meaning. Use your Spelling Dictionary.
14. convinced or pleaded with
15. becoming weak or weary
16. reaching toward a goal
17. taking air into the lungs
18. left with a mark from a healed wound

Spelling-Meaning Connection

Please and *pleasing* have different vowel sounds than *pleasant* and *pleasure*. **Think of this:** A *pleasing* gift gives *pleasure*.

19–20. Write *pleasing* and *pleasant*. Underline the letters that spell the |ē| sound in one word and the |ĕ| sound in the other word.

please
pleasing
pleasant
pleasure

Dictionary

Entry Words as Base Words If you want to know whether *dimmed* has one or two *m*'s, look up the base word *dim*. The dictionary entry shows forms of *dim*.

> **dim** |dĭm| *adj.* **dimmer, dimmest 1.** Somewhat dark.
> **2.** Giving off little light: *a dim lamp.* **3.** Not clearly seen:
> *a dim shape. v.* **dimmed, dimming** To make or become
> dim.

Adjectives and verbs with the endings *-er, -est, -ed,* and *-ing* are usually listed with their base words.

Practice Write the answer to each question.
1–2. What are the *-er* and *-est* forms of the word *dim*?
3–4. Which two words are the verb forms of *dim*?

Write the entry word you would look up to find each word.
5. flipped   **6.** phoning   **7.** joking   **8.** wrapped

Review: Spelling Spree

Adding Endings Write the Basic or Review Word that combines each base word and ending.

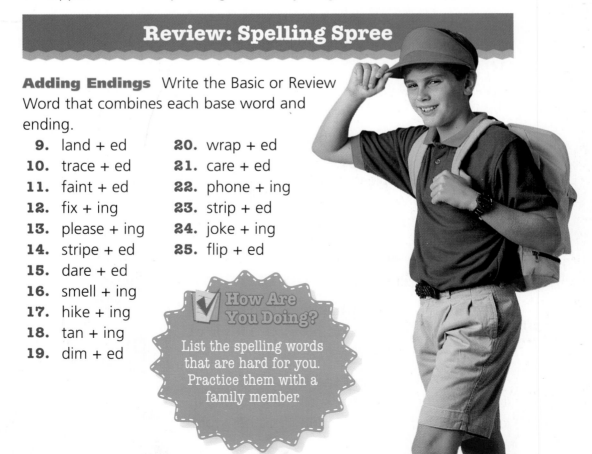

9. land + ed	**20.** wrap + ed
10. trace + ed	**21.** care + ed
11. faint + ed	**22.** phone + ing
12. fix + ing	**23.** strip + ed
13. please + ing	**24.** joke + ing
14. stripe + ed	**25.** flip + ed
15. dare + ed	
16. smell + ing	
17. hike + ing	
18. tan + ing	
19. dim + ed	

How Are You Doing?

List the spelling words that are hard for you. Practice them with a family member.

Proofreading and Writing

Proofread for Spelling Find eight misspelled Basic or Review Words in this journal entry. Write each one correctly.

I walked into the new health club and saw a big room with brightly striped wallpaper. A man at a desk was cheking membership cards. Beyond him people were danceing and snaping their fingers to music. A group of men skiped rope. An instructor was fixing some weights for a woman. The woman was rubing white chalk on her hands. I began taping my feet to the music. Without waisting a moment, I rased to sign up.

Basic

1. dancing
2. skipped
3. hiking
4. flipped
5. snapping
6. raced
7. landed
8. pleasing
9. checking
10. dared
11. dimmed
12. rubbing
13. striped
14. wasting
15. traced
16. stripped
17. tanning
18. smelling
19. phoning
20. fainted

Review
21. cared
22. joking
23. tapping
24. wrapped
25. fixing

Challenge
26. breathing
27. tiring
28. urged
29. scarred
30. striving

Write a List

Write a list of ways to get exercise in school and out of school. What kinds of activities are possible? Try to use five spelling words. You may also want to share your list with a classmate.

A computer spell-checker may find a misspelled word, but you must still know the correct spelling to fix it.

Proofreading Tip

Proofreading Marks

¶ Indent
∧ Add
⌐ Delete
≡ Capital letter
/ Small letter

Expanding Vocabulary

Spelling Word Link

checking

Multiple Meanings for *check* Is a check at a restaurant the same as a check on a shopping list? The word *check* does have more than one meaning, but don't be fooled. Just figure out which meaning of *check* an author is using. Read the four meanings in this dictionary entry.

> **check** |chĕk| *n., pl.* **checks 1.** Something that restrains or controls. **2.** Examination to be sure something is as it should be. **3.** A mark made to show that something has been noted. **4.** A restaurant bill.

Write the meaning of *check* that fits each sentence. Use the dictionary entry above.

1. Please put a <u>check</u> next to your name.
2. Try to keep a <u>check</u> on your enthusiasm.
3. I did a complete <u>check</u> of my homework.
4. When we had finished the meal, we asked for the <u>check</u>.

Work Together With a classmate write a sentence for each thought balloon. Use a different meaning of *check* in each one.

Real-World Connection

Health: Exercise All the words in the box relate to exercise. Look up these words in your Spelling Dictionary. Then write the words to complete this list of tips.

Spelling Word Link

skipped

exercise
energy
fitness
athlete
stretch
strengthen
balance
workout

Welcome to the start of a new season!

Here are some tips from your coach.

✔ Good health and total __(1)__ are important to a trained __(2)__.

✔ Before each game, do warm-up routines to __(3)__ and loosen your muscles.

✔ Eat well to give your body lots of __(4)__.

✔ To get plenty of __(5)__, you can jog and go to a gym for a daily __(6)__.

✔ Take dancing or skating lessons to improve your sense of __(7)__ and to help build and __(8)__ your leg muscles.

Try This CHALLENGE

Yes or No? Write *yes* if the underlined word is used correctly. Write *no* if it is not.

9. The diver lost his <u>balance</u> and fell into the water.
10. Watching the movie was a tough <u>workout</u>.
11. I have lots of <u>energy</u> after a good night's sleep.
12. Taking a nap every day is good <u>exercise</u>.

★★★ Fact File

When you breathe, your body takes in oxygen to give you energy. Aerobic exercises, such as jogging, biking, and fast walking, help your body do a better job of using oxygen.

Final |ē|

|ē|
hungry
turkey
empty

Read and Say

Basic

READ the sentences. **SAY** each bold word.

1. beauty — I love the **beauty** of a rose.
2. ugly — This dirty old hat looks **ugly**.
3. lazy — Our dog is too **lazy** to move.
4. marry — She will **marry** the man she loves.
5. ready — My shirt is clean and **ready** to wear.
6. sorry — I feel **sorry** that I forgot your name.
7. empty — Fill the **empty** box with books.
8. honey — Bees make good **honey**.
9. valley — The **valley** between the hills is pretty.
10. movie — Was the old **movie** shown in color?
11. duty — It is his **duty** to watch the baby.
12. hungry — I am **hungry** for a bite to eat.
13. lonely — The **lonely** child wanted a friend.
14. alley — Is it safe to walk down a dark **alley**?
15. body — The red spots on his **body** were bug bites.
16. plenty — Two hours is **plenty** of time to play.
17. turkey — The biggest bird in this zoo is a **turkey**.
18. hockey — Do you play **hockey** on ice or in the street?
19. fifty — Five dimes equals **fifty** cents.
20. monkey — What a long tail that **monkey** has!

Think and Write

Each word has two syllables and ends with the final |ē| sound:

final |ē| beaut**y**, hon**ey**

• What are the two spelling patterns for the final |ē| sound? What pattern spells the final |ē| sound in the Elephant Word?

Now write each Basic Word under its spelling of final |ē|.

y	ey	Another Spelling

Review
21. pretty
22. sadly
23. friendly
24. city
25. slowly

Challenge
26. fiery
27. envy
28. mercy
29. medley
30. imaginary

Independent Practice

Spelling Strategy When you hear the final |ē| sound in a two-syllable word, think of the spelling patterns *y* and *ey*.

Word Analysis/Phonics Complete the exercises with Basic Words.

1. Write the word with the |yoo| sound spelled *eau*.
2–4. Write the three words that have the |ĕ| sound.
5–8. Write the four words that have double consonants.

Vocabulary: Analogies Write the Basic Word that completes each analogy.

9. *Silkworm* is to *silk* as *bee* is to ___A___ .
10. *Water* is to *thirsty* as *food* is to ___B___ .
11. *Desert* is to *camel* as *jungle* is to ___C___ .
12. *Moo* is to *cow* as *gobble* is to ___A___ .
13. *Ball* is to *soccer* as *puck* is to ___A___ .

Challenge Words Write the Challenge Word that fits each clue. Use your Spelling Dictionary.

14. synonym for *jealousy*
15. describes a dragon's breath
16. kindness a knight would show
17. not real
18. music made up of different songs

Spelling-Meaning Connection

Did you know that the word *movie* comes from the words *moving picture*? *Movie* is related in spelling and meaning to *moving*. **Think of this:** A *movie* shows people *moving*.

19–20. Write *moving*. Then write the Basic Word that is related to *moving* in spelling and meaning.

Review: Spelling Spree

Riddles Write a Basic or Review Word to answer each riddle.

Example: What kind of "T" is nice to look at? *pretty*

1. What kind of "Z" does not like to work?
2. What kind of "T" has streets and buildings?
3. What kind of "T" is half of one hundred?
4. What kind of "D" has arms and legs?
5. What kind of "V" do you watch in a theater?
6. What kind of "T" has nothing in it?
7. What kind of "T" is a lot of something?
8. What kind of "D" is always prepared?
9. What kind of "T" is something you are supposed to do?

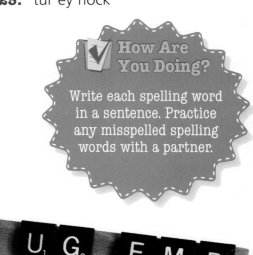

Syllable Scramble Two of the three syllables in each item below form a Basic or Review Word. Write the words correctly.

Example: ty ug emp *empty*

10. ly eve slow
11. sad fif ly
12. ley hon al
13. lone read ly
14. ley fif val
15. mon slow key
16. ry mov mar
17. ty tur beau
18. laz friend ly
19. ty lone pret
20. sor ug ry
21. hock gry hun

22. hon plen ey
23. key beau tur
24. ug cit ly
25. tur ey hock

How Are You Doing?

Write each spelling word in a sentence. Practice any misspelled spelling words with a partner.

Proofreading and Writing

Proofread: Spelling and Abbreviations Each abbreviation for the name of a month begins with a capital letter and ends with a period. (See page 247 for abbreviations of other months.)

April **Apr.**   January **Jan.**   September **Sept.**

Find four misspelled Basic or Review Words and three incorrect abbreviations in this Beast's diary. Write the diary correctly.

Mar. 23   Everyone screams at me in horror.

   I walk the streets slowley and sadly.

aug. 6   I have plenny of gold but no friends.

Sept 9   A girl named Beauty was friendly to me.

oct 26   Beauty wants to marrie me!

Dec. 14   Thanks to Beauty, I am no longer a lonly beast.

Basic

1. beauty
2. ugly
3. lazy
4. marry
5. ready
6. sorry
7. empty
8. honey
9. valley
10. movie
11. duty
12. hungry
13. lonely
14. alley
15. body
16. plenty
17. turkey
18. hockey
19. fifty
20. monkey

Review

21. pretty
22. sadly
23. friendly
24. city
25. slowly

Challenge

26. fiery
27. envy
28. mercy
29. medley
30. imaginary

Write a Story Ending

Think of a familiar fairy tale. Write a new ending for it. For example, what might have happened if Little Red Riding Hood had made friends with the wolf? Try to use five spelling words and at least one abbreviation for a month. You may also want to read your ending to a classmate.

Proofreading Tip   **Check that you wrote any abbreviations for months correctly.**

Proofreading Marks

¶ Indent
∧ Add
⌐ Delete
≡ Capital letter
/ Small letter

Expanding Vocabulary

Spelling Word Link

empty

Thesaurus: Exact Words How would you describe an unused lot with no buildings or trees? Is it *empty* or *vacant*? *Vacant* is another word for *empty*, but it is more exact. *Vacant* describes a place that has been deserted.

vacant

The only thing left on the ~~empty~~ lot was weeds.

Look at the exact words for *empty* and *dark* shown below.

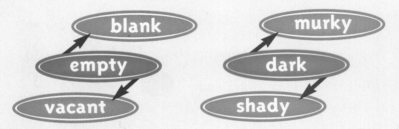

Write the best word to replace *empty* or *dark* in each sentence. Use your Thesaurus.

1. The house was <u>empty</u> long after we moved.
2. I have only three more <u>empty</u> pages to fill in my diary.
3. A frog disappeared into the <u>dark</u> water of the pond.
4. I found relief from the hot sun in the cool, <u>dark</u> forest.

Work Together Find the other synonyms for *empty* and *dark* in your Thesaurus. Write the synonym that best illustrates each picture. Then, with a partner, write a sentence for each synonym you wrote.

5.
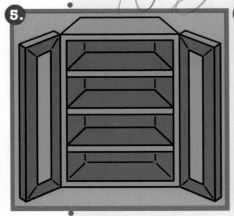

6.

7.

Real-World Connection

Language Arts: Fairy Tales All the words in the box relate to fairy tales. Look up these words in your Spelling Dictionary. Then write the words to complete this part of a fairy tale.

Spelling Word Link

beauty

dungeon
princess
elf
prince
dragon
wicked
wizard
enchanted

The king's daughter Lilla, the __(1)__ of Trinia, quickly followed her tiny fairylike friend, the __(2)__. They had been searching for her brother, the __(3)__, for days. A fire-breathing __(4)__ had locked him in a cold, dark __(5)__ in a faraway castle. This castle had become __(6)__ after an evil __(7)__ named Zin had placed it under a spell. Zin was so __(8)__ that Lilla feared she might never see her brother again if she did not hurry.

Try This CHALLENGE

Clue Match Write a word from the box to match each clue.

9. It could never be mistaken for a giant.
10. It is a home for prisoners.
11. He wears a crown.
12. It would be a good pet to have at a barbecue.

Fact File

Hans Christian Andersen wrote fairy tales based on real feelings. In "The Ugly Duckling," a story of a lonely young swan, Andersen may have been writing about his own life.

18 Review: Units 13–17

railroad

Unit 13   Compound Words   pages 84–89

seat belt	everywhere	background	anything	already
ourselves	forever	breakfast	meanwhile	make-believe

Spelling Strategy   A **compound word** is made up of two or more smaller words. To spell a compound word correctly, you must know if it is written as one word, as two words joined by a hyphen, or as two separate words.

Write the compound word that contains each word below.

1. mean
2. for
3. ready
4. our
5. any
6. back

Write the compound word that completes each analogy.

7. *Nothing* is to *everything* as *nowhere* is to _____.
8. *Nonfiction* is to *real* as *fiction* is to _____.
9. *Sandwich* is to *lunch* as *cereal* is to _____.
10. *Boat* is to *life jacket* as *car* is to _____.

Unit 14   Final |ər| pages 90–95

sailor	cellar	chapter	harbor	sugar
beggar	doctor	feather	collar	motor

Spelling Strategy   When you hear the final |ər| sounds in a two-syllable word, think of the patterns **er**, **or**, and **ar**.

Write a spelling word by adding the second syllable.

11. sail | _____
12. har | _____
13. beg | _____
14. doc | _____
15. mo | _____

Write the word that fits each clue.

16. found in a book
17. found in some foods
18. found on some shirts
19. found on a bird
20. part of some buildings

|ər|
sailor
collar

Unit 15   Final |l| or |əl| pages 96–101

double	special	final	model	eagle
towel	candle	medal	trouble	cattle

Spelling Strategy   When you hear the final |l| or |əl| sounds in a two-syllable word, think of the patterns **el**, **al**, and **le**.

|l| |əl|
medal   **eagle**

Write the word that belongs in each group.

21. hawk, owl, _____

22. single, _____, triple

23. lantern, torch, _____

24. sheep, horses, _____

25. example, copy, _____

Write the word that matches each meaning below.

26. last

27. an award

28. not common

29. difficulty

30. cloth used for wiping something wet

Unit 16   Words with *-ed* and *-ing*   pages 102–107

skipped	snapping	checking	pleasing	raced
fainted	stripped	phoning	striped	rubbing

Spelling Strategy

check + **ing** = check**ing**
race − e + **ed** = rac**ed**
snap + p + **ing** = snap**ping**

Write the word that rhymes with each word below.

31. painted   **33.** teasing

32. paced   **34.** tapping

Write a spelling word by adding *-ed* or *-ing* to each word.

35. phone   **37.** rub   **39.** check

36. skip   **38.** strip   **40.** stripe

|ē|
hungry
turkey
empty

Unit 17 — Final |ē| — pages 108–113

ready	valley	beauty	honey	movie
hockey	lonely	fifty	alley	hungry

Spelling Strategy

final |ē| → **y, ey**

Write the word that completes each sentence.

41. Snow falls more often in the mountains than in the _____.
42. We took a shortcut through the narrow _____.
43. The queen had great charm and _____.
44. Are you _____ to take the test today?

Write the word that completes each phrase.

45. _____ theater
46. _____ puck
47. _____ dollars

48. thirsty and _____
49. sad and _____
50. as sweet as _____

Challenge Words — Units 13–17 — pages 84–113

imaginary	striving	trifle	financial	handkerchief
schooner	medley	tiring	stellar	nationwide

Write the word that fits each clue.

51. has to do with money
52. used when you sneeze
53. has to do with stars

54. something that is sung
55. throughout the whole nation
56. exists only in your mind

Write the word that rhymes with the underlined word.

57. The exercise was _____, and we were all <u>perspiring</u>.
58. I could go on a _____, but a bus would arrive <u>sooner</u>.
59. Open the window a _____, or I will surely <u>stifle</u>.
60. Every swimmer was _____ to win first place in <u>diving</u>.

Spelling-Meaning Strategy

Vowel Changes: Schwa to Short Vowel Sound

metal
metallic

Words from the same word families are often related in both spelling and meaning. Knowing how to spell one word may help you spell other, related words. Read this paragraph.

> Jeremy wore a knight's costume that looked like real **metal**. However, it was really made from stiff silver cloth that looked **metallic** in the light.

Think

- How are *metal* and *metallic* related in meaning?
- What vowel sound does the letter *a* spell in each word?

Here are more related words with the same change in vowel sounds as *metal* and *metallic*. Note that the spelling of the vowel sounds remains the same in each pair.

tot**a**l	med**a**l	form**a**l
tot**a**lity	med**a**llion	form**a**lity

Apply and Extend

Complete these activities on a separate sheet of paper.

1. Use your Spelling Dictionary to look up the words in the box above. Write a short paragraph, using one word pair.
2. With a partner, list as many words as you can that are related to *metal*, *total*, *medal*, and *formal*. Then look at the section "Vowel Changes: Schwa to Short Vowel Sound" beginning on page 275 of your Spelling-Meaning Index. Add to your list any other words that you find in these families.

Summing Up

You can remember how to spell the schwa sound in some words by thinking of a related word with a short vowel sound spelled the same way.

from
Charlotte's Web
by E. B. White

Characters can be people or animals, real or make-believe. What do you learn about a pig named Wilbur in this passage?

One afternoon in June, when Wilbur was almost two months old, he wandered out into his small yard outside the barn. Fern had not arrived for her usual visit. Wilbur stood in the sun feeling lonely and bored.

"There's never anything to do around here," he thought. He walked slowly to his food trough and sniffed to see if anything had been overlooked at lunch. He found a small strip of potato skin and ate it. His back itched, so he leaned against the fence and rubbed against the boards. When he tired of this, he walked indoors and sat down. He didn't feel like going to sleep, he didn't feel like digging, he was tired of standing still, tired of lying down. "I'm less than two months old, and I'm tired of living," he said. He walked out to the yard again.

"When I'm out here," he said, "there's no place to go but in. When I'm indoors, there's no place to go but out in the yard."

"That's where you're wrong, my friend, my friend," said a voice.

Think and Discuss

1 What does this passage tell you about Wilbur, the main **character**? What is Wilbur's problem?

2 What is the **setting** for this part of the story?

3 What do you think will happen next in the **plot**?

The Writing Process
Story

What kinds of stories do you like? Write a story that you would like to read. Keep the guidelines in mind. Follow the Writing Process.

1 Prewriting
- Draw a comic strip to show what happens in your story.

2 Draft
- Use dialogue when the characters talk.

3 Revise
- Take out any parts that do not keep to the main idea of your story.
- Use your Thesaurus to find exact words.
- Have a writing conference.

4 Proofread
- Did you spell each word correctly?
- Did you use the correct forms of *good* and *bad*?

5 Publish
- Make a neat final copy, and add a good title.
- Read your story aloud to classmates.

Super Dog to the Rescue

Guidelines for Writing a Story

✓ Plan a plot that introduces a problem in the beginning. Show how the characters work it out at the end.
✓ Choose characters and settings that fit the story.
✓ Use details and dialogue to bring the story to life.

Composition Words

railroad
trouble
afternoon
skipped
weather
raced
special
sorry

Spelling |k|, |ng|, and |kw|

Read and Say

|k|
shark
jacket

Basic

READ the sentences. **SAY** each bold word.

	Basic	Sentence
1.	shark	What a big jaw the **shark** has!
2.	attack	The ants will **attack** our picnic.
3.	risk	To go outside in a storm is a **risk**.
4.	public	Anyone can use a **public** telephone.
5.	sink	Fill the **sink** and tub with water.
6.	question	Raise your hand to ask a **question**.
7.	electric	Is the **electric** mixer plugged into the wall?
8.	jacket	My new **jacket** keeps me warm.
9.	blank	Please write in the **blank** space.
10.	ache	I feel a dull **ache** in my back.
11.	crooked	The handle on this fork looks **crooked**.
12.	drink	I need a **drink** of water.
13.	topic	A **topic** sentence tells the main idea.
14.	track	Can a train run without a **track**?
15.	blanket	A thick **blanket** was on the bed.
16.	struck	The bat **struck** the baseball hard.
17.	mistake	I want to fix the **mistake** I made.
18.	junk	We threw out some old **junk**.
19.	squirrel	A small **squirrel** ran up the tree.
20.	stomach	This big lunch will fill my **stomach**.

Think and Write

Each word has one of these sounds:

|k| shar**k**, atta**ck**, publi**c** |ng| si**n**k |kw| **qu**estion

• What are three spellings for |k|? What letter spells |ng| before a *k*? What is one spelling for |kw|? How are the Elephant Words different?

Now write each Basic Word under the correct heading. Circle the words with the |ng| sound.

|k| → **ck**	|k| → **k or c**	**Other Spellings for** |k|	|kw|

Review	23. picnic	**Challenge**	28. barracuda
21. quick	24. week	26. aquatic	29. speckled
22. luck	25. sock	27. squid	30. peculiar

Independent Practice

> **Spelling Strategy**   Remember these spelling patterns for the |k|, |ng|, and |kw| sounds:
>
> |k| *k, ck, c* |ng| (before *k*)   n |kw| *qu*

Word Analysis/Phonics   Complete the exercises with Basic Words.

1–2. Write the present tense of *sank* and *drank*.

3–6. Write the word that rhymes with each word below.

   3. dark   **4.** luck   **5.** skunk   **6.** racket

7–8. Write *blank*. Then write another Basic Word that contains *blank*.

Vocabulary: Word Clues   Write the Basic Word that fits each clue.

   9. It eats nuts.   **12.** synonym for *pain*
   10. opposite of *answer*   **13.** A train needs one.
   11. where your food goes

Challenge Words   Write the Challenge Word that fits each meaning. Use your Spelling Dictionary.

   14. a long, narrow fish   **17.** not usual
   15. living in water   **18.** spotted
   16. a sea animal related
          to the octopus

Spelling-Meaning Connection

electric
electricity

How can you remember to spell the |s| sound in *electricity* with a *c*? Think of the related word *electric*. The sound of the *c* changes, but the spelling remains the same.

19–20. Write *electricity*. Then write the Basic Word that is related to *electricity* in spelling and meaning.

Dictionary

Stressed Syllables When you say the word *attack* aloud, which syllable do you stress, or say more strongly? The pronunciation shows the stressed syllable in dark print followed by an **accent mark (').**

at·tack |ə tăk′|

Practice Write each word below. Underline the stressed syllable in each word. Use the dictionary pronunciation.

1. public |**pŭb′** lĭk|
2. doctor |**dŏk′** tər|
3. unpack |ŭn **păk′**|
4. stomach |**stŭm′** ək|

5. blanket |**blăng′** kĭt|
6. crooked |**kroŏk′** ĭd|
7. agree |ə **grē′**|

You say you're full of stress?

Yes! I'm having an |ə tăk′| now!

Review: Spelling Spree

Familiar Phrases Write a Basic or Review Word to complete each phrase.

8. shoe and _____
9. a wish for good _____
10. pile of useless _____
11. bushy-tailed _____
12. sheets, pillow, and _____
13. kitchen _____
14. railroad _____
15. days of the _____
16. a bent and _____ stick
17. an _____ in a tooth
18. fill in the _____
19. the main _____ of a paragraph

20. a _____ basket
21. sleeves of a _____
22. ask a _____

☑ How Are You Doing?

Write each spelling word as a partner reads it aloud. Did you misspell any words?

Proofreading and Writing

Proofread for Spelling Find ten misspelled Basic or Review Words in this movie review. Write each one correctly.

Troubled Waters ★ ★ ★ ½

The movie *Troubled Waters* opened with a quik shot of a publick beach. Then the camera focused on Sue and Lena as they spread their blanket on the sand. Sue lay on her stomack, while Lena reached into the picnic basket for some juice to drik. Suddenly someone yelled that there had been a sharck attach! Panic struk the beach. The air became electrik with fear. Was it a misstake? Was there really a resk of danger?

Basic

1. shark
2. attack
3. risk
4. public
5. sink
6. question
7. electric
8. jacket
9. blank
10. ache
11. crooked
12. drink
13. topic
14. track
15. blanket
16. struck
17. mistake
18. junk
19. squirrel
20. stomach

Review
21. quick
22. luck
23. picnic
24. week
25. sock

Challenge
26. aquatic
27. squid
28. barracuda
29. speckled
30. peculiar

Write a Letter

You are entering your pet shark in a contest for the Pet of the Year. Write a letter to the judges, telling them why your shark should be chosen Pet of the Year. Try to use five spelling words.

SHARK OF THE YEAR

Proofreading Tip

Check for extra letters that have been added to words.

Proofreading Marks

¶ Indent
∧ Add
✂ Delete
≡ Capital letter
/ Small letter

Vocabulary Enrichment

Expanding Vocabulary

Building Words with -et and -let The suffixes -et and -let add the meaning "small" when they are added to the end of nouns. At one time a *jack* was a coat. What is a small or short coat?

jack + **et** = jack**et**

First, read each meaning. Then write a new word by adding -et or -let to each noun. Use your Spelling Dictionary.

a short book	= book +		→1. ?
a small drop	= drop +		→2. ?
a small package	= pack +	-et or -let	→3. ?
a small wave or ripple	= wave +		→4. ?
a small pig	= pig +		→5. ?
a small metal case for a picture	= lock +		→6. ?

Show You Know! For each picture write a sentence, using one word you built with -et or -let.

7.

8.

9.

Vocabulary Enrichment

Real-World Connection

Science: Sea Life All the words in the box relate to sea life. Look up these words in your Spelling Dictionary. Then write the words to complete this book of facts about the sea.

Spelling Word Link

shark

dolphin
octopus
sponge
eel
whale
oyster
clam
coral

Sea animals, like land animals, live in different surroundings.

- The hard-shell or soft-shell __(1)__ burrows in mud.
- The __(2)__ has hundreds of tiny holes.
- The __(3)__ is known for its pearls.
- Many sea animals attach themselves to __(4)__ reefs in warm seas.
- The snakelike __(5)__ and the eight-armed __(6)__ search for food along the ocean floor.
- Sea mammals, such as the giant blue __(7)__ and the smaller __(8)__, use the sea as their playground.

Try This CHALLENGE

Write Sea Similes Writers like to use expressions like "as happy as a clam" to describe people and things. These expressions are called **similes**. Write some sea similes. Use the phrase "as _____ as" in each sentence. Try to use words from the box.

Fact File

Coral reefs are formed from the skeletons of millions of tiny sea creatures. The largest coral reef is the Great Barrier Reef in Australia. It is about 1,250 miles long.

Read and Say

|ĭj| **cottage**
|j| **bridge**
|s| **fence**

Basic

READ the sentences. **SAY** each bold word.

1.	village	This **village** has only one store.
2.	cottage	Our **cottage** is smaller than your house.
3.	bridge	We walked on a **bridge** over the tracks.
4.	fence	Are the farm animals behind a **fence**?
5.	strange	It feels **strange** to eat lunch so late.
6.	chance	I have a good **chance** of winning the race.
7.	twice	Her family went back to the beach **twice**.
8.	cage	My bird needs time out of his **cage**.
9.	change	Do you have **change** for a dollar?
10.	carriage	The twins ride in the same **carriage**.
11.	glance	I took a quick **glance** at the list.
12.	ridge	They reached the **ridge** of the mountain.
13.	manage	The best leader will **manage** the team.
14.	damage	Did the storm **damage** your roof?
15.	since	I have long **since** forgotten the song.
16.	marriage	We wish the bride a happy **marriage**.
17.	edge	The knife has a sharp **edge**.
18.	lodge	How many can sleep in the **lodge**?
19.	cabbage	The salad has carrots and **cabbage**.
20.	dodge	The cars **dodge** in and out of the path.

Think and Write

Each word has a final |j| or |s| sound. Words with more than one syllable, such as *village,* end with the |ĭj| sounds.

|j| bri**dge**, stran**ge**　　　|ĭj| vill**age**　　　|s| fen**ce**

• What are two spelling patterns for |j|? Is the vowel sound long or short before the *dge* pattern? What is one spelling pattern for final |ĭj| in words with more than one syllable? What is one pattern for final |s|?

Now write each Basic Word under the correct heading.

|j| in One-Syllable Words	|ĭj| in Two-Syllable Words	Final |s|→*ce*

Review
21. nice
22. place
23. huge
24. judge
25. page

Challenge
26. fleece
27. fragrance
28. average
29. fringe
30. excellence

Independent Practice

Spelling Strategy

Remember these spelling patterns for the final |j|, |ĭj|, and |s| sounds:

|j| in a one-syllable word   *dge, ge*

|ĭj| in a word of more than one syllable   *age*

|s| *ce*

Word Analysis/Phonics Complete the exercises with Basic Words.

1–2. Write *chance.* Then change one letter in *chance* to write another word.

3–5. Write the three words that have the |ŏ| sound.

6–8. Write the word that begins with each consonant cluster.

    6. str   **7.** br   **8.** tw

Vocabulary: Classifying Write the Basic Word that fits with each group.

  9. city, town, _____   **12.** peak, slope, _____

10. lettuce, carrots, _____   **13.** coop, pen, _____

11. rim, border, _____

Challenge Words Write the Challenge Word that fits each meaning. Use your Spelling Dictionary.

14. usual or ordinary   **17.** high quality

15. a sheep's wool   **18.** shaggy border

16. pleasant scent

Spelling-Meaning Connection

Did you know that *carriage* comes from *carry*? These words are related in spelling and meaning. **Think of this:** The *carriage* will *carry* the people into town.

carry
carriage

19–20. Write *carry.* Then write the Basic Word that comes from *carry.*

Review: Spelling Spree

Puzzle Play Write a Basic or Review Word to fit each clue. Circle the letter that would appear in the box.

Example: part of a book _ _ _ □ *pag(e)*

1. two times □ _ _ _ _
2. possibility _ □ _ _ _ _
3. marks off areas _ _ _ _ □
4. rim or border _ _ □ _
5. giant _ _ _ □
6. quick look _ _ _ □ _ _
7. pleasant _ _ _ □
8. built above rivers _ □ _ _ _ _
9. coins _ _ □ _ _ _
10. to put _ □ _ _ _
11. before now □ _ _ _ _
12. odd _ □ _ _ _ _ _
13. cabin _ □ _ _ _
14. narrow peak □ _ _ _ _
15. jump aside _ _ _ _ □
16. person in a courtroom _ _ _ _ _

Mystery Words Write the circled letters in order. They spell three mystery words that name a building in a village.

_ _ _   _ _ _ _ _ _ _   _ _ _ _
 ?   ?   ?

Using Clues Write a Basic Word or Review Word that fits each clue.

Example: This *age* is round and red, white, or green.   *cabbage*

17. This *age* is in a book.
18. This *age* is in control.
19. This *age* is hurt.
20. This *age* is a small house.
21. This *age* is a vegetable.
22. This *age* carries people.
23. This *age* can keep birds.
24. This *age* is a small town.
25. This *age* joins husband and wife.

How Are You Doing?

Write your spelling words in ABC order. Practice any misspelled words with a family member.

Proofreading and Writing

Proofread: Spelling and Commas in a Series A **series** is a list of three or more items in a sentence. Use a comma after each item except the last.

The houses were made of wood, brick, or stone.

Find four misspelled Basic or Review Words and two missing commas in this travel guide. Write the travel guide correctly.

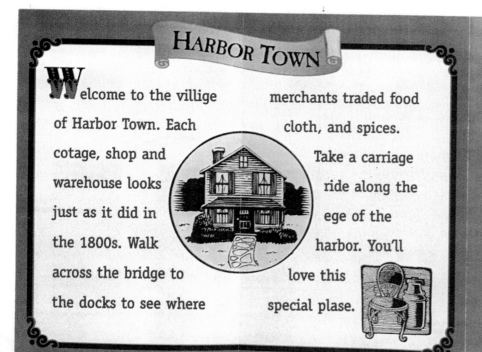

HARBOR TOWN

Welcome to the villige of Harbor Town. Each cotage, shop and warehouse looks just as it did in the 1800s. Walk across the bridge to the docks to see where merchants traded food cloth, and spices. Take a carriage ride along the ege of the harbor. You'll love this special plase.

Basic

1. village
2. cottage
3. bridge
4. fence
5. strange
6. chance
7. twice
8. cage
9. change
10. carriage
11. glance
12. ridge
13. manage
14. damage
15. since
16. marriage
17. edge
18. lodge
19. cabbage
20. dodge

Review

21. nice
22. place
23. huge
24. judge
25. page

Challenge

26. fleece
27. fragrance
28. average
29. fringe
30. excellence

Write an Opinion

Would you rather live in a small village or a big city? Write a paragraph about your choice, giving reasons to support it. Try to use five spelling words and at least one series of three or more items.

Proofreading Marks

¶ Indent
∧ Add
‿ Delete
≡ Capital letter
/ Small letter

Proofreading Tip **Check that you used a comma after each item in a series except the last.**

Unit 20 BONUS

Expanding Vocabulary

Spelling Word Link

change

Multiple Meanings for *change* Like many words, *change* has more than one meaning. The dictionary entry below gives three meanings. Suppose the weather report says "No change." Which of the three definitions of *change* is meant?

> **change** |chānj| *n., pl.* **changes 1.** The act or result of becoming different. **2.** The money returned when the amount given to pay for something is more than what is owed. **3.** Coins.

Write the number of the definition of *change* that goes with each sentence. Use the dictionary entry.

1. We had a change of plans.
2. You will need change to use the public telephone.
3. There will be a change in the weather by Saturday.
4. I counted the change that I got back from the clerk.
5. I put my loose change in a big jar at the end of the week.

6.

Work Together With a partner write a caption for each picture. Use *change* in each sentence.

7.

Vocabulary Enrichment

Real-World Connection

Social Studies: Villages All the words in the box relate to villages. Look up these words in your Spelling Dictionary. Then write the words to complete this part of a story.

Spelling Word Link

village

cobblestones
thatched
steeple
hearth
pasture
ivy
country
latch

ob lifted the ___(1)___ on the wooden gate and left the ___(2)___ where the family's cows grazed. He walked quickly along the village path paved with ___(3)___. The clock in the church ___(4)___ struck six. Already it was getting dark. Autumn came early in this part of the ___(5)___. The ___(6)___ climbing on the cottage walls had already turned red. Rob could see the ___(7)___ roof of his cottage. How he longed for its warm and cozy ___(8)___!

Try This

CHALLENGE

Yes or No? Write *yes* or *no* to answer each question.

9. Could a roof be made of cobblestones?
10. Should a hearth be made of wood?
11. Could you find a pasture in the country?
12. Could a thatched roof catch on fire?

 Fact File

Old Sturbridge Village in Massachusetts shows how people lived and worked between 1790 and 1840. It includes homes, shops, a school, farmland, and other features of village life.

Words with Prefixes

Read and Say

re paint

Basic

READ the sentences. **SAY** each bold word.

1. repaint — We will **repaint** our house red.
2. redo — You cannot **redo** your own work.
3. refill — Please **refill** my glass with milk.
4. rebuild — We can **rebuild** your house after the flood.
5. discolor — Will the sun **discolor** the curtain?
6. untidy — Her **untidy** desk was full of old papers.
7. dislike — I **dislike** the chore of washing dishes.
8. uneven — A bumpy road is very **uneven**.
9. rewind — Turn the key to **rewind** the toy.
10. unlucky — I do not win when I feel **unlucky**.
11. reread — I had to **reread** the page five times.
12. unsure — She feels **unsure** of what to do next.
13. reheat — You can **reheat** the meat in the oven.
14. unpack — Did you **unpack** that box of books?
15. unpaid — Will five dollars cover the **unpaid** bill?
16. distrust — The dogs **distrust** any stranger.
17. recount — I can **recount** every day of our trip.
18. displease — Cold steak will **displease** the chef.
19. unload — Did the men **unload** the moving van?
20. disorder — Noise and **disorder** filled the room.

Think and Write

A **prefix** is added to the beginning of a base word. It adds meaning.

re	+	paint	=	**re**paint	paint again
dis	+	like	=	**dis**like	not like
un	+	even	=	**un**even	not even
un	+	pack	=	**un**pack	opposite of *pack*

• What three prefixes do you see? What do they mean?

Now write each Basic Word under its prefix.

re-	dis-	un-	-

Review
21. remake
22. unclear
23. rewrite
24. unfair
25. unkind

Challenge
26. redecorate
27. unfamiliar
28. unusual
29. rearrange
30. discontinue

Independent Practice

Spelling Strategy A **prefix** is a word part added to the beginning of a base word. It adds meaning to the word. *Un-, re-,* and *dis-* are prefixes. First, find the prefix and the base word. Then remember to spell the word by parts.

Word Analysis/Phonics Complete the exercises with Basic Words.

1–3. Write the three words with the |ē| sound spelled *ea*.

4–7. Write a Basic Word by adding a prefix.

    4. trust   **5.** lucky   **6.** like   **7.** fill

Vocabulary: Synonyms Write the Basic Word that means the same as each word below.

  8. crooked
  9. messy
10. confusion
11. stain
12. uncertain
13. reconstruct

Challenge Words Write the Challenge Words to complete the paragraph. Use your Spelling Dictionary.

    When we decided to __(14)__ our living room, we hired a decorator to help us choose the wallpaper. However, she was __(15)__ with our tastes. She put up wallpaper so __(16)__ that even the factory wants to __(17)__ it. Next time we will just __(18)__ the furniture!

Spelling-Meaning Connection

undo
redo

Did you know that different prefixes can be added to the same base word to form new words that are related in spelling and meaning?
Think of this: Please *undo* the knot, and *redo* it more tightly.

19–20. Write *undo* and *redo*. Then circle the base word that appears in both words.

Dictionary

Prefixes Where can you find the meaning of *unafraid*? Some words with prefixes are not listed as entry words in the dictionary. However, prefixes have separate entries. Look up the prefix and the base word, and combine the two meanings.

> **un-** A prefix that means: **1.** Not: *unable; unbecoming.* **2.** Lack of: *unemployment.* **3.** To do the opposite of: *unlock.*

Which meaning of *un-* is used in the word *unafraid*?

Practice Write the answer to each question.
1. What is the first meaning of *un-*?
2. What sample word is given in the third meaning?

Write the prefix and the base word you would look up to find the meaning of each word below.

3–4. untrue   **5–6.** rewrite   **7–8.** reopen   **9–10.** unbutton

Review: Spelling Spree

Base Word Hunt Write a Basic or Review Word that has the same base word as each word below.

11. kindness	**17.** luckily	**23.** pleased	**26.** unlike
12. writer	**18.** filling	**24.** reader	**27.** clearly
13. reorder	**19.** trusted	**25.** building	**28.** surely
14. repack	**20.** fairness		
15. prepaid	**21.** colorful		
16. discount	**22.** loading		

How Are You Doing?

List the spelling words that are hard for you. Practice them with a family member.

Proofreading and Writing

Proofread for Spelling Find seven misspelled Basic or Review Words in this list. Write each one correctly.

Things to Do Today

- Take out and redoo hem on Nikki's skirt.

- Buy more clay, and remak pot to enter in crafts show.

- Rebuild unevin bookshelf, and repant it.

- Straighten out untidie sewing box. Untangle balls of yarn, and rewinde them.

- Reread instructions on how to reheet wax to make candles.

Basic

1. repaint
2. redo
3. refill
4. rebuild
5. discolor
6. untidy
7. dislike
8. uneven
9. rewind
10. unlucky
11. reread
12. unsure
13. reheat
14. unpack
15. unpaid
16. distrust
17. recount
18. displease
19. unload
20. disorder

Review

21. remake
22. unclear
23. rewrite
24. unfair
25. unkind

Challenge

26. redecorate
27. unfamiliar
28. unusual
29. rearrange
30. discontinue

Write a List

Projects List

Have you noticed things that need to be done at your school or at home? Write a list of these projects. Try to use five spelling words.

Read your paper aloud to a friend. Sometimes you notice mistakes more easily when you hear them.

Proofreading Tip

Proofreading Marks

¶ Indent
∧ Add
ℰ Delete
≡ Capital letter
/ Small letter

Vocabulary Enrichment

Expanding Vocabulary

Building Words with -able The suffix -able can be added to the end of a verb to form an adjective. It means "capable of" or "able to."

refill + able = refill**able**   "capable of being refilled"

Combine each word in the circle with -able. Write the new adjective.

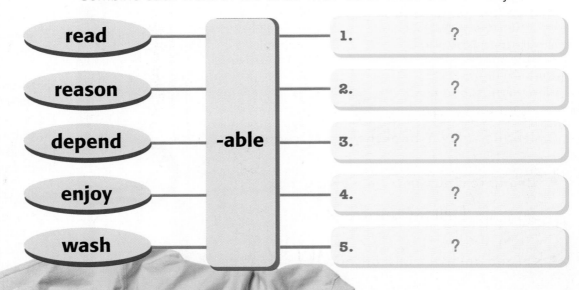

read

reason

depend

enjoy

wash

-able

1.   ?

2.   ?

3.   ?

4.   ?

5.   ?

Show You Know! Complete each sentence by writing a word that you built with -able.

6. You will find a _____ answer if you think things through carefully.
7. If the buses were _____, they would be here on time.
8. Do the children find a sunny day at the beach _____?
9. This shirt is easy to keep clean because it is _____.
10. Print each letter clearly so that your sentences are _____.

Vocabulary Enrichment

Real-World Connection

Art: Crafts All the words in the box relate to crafts. Look up these words in your Spelling Dictionary. Then write the words to complete this part of a letter.

Spelling Word Link

repaint

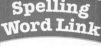

whittling
pottery
collage
quilting
embroidery
weaving
stenciling
batik

Dear Uncle Jim,

I wish you had been here last week. My art class held a crafts fair in the gym. We set up a loom for __(1)__. Kim brought in some clay to make __(2)__. We had materials for pasting together a __(3)__. Joe displayed cutouts for __(4)__ letters and designs with ink. We also provided carving tools and wood for __(5)__. I sewed together padded squares of cloth to show how __(6)__ is done. Jane used tiny stitches to make an __(7)__ of a house. Cara used melted wax and colorful dyes to show the art of __(8)__.

You would have enjoyed seeing the talents of our class.

Love,
Teresa

Try This CHALLENGE

Clue Match Write the word that names the craft in which each tool or material is used.

9. wax   **10.** wood   **11.** paste   **12.** kiln or oven

⭐ **Fact File**

The Pennsylvania Dutch are a group of people known for their simple way of life and fine crafts. Colorful designs of birds, hearts, and tulips decorate their barns and handicrafts.

VCCV Pattern

Read and Say

vc|cv
hel|met
pic|ture

Basic

READ the sentences. **SAY** each bold word.

1.	picture	Draw a **picture** of your family.
2.	person	Every **person** has the right to speak.
3.	perfect	The mirror shows a **perfect** reflection.
4.	attend	Ten people will **attend** the meeting.
5.	number	Is the **number** greater than five?
6.	support	He uses a cane to **support** himself.
7.	common	Bicycles are **common** in the park.
8.	welcome	Who will greet and **welcome** visitors?
9.	offer	I **offer** you this homemade bread.
10.	expert	The chef is an **expert** on baking fish.
11.	harvest	The farmer will **harvest** the corn crop.
12.	survive	Roses cannot **survive** a frost.
13.	suppose	I am not sure, but I **suppose** I can go.
14.	perform	You must **perform** your duties quickly.
15.	escape	The bird will **escape** if you open the door.
16.	helmet	A **helmet** protects a football player's head.
17.	allow	Please **allow** me to carry your books.
18.	fellow	Is this **fellow** the man you met in China?
19.	barber	My hair was cut by a **barber**.
20.	tender	Grandmother gave me a **tender** hug.

Think and Write

Each word has the vowel-consonant-consonant-vowel (VCCV) pattern.
Divide between the consonants to find the syllables.

VC	CV	VC	CV
per	**son**	**at**	**tend**

• Where is each word in the list divided into syllables?

**Now write each Basic Word under the heading that tells where
its syllables divide. Draw a line between its syllables.**

Between Double Consonants	Between Different Consonants

Review			**Challenge**	
21. lesson	23. yellow		26. filter	28. disturb
22. until	24. hello		27. candid	29. narrate
	25. garden			30. rascal

Independent Practice

Spelling Strategy   To spell a word with the VCCV syllable pattern, divide the word between the consonants. Look for patterns you have learned, and spell the word by syllables.

Word Analysis/Phonics Complete the exercises with Basic Words.

1–2. Write the two words that have a double *l*.

3–5. Write the three words that have a long vowel sound spelled vowel-consonant-*e*.

Vocabulary: Definitions Write the Basic Word that fits each meaning.

6. usual or ordinary

7. a human being

8. to bring in crops

9. a numeral

10. a photograph or drawing

11. to hold something up

12. someone who cuts hair

13. something worn to protect the head

Challenge Words Write the Challenge Word that completes each sentence. Use your Spelling Dictionary.

14. Do not _____ me while I am taking the picture.

15. Look at the pictures as I _____ the story.

16. Your surprise is really captured in this _____ picture.

17. You looked like such a _____ when you made that face!

18. I used a red _____ to block out red light waves.

Spelling-Meaning Connection

How can you remember how to spell the |ĭ| sound in *perfect*? Think of the |ĕ| sound in the related word *perfection*.

19–20. Write *perfect* and *perfection*. Then underline the letter in *perfection* that helps you spell the |ĭ| sound in *perfect*.

perfect
perfection

Review: Spelling Spree

Syllable Addition Write a Basic or Review Word by combining the underlined syllables in each pair of words.

Example: <u>at</u>tack + pre<u>tend</u>   *attend*

1. <u>sup</u>ply + re<u>port</u>
2. <u>sur</u>face + re<u>vive</u>
3. <u>per</u>fume + in<u>fect</u>
4. <u>per</u>mit + in<u>form</u>
5. <u>gar</u>lic + sud<u>den</u>
6. <u>of</u>fice + pre<u>fer</u>
7. <u>ten</u>nis + <u>un</u>der
8. <u>pic</u>nic + na<u>ture</u>

Code Breaker Some Basic and Review Words are written in code. The slides will help you crack the code. First, find the code on the slides. Then use the letters inside the slides to write the words correctly.

Example: ftdbqf   *escape*

9. ifmmp
10. voujm
11. gfmmpx
12. tvqqptf
13. ibswftu
14. ovncfs
15. dpnnpo
16. buufoe
17. qfstpo
18. zfmmpx
19. cbscfs
20. ifmnfu
21. bmmpx
22. fyqfsu
23. xfmdpnf
24. ftdbqf
25. mfttpo

How Are You Doing?

Write each spelling word in a sentence. Practice any misspelled spelling words with a partner.

Proofreading and Writing

Proofread: Spelling and Introductory Words Use a comma to set off *yes, no,* and *well* at the beginning of a sentence. Otherwise, the meaning of the sentence may change.

No, photos should be saved.　　No photos should be saved.

Find four misspelled Basic or Review Words and two missing commas in this part of Andy's letter. Write the letter correctly.

Dear Tom,

Yes I finally entered a picher in the photo contest. The prize is a lessen with an exspert. Well I suppose that I would welcome the advice. My photos are hardly perfict!

Your friend,

Andy

Basic

1. picture
2. person
3. perfect
4. attend
5. number
6. support
7. common
8. welcome
9. offer
10. expert
11. harvest
12. survive
13. suppose
14. perform
15. escape
16. helmet
17. allow
18. fellow
19. barber
20. tender

Review

21. lesson
22. until
23. yellow
24. hello
25. garden

Challenge

26. filter
27. candid
28. disturb
29. narrate
30. rascal

Write a Note

You received a birthday invitation. Write a note, telling whether or not you can go. Try to use five spelling words and at least one introductory word.

Proofreading Tip **Check that you used commas correctly after the introductory words *yes*, *no*, and *well*.**

Proofreading Marks

¶　Indent
∧　Add
⌒　Delete
≡　Capital letter
／　Small letter

Expanding Vocabulary

Spelling Word Link

attend

Building Word Families: attend You can build several words from the base word *attend*. In some words, however, the spelling of the final *d* changes to *t* when a suffix is added.

Copy the "web." Write a word to combine *attend* and the suffix inside each arrow. Use your Spelling Dictionary. (The first one has been done for you.) Then write a sentence for each new word.

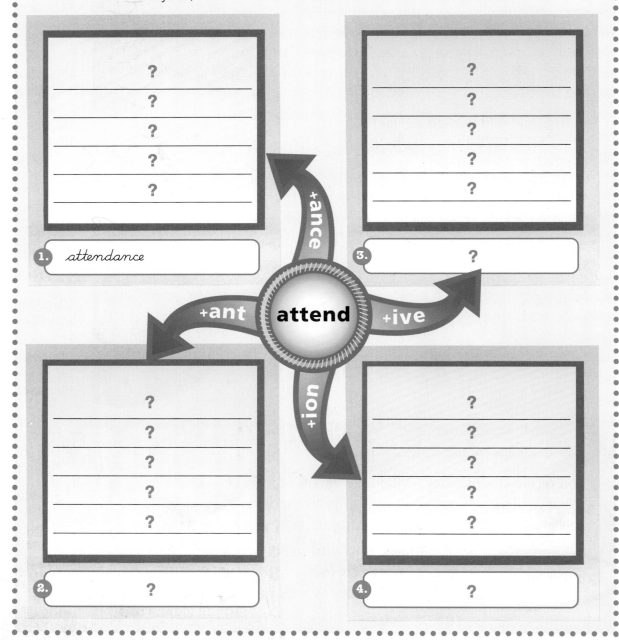

1. attendance

?
?
?
?
?

3. ?

?
?
?
?
?

+ance

+ant   attend   +ive

+ion

2. ?

?
?
?
?
?

4. ?

?
?
?
?
?

Real-World Connection

Art: Photography All the words in the box relate to photography. Look up these words in your Spelling Dictionary. Write the words to complete this page from a book and label the diagram.

Spelling Word Link

picture

portrait
lens
shutter
film
pose
flash
develop
darkroom

The Art of Photography

In the business world, photographers are masters in their studios. They do not just take a picture. They create a ___(1)___. These experts know how to set up their equipment perfectly and make sure that their subjects sit in a natural ___(2)___. Then once they take the shots, the real work begins.

In the total darkness of a well-equipped ___(3)___, they ___(4)___ each shot. Suddenly an image appears just like magic!

5. **Load each roll into the camera carefully.**
6. **Attach this when you need more light.**
7. **This allows light to come inside the camera.**
8. **Focus this so that pictures are clear and bright.**

Try This CHALLENGE

Yes or No? Write *yes* if the underlined word is used correctly. Write *no* if it is not.

9. My father <u>lens</u> me his camera sometimes.
10. Brett mixed chemicals to <u>develop</u> the film.
11. My mother bought a pretty frame for my <u>pose</u>.
12. The wrong <u>shutter</u> speed may let in too much light.

 Fact File

Dorothea Lange was a photographer who became famous for her pictures of people. Her photos showed the problems of the poor and the hardships of wartime.

VCCV Pattern

Read and Say

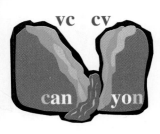

vc cv

can yon

Basic

READ the sentences. **SAY** each bold word.

1. current — Is the **current** of the river flowing east?
2. danger — Cars are a **danger** to deer in the park.
3. canyon — At the base of the **canyon** is a creek.
4. plastic — The **plastic** flowers look real.
5. bottom — Fish swim on the **bottom** of ponds.
6. hollow — The tree trunk is **hollow**.
7. member — She is a new **member** of our team.
8. borrow — May I **borrow** a book just for today?
9. organ — An **organ** has keys like a piano does.
10. compose — Artists and poets **compose** their work.
11. lumber — The **lumber** was cut from oak trees.
12. seldom — He **seldom** bothers to ask for help.
13. engine — The new car has a quiet **engine**.
14. pillow — Rest your head on a **pillow**.
15. carpet — Do not cover the floor with a **carpet**.
16. garbage — Throw the **garbage** into a trash can.
17. master — Will the cats listen to their **master**?
18. arrow — The tip of an **arrow** is sharp.
19. army — The **army** trains its new troops.
20. thirty — Three times ten is **thirty**.

Think and Write

Each two-syllable word has the VCCV pattern. Divide each word into syllables between the consonants. Look for patterns you have learned. Spell the words by syllables.

VC | CV	VC | CV	VC | CV
cur | rent	**dan | ger**	**can | yon**

• Where is each word in the list divided into syllables?

Now write each Basic Word under the heading that tells where its syllables are divided. Draw a line between its syllables.

Between Double Consonants   **Between Different Consonants**

Review   23. enjoy
21. sudden   24. happen
22. follow   25. forget

Challenge   28. submerge
26. challenge   29. eddy
27. vessel   30. venture

Independent Practice

 **Spelling Strategy**   To spell a word with the VCCV syllable pattern, divide the word between the consonants. Look for patterns you have learned, and spell the word by syllables.

Word Analysis/Phonics Complete the exercises with Basic Words.

1–4. Write the four words that end with the |ər| sounds spelled *er*.

5–8. Write the word that rhymes with each word below.

    5. follow   **6.** narrow   **7.** willow   **8.** sorrow

Vocabulary: Analogies Write the Basic Word that completes each analogy.

  9. *Always* is to *never* as *often* is to _____.

10. *Sailors* are to *navy* as *soldiers* are to _____.

11. *Table* is to *tablecloth* as *floor* is to _____.

12. *Nine* is to *ten* as *twenty-nine* is to _____.

13. *Attic* is to *top* as *basement* is to _____.

Challenge Words Write the Challenge Word that fits each meaning. Use your Spelling Dictionary.

14. a task that is risky   **17.** a current of water or air

15. to cover with water   **18.** a call to take part in a contest

16. a large boat

Spelling-Meaning Connection

compose

composition

How can you remember that the first schwa sound in *composition* is spelled with an *o*?
Think of the |ō| sound in the related word *compose*.

19–20. Write *composition*. Then write the Basic Word that is related to *composition* in spelling and meaning.

Dictionary

Word Histories How can you find out where a word comes from? A dictionary may give a **word history** that tells what language or languages a word comes from and what it originally meant.

> **History**
>
> **Current** comes from a Latin word meaning "running." A current is something that runs or flows, such as a river current.

Practice Write the answer to each question.
1. What language does the word *current* come from?
2. What did the word originally mean?

Look up each word below in your Spelling Dictionary. Read the word history. First, write the language the word comes from. Then write the original meaning of the word.

3–4. magazine   **5–6.** porcupine

Review: Spelling Spree

Alphabet Puzzler Write the Basic or Review Word that would appear alphabetically between each pair of words below.

7. both, _____, bought
8. swap, _____, under
9. arrive, _____, art
10. found, _____, hair
11. sand, _____, submarine
12. know, _____, lump
13. never, _____, person
14. camp, _____, cap
15. pile, _____, pilot
16. folder, _____, fool
17. armor, _____, arrange
18. many, _____, match
19. cape, _____, cat
20. end, _____, engulf

21. collar, _____, cost
22. holiday, _____, icy
23. border, _____, boss
24. plain, _____, platter

How Are You Doing?

Write each spelling word as a partner reads it aloud. Did you misspell any words?

Proofreading and Writing

Proofread for Spelling Find seven misspelled Basic or Review Words in this journal entry. Write each one correctly.

June 27

I will never ferget today. I have seldom had more fun. I went rafting on Big River. First, each group membor put on a life jacket. Our guide told us to follow her directions to avoid danjer. She said to hold on and injoy what was about to hapen. All of a suddin, the curent pulled us into white water. I was soaked!

Basic

1. current
2. danger
3. canyon
4. plastic
5. bottom
6. hollow
7. member
8. borrow
9. organ
10. compose
11. lumber
12. seldom
13. engine
14. pillow
15. carpet
16. garbage
17. master
18. arrow
19. army
20. thirty

Review

21. sudden
22. follow
23. enjoy
24. happen
25. forget

Challenge

26. challenge
27. vessel
28. submerge
29. eddy
30. venture

Write Bumper Stickers

Travel to the canyon with
Joe's Canoe Service.

Write sentences that can be used as bumper stickers. Try to use five spelling words. You may want to share your work with a classmate.

Proofreading Tip

Circle any word that you think might be misspelled. Then look up its spelling in the dictionary.

Proofreading Marks

- ¶ Indent
- ∧ Add
- Delete
- ≡ Capital letter
- / Small letter

Expanding Vocabulary

alligator
ranch
vanilla
lasso
hurricane
burro

Words from Spanish Do you know where the word *canyon* comes from? Many English words were borrowed from Spanish.

English word: **canyon**   Spanish word: **cañon**

Write a word from the box to match each picture. Use the numbered clues, the Spanish word in ( ), and your Spelling Dictionary for help.

1. It means "a long rope."   (*el lazo*)
2. It means "a special kind of farm."   (*el rancho*)
3. It means "a large reptile."   (*el lagarto*)
4. It means "a strong windstorm."   (*el huracán*)
5. It means "a small donkey."   (*el borrico*)
6. It means "a flavoring."   (*la vainilla*)

1. ?

2. ?

3. ?

4. ?

5. ?

6. ?

Work Together With a partner write a sentence for each picture, using the word you wrote.

Real-World Connection

Recreation: White-Water Rafting All the words in the box relate to white-water rafting. Look up these words in your Spelling Dictionary. Then write the words to complete this ad.

Spelling Word Link

current

raft
rapids
paddle
whirlpool
swift
gorge
steer
launch

WHITEWATER RAFTING • WHITEWATER RAFTING

With a shove of a long plastic ___(1)___, your experienced guide helps you move the large rubber ___(2)___ into the water to ___(3)___ it. Your guide then jumps in and begins to guide and ___(4)___ the boat into the ___(5)___ current. She may have to pull quickly to one side to avoid a spinning ___(6)___. Your real adventure lies up ahead when the river rounds a bend and enters a narrow ___(7)___. Beyond the bend are the biggest ___(8)___ your team will ever face. You will need to brace yourself for the rough ride.

WHITEWATER RAFTING • WHITEWATER RAFTING • WHITEWATER RAFTING

Try This CHALLENGE

Clue Match Write a word from the box to match each clue.

9. If a rowboat needs oars, a canoe needs this.
10. It has high walls on both sides.
11. Its rotating water could make you dizzy.
12. If you do not do this, your boat will stay on land.

★★ Fact File

The Colorado River is a popular river for white-water rafting, especially through the Grand Canyon. Its big rapids have such names as Last Chance Rapid.

24 Review: Units 19–23

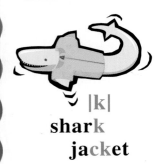

|k|
shark
jacket

Unit 19   Spelling |k|, |ng|, and |kw| pages 120–125

electric	question	jacket	sink	ache
blanket	mistake	squirrel	track	stomach

Spelling Strategy

|k| → **k, ck, c** |ng| → **n** before **k** |kw| → **qu**

Write the word that fits each clue below.

1. something asked
2. used on a bed
3. climbs trees
4. a short coat
5. rhymes with *rink*
6. rhymes with *stack*

Write the word that completes each sentence.

7. Joshua ate apples until his _____ was full.
8. Did your legs _____ after all that walking?
9. Our kitchen has an _____ stove instead of a gas stove.
10. I made a careless _____ on my homework.

|ĭj| **cottage**
|j| **bridge**
|s| **fence**

Unit 20   Final |j| and |s| pages 126–131

change	bridge	twice	strange	carriage
damage	edge	glance	since	lodge

Spelling Strategy

|j| → **dge**, **ge** (one-syllable words) |s| → **ce**
|ĭj| → **age** (two-syllable words)

Write the word that rhymes with each word below.

11. hedge   12. mice   13. mince   14. dodge   15. chance

Write the word that fits each meaning.

16. to make different
17. to harm
18. a vehicle with wheels that is used for carrying passengers
19. unfamiliar
20. a structure built over a river so that people or cars can cross from one side to the other

Unit 21   Words with Prefixes   pages 132–137

| unlucky | uneven | rebuild | dislike | repaint |
| recount | unload | disorder | unsure | displease |

Spelling Strategy   A **prefix** is a word part added to the beginning of a base word. It adds meaning to the word. **Un-**, **re-**, and **dis-** are prefixes.

Write a word by changing the underlined prefix.
21. <u>re</u>order   **22.** <u>un</u>like   **23.** <u>mis</u>count   **24.** <u>re</u>load

Write a word by adding a prefix to each base word.
25. lucky   **26.** sure   **27.** please

Write the word that completes each sentence.
28. Those pieces of lumber are rough and _____.
29. We will _____ the porch so that it will be sturdy.
30. Can you _____ the woodwork to match the wallpaper?

Unit 22   VCCV Pattern   pages 138–143

| expert | common | picture | welcome | perfect |
| barber | allow | escape | perform | survive |

vc|cv
hel|met
pic|ture

Spelling Strategy   To spell a word with the VCCV syllable pattern, divide the word between the consonants.

Write the word that completes each analogy.
31. *Teeth* is to *dentist* as *hair* is to _____.
32. *Writer* is to *story* as *artist* is to _____.
33. *Appearance* is to *appear* as *performance* is to _____.
34. *Rough* is to *smooth* as *unusual* is to _____.

Write the word that matches each meaning.
35. to stay alive   **37.** to permit   **39.** having no mistakes
36. to get free   **38.** to greet   **40.** having special skills

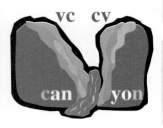

Unit 23 **VCCV Pattern** pages 144–149

canyon	organ	compose	danger	borrow
army	carpet	garbage	seldom	arrow

Spelling Strategy To spell a word with the VCCV syllable pattern, divide the word between the consonants. Look for patterns you have learned, and spell the word by syllables.

Write the word that completes each phrase.

41. to take out the _____

42. a bow and _____

43. lend and _____

44. a soldier in the _____

45. the steep walls of a _____

Write the word that belongs in each group.

46. write, create, _____

47. often, _____, never

48. risk, hazard, _____

49. trumpet, piano, _____

50. tile, rug, _____

Challenge Words **Units 19–23** pages 120–149

unfamiliar	redecorate	challenge	average	narrate
excellence	barracuda	speckled	submerge	disturb

Write the word that means the opposite of each phrase.

51. well known

52. to leave in peace

53. not ordinary

54. to surface

55. a task of little difficulty

Write the word that fits each clue.

56. It is a way to tell a story.

57. It stands for the highest quality.

58. It describes a sparrow's spotted feathers.

59. It has sharp teeth.

60. It is something you do to a room.

Spelling-Meaning Strategy

Vowel Changes: Schwa to Long Vowel Sound

supposition
suppose

Unfamiliar words that at first seem difficult to spell may seem easier if you think about related words that you already know. Read this paragraph.

> Let's **suppose** that each child in the school will bring two people to the fair. Based on that **supposition**, how many people should we expect?

Think

- What does *suppose* mean? What does *supposition* mean? How are they related in meaning?
- What vowel sound does the letter *o* spell in each word?

Here are more related words in which the same letter spells a schwa sound in one word and a long vowel sound in the other.

adm**i**ration	rel**a**tive	def**i**nition
adm**i**re	rel**a**te	def**i**ne

Apply and Extend

Complete these activities on a separate sheet of paper.

1. Use your Spelling Dictionary to look up the words in the box above. Write six sentences, using each word.
2. With a partner, list as many words as you can that are related to *suppose*, *admire*, *relate*, and *define*. Then look at the section "Vowel Changes: Schwa to Long Vowel Sound" beginning on page 274 of your Spelling-Meaning Index. Add to your list any other words that you find in these families.

Summing Up

You can remember how to spell the schwa sound in some words by thinking of a related word with a long vowel sound spelled the same way.

from

The
Once-A-Year Day

by Eve Bunting

Annie could have an orange only once a year—on the special day when supplies came to her Alaskan village. What did the orange taste like to Annie?

Annie cradled the orange in her hands. She walked slowly behind the store and sat facing the bay. Then she closed her eyes, lifted the orange to her nose, and breathed of it. "California," she thought. In her hands, she held the sunshine, the warmth, the groves of orange trees, the blue of the ocean, and the wonder of the land she had learned of in school but might never see.

The day was shimmering to an end, the special day. She bit into the peel, tasting the first bitter oil, feeling it sting her tongue. She nibbled at the white beneath the peel and then placed the piece of skin carefully in her pocket. Later, she could take it out, smell, and remember. Little by little, she peeled the orange till its pale, tender roundness lay free in her hand. She pulled off one section and sank her teeth in. Oh, it was good. It was good beyond believing! Drops stung her chin, stickied her fingers. It was like eating summer.

Think and Discuss

1 Sense words appeal to the five senses. What sense words help you taste the orange? feel the juice?

2 What exact words tell you that Annie did not hurry to eat the orange?

3 What details about the orange does the author tell first? next?

The Writing Process

Description

Think of your favorite people, animals, places, or things. Write a description of one of them. Keep the guidelines in mind, and follow the Writing Process.

1 Prewriting
- Make a chart naming the five senses. List sense words to describe your subject.

2 Draft
- Write sentences that describe your subject. Put them in an order that makes sense.

3 Revise
- Write two more opening sentences. Choose the most interesting one.
- Use your Thesaurus to find exact words.
- Have a writing conference. Draw pictures of each other's descriptions. Are the details clear?

4 Proofread
- Did you spell each word correctly?
- Did you use commas correctly?

5 Publish
- Make a neat final copy, and add a good title.
- Record your description with sound effects.

Guidelines for Writing a Description

✓ Open with an interesting topic sentence.
✓ Use details to create a clear picture.
✓ Use sense words, exact words, and comparisons.
✓ Put the details in an order that is clear.

Composition Words

crooked
picture
mistake
number
uneven
hollow
untidy
perfect

My Favorite Mountain Memories

CASSETTE
3

LADO
B

© 1997 Houghton Mifflin Company. All rights reserved. 1-55093-2

Changing Final *y* to *i*

Read and Say

Basic

READ the sentences. **SAY** each bold word.

1. sunnier — It will be **sunnier** after the clouds pass.
2. cloudier — It will rain if the sky grows **cloudier**.
3. windier — You need a much **windier** day to fly a kite.
4. cities — Are **cities** larger than towns?
5. heaviest — This box is the **heaviest** one to lift.
6. prettiest — Roses are the **prettiest** flowers of all.
7. studied — We read and **studied** all about foods.
8. easier — Work is **easier** if you ask for help.
9. noisier — Barking dogs are **noisier** than cats.
10. families — Each of the **families** has one child.
11. ferries — People cross the river on **ferries**.
12. crazier — Monkeys act **crazier** than a clown.
13. funnier — Is my joke **funnier** than yours?
14. earlier — I leave five minutes **earlier** than you.
15. copied — She **copied** every word by hand.
16. hobbies — One of his **hobbies** is fishing.
17. angriest — The **angriest** workers quit their jobs.
18. emptied — A dump truck **emptied** the dirt here.
19. worried — The storm **worried** my father.
20. happiest — The **happiest** child laughs and plays.

Think and Write

Each word has the ending *-es*, *-ed*, *-er*, or *-est*.

city + es = cit**ies**   study + ed = stud**ied**
sunny + er = sunn**ier**   heavy + est = heav**iest**

• Does a vowel or a consonant come before the final *y* in each base word? How does the spelling of the base word change when an ending is added?

Now write each Basic Word under its ending.

-es or *-ed*	*-er* or *-est*

Review
21. hurried
22. stories
23. carried
24. pennies
25. babies

Challenge
26. iciest
27. hazier
28. breezier
29. categories
30. qualities

Independent Practice

Spelling Strategy If a word ends with a consonant and *y*, change the *y* to *i* when adding *-es*, *-ed*, *-er*, or *-est*.

Word Analysis/Phonics Complete the exercises with Basic Words.

1–3. Write the past tense of each word below.

    1. study   **2.** copy   **3.** worry

4–7. Write the plural of each word below.

    4. city   **5.** ferry   **6.** family   **7.** hobby

Vocabulary: Opposites Write the Basic Word that means the opposite of each word below.

  8. filled

  9. quieter

10. lightest

11. ugliest

12. saddest

13. harder

Challenge Words Write the Challenge Word that completes each sentence. Use your Spelling Dictionary.

14. Because of the sea winds, it is _____ near the ocean.

15. The fog from the sea made the air even _____.

16. Different kinds of clouds can be classified into _____.

17. The types of clouds have different features, or _____.

18. When it snows, this back road is the _____ one in town.

Spelling-Meaning Connection

easy
easier
easiest
easily

Endings can be added to *easy* to form *easier*, *easiest*, and *easily*. These new words are related to *easy* in spelling and meaning.

Think of this: You can complete an *easy* chore *easily*.

19–20. Write *easy*. Then write the Basic Word that is related to *easy* in spelling and meaning.

Review: Spelling Spree

Adding Endings Write the Basic or Review Word that combines each base word and ending.

Example: study + ed   *studied*

1. carry + ed
2. noisy + er
3. copy + ed
4. angry + est
5. funny + er

6. easy + er
7. windy + er
8. sunny + er
9. hurry + ed
10. empty + ed

11. happy + est
12. crazy + er
13. family + es
14. pretty + est
15. cloudy + er

Silly Titles Write a Basic or Review Word to complete each book title. Remember that the first, last, and each important word in a title begins with a capital letter.

Example: *Louder and _____ by Willie B. Quiet   Noisier*

16. *Dimes, Nickels, and _____ by Count U. R. Change*
17. *Big _____ and Small Towns by Sid E. Slicker*
18. *Small Boats and _____ by Shep O. Hoy*
19. *_____ About the Future by Ima Worrywart*
20. *Feeding _____ and Children by Hoo Flung Chow*
21. *Books and _____ About Fishing by Rod N. Reel*
22. *Woodworking and Other _____ by Whit Ling*
23. *I _____ for Tests While Sleeping by Betty Failed*
24. *The _____ Weight by Meg A. Ton*
25. *How to Wake Up _____ in the Morning by Earl E. Bird*

How Are You Doing?

List the spelling words that are hard for you. Practice them with a family member.

Proofreading and Writing

Proofread: Spelling and Direct Address Use a comma or commas to set off the name of a person who is directly spoken to, or addressed.

Jim, today will be cold.   You, Kate, need a sweater today.

Find four misspelled Basic or Review Words and three missing commas in this script for a radio weather report. Write the script correctly.

Al: Have you studyed tomorrow's forecast, Lin?

Lin: I think Al, that it will be cloudier and windyer than it was today.

Al: Are you worred about heavy rain, Lin?

Lin: Al it may rain lightly earlier in the day until the clouds are carryed out to sea.

Al: Thank you, Lin for your report.

Basic

1. sunnier
2. cloudier
3. windier
4. cities
5. heaviest
6. prettiest
7. studied
8. easier
9. noisier
10. families
11. ferries
12. crazier
13. funnier
14. earlier
15. copied
16. hobbies
17. angriest
18. emptied
19. worried
20. happiest

Review
21. hurried
22. stories
23. carried
24. pennies
25. babies

Challenge
26. iciest
27. hazier
28. breezier
29. categories
30. qualities

Write a Script

Write a radio or TV script for your own weather broadcast. Try to use five spelling words and at least one noun in direct address. You may want to have your script read aloud.

Proofreading Tip

Check that you used commas correctly with nouns in direct address.

Proofreading Marks

¶ Indent
∧ Add
⌒ Delete
≡ Capital letter
/ Small letter

159

Expanding Vocabulary

Spelling Word Link

noisier

blare
racket
roar
patter
clang

Thesaurus: Exact Words for _noise_ Which sentence below helps you hear the sound of a bell?

I heard the **noise** of the bell.   I heard the **clang** of the bell.

Clang is an exact word that describes the sound of metal hitting metal.

Write the best word from the box to replace _noise_ in each sentence. Use your Thesaurus.

1. Crows make a <u>noise</u> each morning in our back yard.
2. The <u>noise</u> of the kitten's paws scared the mouse away.
3. The <u>noise</u> of the lion was heard throughout the zoo.
4. We heard the <u>noise</u> of the trumpets in the band.
5. I listened for the <u>noise</u> of the schoolyard bell.

Work Together With a partner write captions for these pictures. Use a different word for _noise_ in each one.

6.

7.

8.

Real-World Connection

Science: Weather All the words in the box relate to weather. Look up these words in your Spelling Dictionary. Write the words to complete this page from an almanac.

Spelling Word Link

sunnier

lightning
thunder
hurricane
blizzard
frost
drought
monsoon
hail

Weather Extremes ☀ ☀ ☀ ☀ ☀ ☀

Around the globe you will find some extreme weather conditions.

- Africa has periods of __(1)__ with no water.
- In Asia there are heavy __(2)__ rains in April.
- The tropics have a __(3)__ season with rain and strong winds.
- New England can be hit by a __(4)__ with heavy snow.
- Hard balls of __(5)__ fall in Colorado.
- Fruit growers in Florida must guard crops against an icy __(6)__.
- Rainstorms with loud __(7)__ and flashes of __(8)__ are common in New Mexico.

Try This CHALLENGE

Clue Match Write the word from the box that matches each clue.

9. Crops need rain. They can't grow during one of these.
10. It is caused by a charge of electricity.
11. You would be snowed in by one of these.
12. It can be as small as peas or as large as baseballs.

⭐ **Fact File**

Dog days are hot days in July and August. The star Sirius, or Dog Star, appears in those months. Long ago, people thought that the heat from the star caused the hot weather.

VCV Pattern

Read and Say

v|cv
pi|lot

Basic

READ the sentences. SAY each bold word.

1.	pilot	The **pilot** landed our plane safely.
2.	pupil	The teacher helps each **pupil**.
3.	navy	Which shade of blue is **navy**?
4.	female	Is the baby male or **female**?
5.	silent	You can whisper or stay **silent**.
6.	human	A monkey seems **human** at times.
7.	chosen	Has the team **chosen** its leader?
8.	music	The band played jazz **music**.
9.	paper	The copy machine has no **paper**.
10.	reason	What is your **reason** for being late?
11.	tiger	The **tiger** is a wild cat with stripes.
12.	spider	A **spider** walks on eight legs.
13.	tiny	The eye of the needle is so **tiny**.
14.	tuna	They went fishing for **tuna**.
15.	fever	She is sick with a cold and a **fever**.
16.	frozen	The water is **frozen** into ice cubes.
17.	moment	A **moment** of time is very brief.
18.	season	Spring is a pretty **season** of the year.
19.	stolen	Was your wallet **stolen** from you?
20.	basic	The engine is a **basic** part of a car.

Think and Write

Each two-syllable word has the vowel-consonant-vowel (VCV) pattern. Divide the word into syllables before the consonant. Look for patterns you have learned, and spell the word by syllables.

V | CV :   **pi | lot   si | lent**

• In the examples does the first syllable have a long or a short vowel sound? Where would you divide each Basic Word into syllables?

Now write each Basic Word. Draw a line between its syllables.

Review	23. knew	**Challenge**	28. waver
21. bird	24. straight	26. license	29. feature
22. once	25. through	27. radar	30. diesel

Independent Practice

Spelling Strategy When the first vowel sound in a VCV word is long, divide the word into syllables before the consonant. Remember to look for patterns you have learned, and spell the word by syllables.

Word Analysis/Phonics Complete the exercises with Basic Words.

1–2. Write the two words that have the |ē| sound spelled *ea*.

3–5. Write the Basic Word that contains each base word below.

    3. froze   **4.** stole   **5.** chose

Vocabulary: Making inferences Write the Basic Word that fits each clue.

  6. This person flies planes.

  7. It is used to write on.

  8. It growls.

  9. It spins a web.

10. It describes the *k* in *knit*.

11. It lives in the sea.

12. A band plays it.

13. This person is in school.

Challenge Words Write the Challenge Word that fits each meaning. Use your Spelling Dictionary.

14. used to locate airplanes

15. legal permission

16. a special part or quality

17. to be uncertain

18. powered by an engine that burns oil

Spelling-Meaning Connection

How can you remember how to spell the schwa sound in *human*? Think of the |ă| sound in the related word *humanity*.

19–20. Write *human* and *humanity*. Then underline the letter in *humanity* that helps you remember how to spell the schwa sound in *human*.

Dictionary

Parts of Speech A dictionary entry has a **part-of-speech label**, such as *n.* (noun), *v.* (verb), or *adj.* (adjective). The label tells how the word can be used in a sentence. Some words have more than one part-of-speech label.

part-of-speech label

> **pa·per** |pā′ pər| *n., pl.* **papers** **1.** A material made in thin sheets from pulp. **2.** A single sheet of paper. *v.* **papered**, **papering** To cover with wallpaper.

Practice Write *noun, verb,* or *adjective* to tell how each word below can be used. Use your Spelling Dictionary.

1. reason
2. welcome

Write *noun* or *verb* to show how *reason* is used.

3. I have a good <u>reason</u> for being late.
4. Jay tried to <u>reason</u> with Jenny to get her vote.

Review: Spelling Spree

Alphabet Puzzler Write the Basic or Review Word that comes in the alphabet between each pair of words.

5. straggly, _____ , strain
6. reach, _____ , recent
7. stock, _____ , stomach
8. timid, _____ , tiptoe
9. tide, _____ , tight
10. motor, _____ , mustard
11. fell, _____ , fence
12. jar, _____ , matter
13. tulip, _____ , tune
14. sniffle, _____ , stand
15. panda, _____ , parade
16. glad, _____ , ink
17. barrel, _____ , basket

18. forget, _____ , fruit
19. poster, _____ , race
20. nature, _____ , neat
21. fern, _____ , fewer
22. nest, _____ , pale

How Are You Doing?

Write each spelling word in a sentence. Practice any misspelled spelling words with a partner.

Proofreading and Writing

Proofread for Spelling Find seven misspelled Basic or Review Words in this ad. Write each one correctly.

Airplane Rides

$100 for one Hour

Come fly throw the air like a brid. An experienced pilet, who has been choosen for her skill, will take you straight up into the wild blue yonder. High above the clouds, the world is silant and peaceful. The world below and all your problems will seem tiny. Once you have flown, you will catch the flying fever. Don't waste a momant.

The seson ends November 1.

Fly now!

Basic

1. pilot
2. pupil
3. navy
4. female
5. silent
6. human
7. chosen
8. music
9. paper
10. reason
11. tiger
12. spider
13. tiny
14. tuna
15. fever
16. frozen
17. moment
18. season
19. stolen
20. basic

Review

21. bird
22. once
23. knew
24. straight
25. through

Challenge

26. license
27. radar
28. waver
29. feature
30. diesel

Write Questions

Interview Questions

You are planning to interview a pilot. Write a list of questions you will ask. Try to use five spelling words.

Proofreading Tip

If you are using a word processor, you can boldface any words that you think are misspelled. Then look them up in a dictionary.

Proofreading Marks

¶ Indent
∧ Add
⤴ Delete
≡ Capital letter
/ Small letter

Expanding Vocabulary

Spelling Word Link

silent

frozen
big
boiling
firm
begin
end
tiny
soft

Thesaurus: Synonyms and Antonyms Many words have both synonyms and antonyms. Synonyms are words with similar meanings. Antonyms are words with opposite meanings.

Make three columns. In the middle column, write the word from each plane. Then find a synonym for that word from the box, and write it in the left column. In the right column, write an antonym from the box. Use your Thesaurus.

SYNONYM	WORD	ANTONYM
quiet	silent	noisy

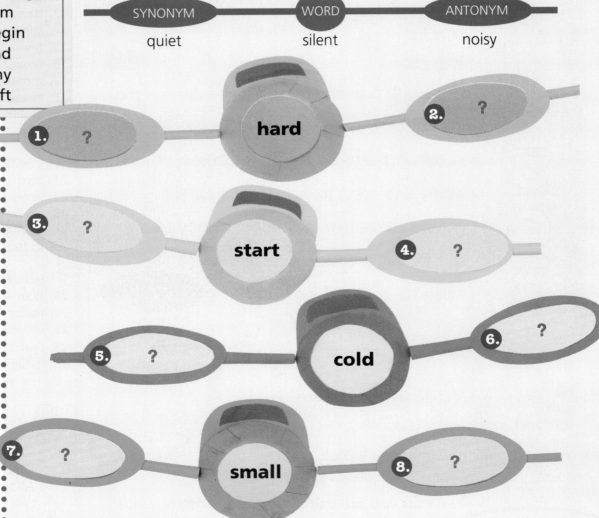

1. ?   **hard**   2. ?

3. ?   **start**   4. ?

5. ?   **cold**   6. ?

7. ?   **small**   8. ?

Show You Know! Write a sentence for each synonym and antonym you wrote. Use both the antonym and the synonym in each sentence.
Example: At band rehearsal the quiet room became very noisy.

Real-World Connection

Careers: Flying All the words in the box relate to flying. Look up these words in your Spelling Dictionary. Then write the words to complete this schedule for a Career Day visit to an airport.

Spelling Word Link

pilot

helicopter
runway
hangar
control tower
glider
parachute
aviation
terminal

Career Day Schedule

9:00 Begin a tour of the airport since our class is studying __(1)__ .

9:30 Observe passengers and planes arriving and departing from a __(2)__ .

10:30 Observe an air traffic controller in the __(3)__ telling a pilot which __(4)__ to use for takeoff.

11:30 Lunch

12:45 Visit a __(5)__ to see where planes are kept and repaired.

1:30 Listen to a worker explain how to fix the blades of a __(6)__ .

2:00 Observe a test pilot packing a __(7)__ in case of an emergency.

2:30 Observe a __(8)__ land silently in a field.

Try This CHALLENGE

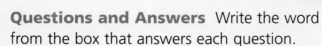

Questions and Answers Write the word from the box that answers each question.

9. Which needs an engine: a <u>glider</u> or a <u>helicopter</u>?
10. Which is larger: a <u>hangar</u> or a <u>glider</u>?
11. Does a <u>parachute</u> or a <u>runway</u> help a plane to land?
12. Do passengers wait in a <u>terminal</u> or in a <u>hangar</u>?

⋆⋆⋆ Fact File

The Concorde, a French airplane, travels faster than the speed of sound. It sends shock waves through the air that make an explosive sound called a sonic boom.

VCV Pattern

vc|v
rob|in
cab|in

Basic

READ the sentences. **SAY** each bold word.

1. cabin	This **cabin** is smaller than our house.	
2. robin	A **robin** built a nest in the tree.	
3. cover	Put the **cover** back on the honey jar.	
4. planet	Which **planet** is closest to the sun?	
5. visit	Maria stopped by for a short **visit**.	
6. finish	The race was close until the **finish**.	
7. salad	Eat a **salad** for lunch.	
8. seven	A week has **seven** days in it.	
9. magic	Her tricks of **magic** made us smile.	
10. exact	Do I need **exact** change to ride the bus?	
11. talent	She has the **talent** to play the drums.	
12. modern	The cars you see today are **modern**.	
13. limit	Drive the car within the speed **limit**.	
14. cousin	My **cousin** Tom is the son of my aunt.	
15. oven	I will bake a cake in the **oven**.	
16. prison	He locked them inside a **prison** cell.	
17. punish	How will the judge **punish** the robber?	
18. habit	I have a bad **habit** of biting my nails.	
19. never	I have **never** been here in my life.	
20. busy	His toys keep him **busy** all day.	

Think and Write

Each word has the VCV pattern and is divided into syllables after the consonant.

VC | V : **cab | in   plan | et**

• Do you hear a long or a short vowel sound in the first syllable of each word? Does that syllable end with a vowel or a consonant sound? Where would you divide each word into syllables?

Now write each Basic Word. Draw a line between its syllables.

Review	23. orange	**Challenge**	28. hazard
21. travel	24. ever	26. pheasant	29. vivid
22. would	25. second	27. quiver	30. jealous

Independent Practice

Spelling Strategy When the first syllable of a VCV word has a short vowel sound followed by a consonant sound, divide the word into syllables after the consonant. Remember to look for patterns you have learned, and spell the word by syllables.

Word Analysis/Phonics Complete the exercises with Basic Words.

1–4. Write the four words with the |z| sound spelled *s*.

5–8. Write four words by adding the missing syllables.

5. tal | _____   **7.** lim | _____

6. _____ | act   **8.** cov | _____

Vocabulary: Classifying Write the Basic Word that fits in each group.

9. five, six, _____

10. sparrow, jay, _____

11. hut, lodge, _____

12. sun, moon, _____

13. soup, sandwich, _____

Challenge Words Write the Challenge Word that fits each meaning. Use your Spelling Dictionary.

14. brightly colored game bird

15. bright and strong

16. envious

17. to tremble

18. something that may cause injury or harm

Spelling-Meaning Connection

How can you remember to spell the |sh| sound in *magician* with a *c*? Think of the related word *magic*. **Think of this**: A *magician* is a person who performs *magic*.

magic
magician

19–20. Write *magic* and *magician*. Underline the letter in *magic* that helps you spell the |sh| sound in *magician*.

Review: Spelling Spree

Silly Rhymes Write the Basic or Review Word that completes each sentence. Each answer rhymes with the underlined word.

1. It is <u>tragic</u> that the wizard forgot his _____.
2. Elephants do not _____ say the word <u>never</u>.
3. The baby bird <u>could</u> fly if it _____ only try.
4. We could not <u>unravel</u> the plans we made to _____.
5. Do four and _____ make <u>eleven</u>?
6. Kim tried but could _____ lift the <u>lever</u>.

Familiar Phrases Write the Basic or Review Word that completes each phrase.

7. an apple and an _____
8. first, _____, third
9. a log _____
10. a wren and a _____
11. break a bad _____
12. aunt and _____
13. a sweet _____ dressing
14. give the _____ change
15. the _____ line of a race
16. bake in the _____
17. behind the bars of a _____
18. as _____ as a bee
19. the _____ Earth
20. to drive at the speed _____
21. a special skill or _____
22. a new and _____ building
23. a short _____ with friends
24. to judge a book by its _____
25. reward the good and _____ the bad

How Are You Doing?

Write your spelling words in ABC order. Practice any misspelled words with a family member.

Proofreading and Writing

Proofread: Spelling and Quotations Use quotation marks before and after a speaker's exact words. Begin the first word with a capital letter. Put punctuation marks inside the last quotation marks.

Lou exclaimed, "These woods are beautiful**!**"

Find four misspelled Basic or Review Words, two missing quotation marks, and two letters that need capitalizing in this conversation from a story. Write the story correctly.

Pete said, "I am going to visit my cusin today."

"Is she the one who lives in a log caben?

asked Lou.

"yes, I travle to see her every year, replied Pete.

"I have never seen those woods," sighed Lou.

Pete said, "maybe you woud like to come along."

Basic

1. cabin
2. robin
3. cover
4. planet
5. visit
6. finish
7. salad
8. seven
9. magic
10. exact
11. talent
12. modern
13. limit
14. cousin
15. oven
16. prison
17. punish
18. habit
19. never
20. busy

Review
21. travel
22. would
23. orange
24. ever
25. second

Challenge
26. pheasant
27. quiver
28. hazard
29. vivid
30. jealous

Write a Story Beginning

Rewrite the beginning of a fairy tale you know, or make up a story beginning. Try to use five spelling words, and include at least one conversation. You may want to act out your story with a classmate.

Beauty and the Birds

Proofreading Tip Check that you have capitalized and punctuated quotations correctly.

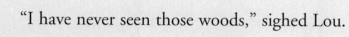

Proofreading Marks

¶ Indent
∧ Add
⌐ Delete
≡ Capital letter
/ Small letter

Expanding Vocabulary

Spelling Word Link

cover

Building Words with Prefixes You can build new words by adding different prefixes to the base word *cover*.

Add each prefix on the branches to *cover*. Write the new words. Then write a sentence for each new word.

1. ?

2. ?

under +

re +

dis +

cover

un +

4. ?

3. ?

Real-World Connection

Science: A Nature Walk All the words in the box relate to nature walks. Look up these words in your Spelling Dictionary. Then write the words to complete this journal entry.

I thought my job as a nature guide would be easy. After all, I know the difference between a six-legged __(1)__ and a fuzzy __(2)__. I can identify an __(3)__ by its hoot and a __(4)__ by its stripes. I can identify the needles of a __(5)__ tree and the leaves of a __(6)__. But I did not expect that one child would try to pet the sharp quills of a __(7)__, or that another child would try to go near a dangerous __(8)__. This is not an easy job!

Spelling Word Link

robin

porcupine
spruce
maple
caterpillar
owl
chipmunk
rattlesnake
insect

Try This CHALLENGE

Write a Description Write a description of a park or another outdoor place. Try to use words from the box. You may also want to draw the place you described.

Fact File

Deciduous trees lose their leaves in the fall. Deciduous trees, such as maple trees, have broad leaves. Evergreen trees, such as spruce trees, keep their needle-shaped leaves.

Words with Suffixes

ill   ness
sick   ness

Basic

READ the sentences. **SAY** each bold word.

1. sickness	The doctor cured his **sickness**.
2. illness	Will medicine help your **illness**?
3. treatment	What **treatment** do you have for a cold?
4. painful	Her broken leg is **painful**.
5. careless	It was **careless** of me to forget my hat.
6. fearful	A noise made the **fearful** baby cry.
7. colorful	A bright sunset is **colorful**.
8. endless	Our long car trip seemed **endless**.
9. beautiful	We danced to the **beautiful** music.
10. awful	The heavy rains were **awful**.
11. movement	Jay threw the ball in a swift **movement**.
12. restless	I had a **restless** night with no sleep.
13. darkness	I can see nothing in the **darkness**.
14. useless	Is the broken tool **useless**?
15. kindness	Sending a card is an act of **kindness**.
16. hopeless	Did the lost children feel **hopeless**?
17. statement	His **statement** delighted the crowd.
18. powerful	Horses are **powerful** animals.
19. friendliness	Every guest felt his warm **friendliness**.
20. peaceful	This quiet room is so **peaceful**.

Think and Write

Each word is made up of a base word and a suffix. A **suffix** is a word part added to the end of a base word. A suffix adds meaning.

sick**ness**   treat**ment**   beauti**ful**   care**less**

• What four suffixes do you see in the list? How does the spelling of base words that end with *y* change when the suffix is added? Which word has the base word *awe*?

Now write each Basic Word under its suffix.

-ness	-ment	-ful	-less

Review
21. hopeful
22. useful
23. careful
24. thankful
25. singer

Challenge
26. ailment
27. appointment
28. resourceful
29. numbness
30. cleanliness

Independent Practice

Spelling Strategy

A **suffix** is a word part added to the end of a base word. It adds meaning to the base word. When a suffix begins with a consonant, remember that the spelling of the base word usually does not change. When the base word ends with *y*, you must change the *y* to *i* before adding the suffix.

Word Analysis/Phonics Complete the exercises with Basic Words.

1–2. Write the two words ending with *-ness* that are synonyms.

3–7. Write the word that has each underlined base word.

3. <u>hope</u>ful
4. <u>use</u>ful
5. <u>fear</u>less
6. <u>color</u>less
7. <u>power</u>less

Vocabulary: Word Clues Write the Basic Word that fits each clue.

8. synonym for *horrible*
9. antonym for *ugly*
10. unable to sit still
11. synonym for *calm*
12. having no light
13. never finishing

Challenge Words Write the Challenge Word that fits each clue. Use your Spelling Dictionary.

14. an arrangement to meet
15. free from dirt
16. an illness
17. clever and capable
18. lacking the power to feel or move

Spelling-Meaning Connection

Can you see *pain* in *painful* and *painless*? Different suffixes can be added to the same base word to form new related words.

19–20. Write *painless*. Then write the Basic Word that is related to *painless* in spelling and meaning.

Dictionary

Suffixes Some words with suffixes are not listed as entry words. However, suffixes have separate entries. Look up the base word and the suffix, and combine the two meanings.

> **-less** A suffix that forms adjectives and means "not having" or "without": *harmless*.

Practice Look up the base word in your Spelling Dictionary and the suffix of each word below. Write a short definition of each word.

1. firmness   2. flavorful   3. friendless   4. accomplishment

Review: Spelling Spree

Suffix Match Write Basic or Review Words by matching the base words and suffixes. Be careful of the word that ends with *y*!

5. hope	**9.** rest	**13.** care	**17.** end
6. dark	**10.** color	**14.** thank	**18.** fear
7. friendly	**11.** pain	**15.** peace	**19.** power
8. state	**12.** kind	**16.** move	**20.** use

✓ **How Are You Doing?**

Write each spelling word as a partner reads it aloud. Did you misspell any words?

Proofreading and Writing

Proofread for Spelling Find nine misspelled Basic or Review Words in this TV script. Write each one correctly.

1

Doctor: Aren't you the famous singor Johnny Jazz? What happened to your beutiful voice? You sound awecul!

2

Patient: I was carless with my health, and now I have a painful sore throat. Can you give me some powerful medicine to cure my sikness? I have to perform tonight.

3

Doctor: I am afraid it is hopeliss. The only usefull treetment for your ilness is to rest your voice.

Basic

1. sickness
2. illness
3. treatment
4. painful
5. careless
6. fearful
7. colorful
8. endless
9. beautiful
10. awful
11. movement
12. restless
13. darkness
14. useless
15. kindness
16. hopeless
17. statement
18. powerful
19. friendliness
20. peaceful

Review

21. hopeful
22. useful
23. careful
24. thankful
25. singer

Challenge

26. ailment
27. appointment
28. resourceful
29. numbness
30. cleanliness

Write a Personal Story

Were you ever too sick to do something you wanted to do? Did you ever pretend to be sick? Write a paragraph about that time. Try to use five spelling words.

Proofreading Tip

Check that your *a*'s are written clearly so that they do not look like *o*'s or *u*'s.

Proofreading Marks

¶ Indent
∧ Add
⌐ Delete
≡ Capital letter
/ Small letter

Expanding Vocabulary

Spelling Word Link

colorful

scarlet
lavender
amber
tangerine
turquoise

Thesaurus: Color Words Which phrase better describes colorful autumn leaves of yellow and bright red?

yellow and **red** leaves   **gold** and **scarlet** leaves

Gold and *scarlet* are exact words that describe specific shades of yellow and bright red.

Look up *yellow*, *red*, *green*, *orange*, and *purple* in your Thesaurus. Then write a word from the box to replace the underlined word or words in each sentence.

1. The brownish-yellow cider looked refreshing.
2. The marching band wore cherry-red uniforms.
3. I bought a blue-green bracelet at the crafts fair.
4. Jacob used the orange crayon to add color to his picture.
5. Anika decided to paint her room purple.

Work Together Look up the color words *red*, *green*, and *yellow* in your Thesaurus. Find the subentries that you have not yet practiced. Then, with a partner, write the subentry that matches each paint color.

Real-World Connection

Health: Medicine All the words in the box relate to medicine. Look up these words in your Spelling Dictionary. Then write the words to complete this description.

Spelling Word Link

sickness

medicine
patient
infected
disease
surgery
clinic
wound
prescription

CITY HOSPITAL

Dr. Davis runs the only __(1)__ for miles around, and every __(2)__ who comes in is important to her. Whether she is writing a __(3)__ for a child with a fever, cleaning a bleeding __(4)__ so it does not become __(5)__, or treating someone with a serious __(6)__, such as cancer, she is always kind and gentle. She has even performed emergency __(7)__ on a cat! Dr. Davis knows that to be a good doctor you must do more than just give out __(8)__.

Dr. Davis

Try This — CHALLENGE

Yes or No? Write *yes* if the underlined word or phrase is used correctly. Write *no* if it is not.

9. The <u>wound</u> on Paula's finger was not deep.
10. The doctor's <u>prescription</u> was that I had the flu.
11. The nurse put a bandage on my <u>disease</u>.
12. The doctor operated on the <u>patient</u>.

 Fact File

Doctors promise to serve patients well when they take the Hippocratic oath. This oath is named after Hippocrates, a doctor in ancient Greece, called the father of modern medicine.

VCCV Pattern

Read and Say

vcc|v
chick|en
rock|et

Basic

READ the sentences. **SAY** each bold word.

1.	rocket	Can a **rocket** move faster than a jet?
2.	achieve	We are proud of goals we **achieve**.
3.	afraid	I am **afraid** that a bee will sting me.
4.	machine	A blender is a simple **machine**.
5.	secret	Do not tell anyone the **secret**.
6.	gather	You can **gather** the shoes together.
7.	other	This car is older than the **other** one.
8.	package	Mail the **package** at the post office.
9.	declare	I **declare** that you are the winner.
10.	asleep	I dream when I am **asleep**.
11.	agree	Nod your head if you **agree** with me.
12.	apron	The cook wears a white **apron**.
13.	bucket	The water **bucket** holds six gallons.
14.	pocket	Please carry the key in your **pocket**.
15.	ticket	The bus **ticket** costs one dollar.
16.	chicken	The farmer fed corn to his **chicken**.
17.	degree	We brag about each **degree** of success.
18.	bother	Will the noise **bother** the baby?
19.	rather	The joke is **rather** silly.
20.	whether	He knows **whether** or not the door is open.

Think and Write

In this VCCV pattern, the two consonants form a cluster, like the *fr* in *afraid*, or spell one sound, like the *ck* in *rocket*. Divide the word into syllables before or after the two consonants.

V | CCV : **a | fraid**   VCC | V : **rock | et**

• Does the first syllable of each example word end with a vowel sound or a consonant sound? Where is each word divided into syllables? **Now write each Basic Word under the heading that tells where its syllables are divided. Draw a line between the syllables.**

Before the Consonants   After the Consonants

Review   23. teacher
21. nothing   24. helper
22. between   25. farmer

Challenge   28. method
26. descent   29. reflect
27. vibrate   30. abrupt

Independent Practice

Spelling Strategy   If the consonants in a VCCV word are different and form a cluster or spell one sound, divide the word before or after the two consonants. Look for patterns you have learned, and spell the word by syllables.

Word Analysis/Phonics Complete the exercises with Basic Words.

1. Write the word that is a homophone for *weather*.

2–5. Write the four words that begin with the schwa sound spelled *a*.

6–7. Write the two words that rhyme with *locket*.

Vocabulary: Synonyms Write the Basic Word that is a synonym for each word below.

8. somewhat
9. disturb
10. pail
11. bundle
12. hen
13. collect

Challenge Words Write the Challenge Word that fits each meaning. Use your Spelling Dictionary.

14. to give back an image of
15. a downward slope
16. taking place without warning
17. to move back and forth rapidly
18. a regular way of doing something

Spelling-Meaning Connection

Can you see *declare* in the word *declaration*? These words are related in spelling and meaning. **Think of this:** The countries will *declare* peace in the *declaration*.

declare
declaration

19–20. Write *declaration*. Then write the Basic Word that is related to *declaration* in spelling and meaning.

Review: Spelling Spree

Syllable Scramble Two of the three syllables in each item below form a Basic or Review Word. Write the words correctly.

Example: ing be noth   *nothing*

1. er et help
2. de er both
3. buck ma et
4. a gath sleep
5. cret se pock

6. fraid de a
7. se clare de
8. er buck wheth
9. pock cret et
10. clare et rock

11. er age gath
12. ma rock chine
13. chieve both a
14. age pack cret

Word Search Write the Basic or Review Word that is hidden in each sentence.

Example: I made <u>both er</u>rors.   *bother*

15. It is hot here.
16. I see no thin goats.
17. I bet we enter there.
18. I bought each eraser.
19. You are far merrier today.
20. What is a pronoun?
21. He is a greedy man.
22. I need a plastic kettle.
23. There was no rat here.
24. The chick enjoys its food.
25. We made green beans.

How Are You Doing?

List the spelling words that are hard for you. Practice them with a family member.

Proofreading and Writing

Basic

Proofread: Spelling and Friendly Letters Be sure to use commas and capital letters correctly in friendly letters.

DAY AND YEAR: **May 9, 1998**
CITY AND STATE: **Bath, Maine**
GREETING: **Dear Sam,**
CLOSING: **Your friend,**

Find four misspelled Basic or Review Words, one letter that needs capitalizing, and two missing commas in this part of Michael's letter. Write the letter correctly.

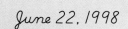

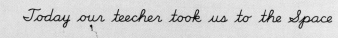
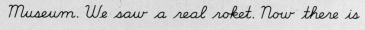

June 22, 1998

dear Lisa

Today our teecher took us to the Space Museum. We saw a real roket. Now there is nuthing I would rather do than travel in space! I would not be afrade.

Your brother

Michael

Basic

1. rocket
2. achieve
3. afraid
4. machine
5. secret
6. gather
7. other
8. package
9. declare
10. asleep
11. agree
12. apron
13. bucket
14. pocket
15. ticket
16. chicken
17. degree
18. bother
19. rather
20. whether

Review

21. nothing
22. between
23. teacher
24. helper
25. farmer

Challenge

26. descent
27. vibrate
28. method
29. reflect
30. abrupt

Write a Letter

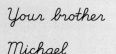

Dear Michael, How are you? I am ...

Write a friendly letter. Describe a trip you took to a museum or some other special place. Try to use five spelling words. Do you want to mail your letter?

Proofreading Tip

Check the parts of your friendly letter for correct use of commas and capital letters.

Proofreading Marks

¶ Indent
∧ Add
⌐ Delete
≡ Capital letter
/ Small letter

Expanding Vocabulary

Spelling Word Link

bucket

bureau
seesaw
faucet
elastic
pocketbook
poke
skillet
bucket

Regional Differences

People who live in different parts of the United States call some things by different names. What do you call this item where you live?

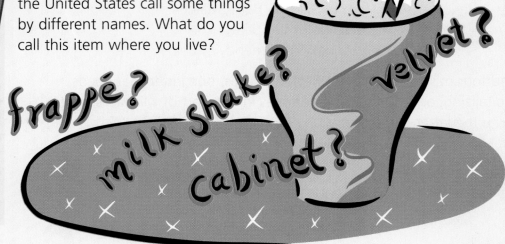

frappé?

milk shake?

cabinet?

velvet?

Write a word from the box that has the same meaning as each numbered word. Use your Spelling Dictionary.

1. teeter-totter
2. purse
3. rubber band
4. spider
5. spigot
6. pail
7. sack
8. dresser

★★★ Fact File

Speakers in Rhode Island call the drink that is made with milk and syrup a milk shake. However, if ice cream is included, they call it a cabinet, possibly because ice cream shops used to store the mixer in a square wooden cabinet. In northern New England, this same drink is a velvet or a frappé.

Real-World Connection

Science: Space Exploration All the words in the box relate to space exploration. Look up these words in your Spelling Dictionary. Write the words to complete this encyclopedia article.

Spelling Word Link

rocket

satellite
space shuttle
galaxy
astronaut
orbit
gravity
capsule
booster

Spacecraft

In 1962 John Glenn became the first American __(1)__ to go into __(2)__ around the earth. He viewed outer space from the small __(3)__ of his spacecraft. Now a vehicle called the __(4)__ goes back and forth between Earth and space. Its strong __(5)__ rockets thrust it away from the pull of Earth's __(6)__. It can carry an information-gathering __(7)__ into space. Someday an even more advanced vehicle may take us across the Milky Way, our __(8)__.

Try This CHALLENGE

Yes or No? Write *yes* if the underlined word is used correctly. Write *no* if it is not.

9. The rocket used up a lot of <u>gravity</u> during takeoff.
10. The weather <u>satellite</u> circled Earth.
11. The <u>space shuttle</u> returned after a two-week flight.
12. The astronaut needed a <u>booster</u> to board the capsule.

30 Review: Units 25–29

Unit 25   Changing Final *y* to *i*   pages 156–161

cities	prettiest	studied	families	easier
earlier	angriest	ferries	happiest	worried

Spelling Strategy   If a word ends with a consonant and **y**, change the **y** to **i** when adding **-es, -ed, -er,** or **-est**.

Write the word that fits each group.

1. study, studying, _____
2. pretty, prettier, _____
3. early, _____, earliest
4. easy, _____, easiest
5. worry, worrying, _____
6. angry, angrier, _____
7. happy, happier, _____

Write the word that completes each phrase.

8. towns and _____
9. parents and _____
10. sailboats and _____

v|cv
pi|lot

Unit 26   VCV Pattern   pages 162–167

pupil	female	chosen	reason	paper
season	tiny	tiger	spider	frozen

Spelling Strategy   When the first vowel sound in a VCV word is long, divide the word into syllables before the consonant. Remember to look for patterns you have learned, and spell the word by syllables.

Write a word by adding the missing syllable.

11. fro | ___
12. cho | ___
13. rea | ___
14. pu | ___
15. fe | ___

Write the word that matches each clue.

16. has eight legs
17. has stripes
18. used to write on
19. describes an ant
20. summer or winter

Unit 27   VCV Pattern   pages 168–173

cover	exact	robin	finish	cabin
oven	cousin	prison	busy	modern

Spelling Strategy   When the first syllable of a VCV word has a short vowel sound followed by a consonant sound, divide the word into syllables after the consonant. Remember to look for patterns you have learned, and spell the word by syllables.

vc|v
rob|in
cab|in

Write a word by adding the missing syllable.

21. rob | ___   **23.** pris | ___   **25.** ___ | y

22. cous | ___   **24.** ___ | ern

Write the spelling word that you find in each word below.

26. refinish   **29.** cabinet

27. coverlet   **30.** ovenproof

28. exactly

Unit 28   Words with Suffixes   pages 174–179

illness	beautiful	careless	treatment	awful
useless	friendliness	peaceful	powerful	movement

Spelling Strategy

beau**ty** + **ful** = beaut**iful**

care + **less** = care**less**

ill   ness
sick   ness

Write the word that contains each base word below.

31. ill   **34.** move

32. treat   **35.** friendly

33. care

Write a word that is a synonym for each word.

36. quiet   **38.** mighty   **40.** terrible

37. lovely   **39.** worthless

vcc|v
**chick|en
rock|et**

declare	package	achieve	afraid	rocket
degree	chicken	bother	agree	whether

Spelling Strategy   If the consonants in a VCCV word are different and form a cluster or spell one sound, divide the word before or after the two consonants. Look for patterns you have learned, and spell the word by syllables.

Write the word that fits each meaning.

41. to share the same opinion   **44.** a step in a series

42. to give trouble to   **45.** if

43. a hen or a rooster   **46.** a bundle of things

Write the word that rhymes with each word below.

47. locket   **49.** believe

48. beware   **50.** braid

Challenge Words   **Units 25–29**   **pages 156–185**

appointment	categories	breezier	feature	quiver
resourceful	license	pheasant	method	descent

Write the word that completes each phrase.

51. a special _____   **54.** to make an _____ with a dentist

52. to _____ with fear   **55.** the feathers of a _____

53. a steep _____

Write the word that can replace the underlined word or words.

56. a <u>way</u> of cooking chicken

57. a <u>clever</u> problem solver

58. organized into <u>groups</u>

59. legal <u>permission to drive</u>

60. a <u>windier</u> day than yesterday

Spelling-Meaning Strategy

Consonant Changes The Sounds of *c*

Words that end with *c* may have related words in which the *c* spells a different sound. Read these sentences.

> The school band played some beautiful classical **music** during the concert in the high school auditorium. All of the young **musicians** played with great skill and feeling.

music
musician

Think

- How are *music* and *musician* related in meaning?
- What sound does *c* spell in each word?

Here are more related words in which the letter *c* spells different sounds.

electri**c**	mathemati**c**s
electri**ci**an	mathemati**ci**an

Apply and Extend

Complete these activities on a separate sheet of paper.

1. Use your Spelling Dictionary to look up the meaning of each word in the box above. Write four sentences, using each word in one sentence.

2. With a partner, list as many words as you can that are related to *music, electric,* and *mathematics*. Then look at the section "Consonant Changes: The Sound of *c*" beginning on page 272 of your Spelling-Meaning Index. Add to your list any other words that you find in these families.

Summing Up

The |k| sound of *c* may change to |sh| when the suffix *-ian* is added. Thinking of a related word can help you remember that the |sh| sound is spelled *c*.

Literature and Writing

Ben's class needed to raise money. Ben remembered the story *Ernie and the Mile-Long Muffler* by Marjorie Lewis. The students in that story learned to knit and sold the things they made at a fair. Ben decided to write a persuasive letter to his neighbor. What did Ben want Mrs. Hendriks to do?

1135 Greenway Ave.
Palo Alto, CA 94555
November 8, 1998

Dear Mrs. Hendriks,

I would like you to teach me to quilt. My class is going to have a crafts fair in May to raise money for the school library. If I learn to quilt, I will be able to teach my friends. Then we could make pillows, pot holders, and other things to sell at the fair. Last year we earned almost $200 from the fair. I also know how to use a sewing machine, so you wouldn't have to teach me. I've sewed a cover for my bike.

I am sure that with your help, we will be able to earn lots of money for the library.

Sincerely yours,

Ben Gardner

Ben Gardner

Think and Discuss

1 What did Ben want to persuade Mrs. Hendriks to do?

2 What reasons did Ben use to try to persuade her?

3 What facts and examples did Ben use to support his reasons?

4 What is included in the five parts of a letter? Use the model on page 252 if you need help.

The Writing Process
Persuasive Letter

What would you like to persuade someone to do? Write a friendly letter to that person. Follow the guidelines and the Writing Process.

1 Prewriting
- List several reasons that would persuade your audience.
- Ask a group of classmates to rate each reason from 1 (weak) to 5 (strong). Use the strongest reasons.

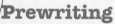

2 Draft
- Write about one reason at a time.

3 Revise
- Support each reason with at least one fact or example.
- Use your Thesaurus to find exact words.
- Have a writing conference.

4 Proofread
- Did you spell each word correctly?
- Did you use capital letters and punctuation marks correctly?

5 Publish
- Mail a neat final copy of your letter.

Guidelines for Persuading

✓ Introduce the problem or your goal.
✓ State your goal clearly.
✓ Give strong reasons. Support them with facts and examples.
✓ Conclude by encouraging an action.

Composition Words
families
worried
human
basic
planet
talent
achieve
agree

UNIT 31 VCV Pattern

v|cv
si|ren

Read and Say

Basic

READ the sentences. **SAY** each bold word.

1.	ocean	We sail our boat on the **ocean**.
2.	police	Can the **police** solve the crime?
3.	depend	Farmers **depend** on a good crop.
4.	siren	The fire truck blew its **siren**.
5.	defend	The army will **defend** the fort.
6.	today	Can we call now or later **today**?
7.	parent	Which **parent** found the lost child?
8.	become	The bud will **become** a flower.
9.	below	The pilot pointed to the city **below**.
10.	relate	The reporter will **relate** the story.
11.	exit	I left through the door at the **exit**.
12.	polite	The kind man gave a **polite** answer.
13.	open	The shop will **open** its doors at noon.
14.	figure	A dark **figure** stood in the shadows.
15.	event	Are these flowers for a special **event**?
16.	belong	In which closet do the toys **belong**?
17.	award	The winner of the race gets an **award**.
18.	palace	The king and queen live in a **palace**.
19.	delay	The shower will **delay** our picnic.
20.	clever	Anyone who finds the answer is **clever**.

Think and Write

If a VCV word begins with the short vowel pattern, divide it after the consonant. Other VCV words are divided before the consonant.

VC | V :   **par | ent**   V | CV :   **si | ren**

• Which Basic Words have first syllables with the short vowel pattern? Which ones have first syllables ending with a vowel sound?
Now write each Basic Word under the heading that tells where its syllables are divided.

VC|V	V|CV

Review | 23. alive
21. before | 24. begin
22. away | 25. giraffe

Challenge | 28. cadet
26. peril | 29. rival
27. marine | 30. alert

192

Independent Practice

Spelling Strategy   Remember that a two-syllable word with the VCV pattern can be divided into syllables before or after the consonant. Look for familiar patterns, and spell the word by syllables.

Word Analysis/Phonics   Complete the exercises with Basic Words.

1. Write the word with the |sh| sound.
2–3. Write the two words that end with the |s| sound.
4–6. Write the three words with the first syllable *be*.
7–8. Write the two words that rhyme with *send*.

Vocabulary: Classifying   Write the Basic Word that belongs in each group.

9. yesterday, tomorrow, _____
10. symbol, number, _____
11. son, daughter, _____
12. bell, whistle, _____
13. medal, prize, _____

Challenge Words   Write the Challenge Word that fits each meaning. Use your Spelling Dictionary.

14. quick to notice or act
15. condition of being in danger
16. relating to the sea
17. someone who competes
18. student at a naval school

Spelling-Meaning Connection

relate
relation

How can you remember how to spell the |sh| sound in *relation*? Think of the word *relate*. The *t* in *relate* is kept in *relation* even though the sound changes.

19–20. Write *relate* and *relation*. Then underline the letter in *relate* that helps you spell the |sh| sound in *relation*.

Review: Spelling Spree

Questions Write a Basic or Review Word to answer each question.

1. What animal has a very long neck?
2. What do you do at the start of something?
3. How could you describe someone who is breathing?
4. What is the opposite of *after*?
5. What do you call someone who is smart?
6. Where does a king live?
7. What is another name for a shape?
8. What makes a loud warning noise?
9. Who keeps law and order in a city or a town?
10. Where do whales live?
11. What do you call someone who says *please*?

Syllable Addition Write a Basic or Review Word by adding the underlined syllable of the first word to the underlined syllable of the second word.

12. <u>de</u>mand + sus<u>pend</u>
13. <u>to</u>morrow + birth<u>day</u>
14. <u>be</u>tween + wel<u>come</u>
15. <u>re</u>move + trans<u>late</u>
16. <u>o</u>dor + hap<u>pen</u>
17. <u>e</u>rase + pre<u>vent</u>
18. <u>a</u>mong + for<u>ward</u>

19. <u>de</u>part + of<u>fend</u>
20. <u>par</u>rot + tal<u>ent</u>
21. <u>be</u>hind + fol<u>low</u>
22. <u>ex</u>tra + lim<u>it</u>
23. <u>de</u>light + re<u>lay</u>
24. <u>be</u>lieve + a<u>long</u>
25. <u>a</u>head + sub<u>way</u>

How Are You Doing?

Write your spelling words in ABC order. Practice any misspelled words with a family member.

Proofreading and Writing

Proofread for Spelling and Book Titles Remember to capitalize the first, last, and each important word in a book title. Underline the title.

My favorite book is <u>This Is the Story of the Sea</u>.

Find four misspelled Basic or Review Words, one word that needs a capital letter, and a missing underline in Yoko's book list. Write the book list correctly.

1. In the book <u>Sea Stories</u>, a sailor is found aliv after being lost on the ochen for weeks.

2. The books <u>The World Below</u> and <u>Underwater</u> relat true stories of underwater exploration.

3. In <u>All Hands on deck</u>, young sailors difend their ship and drive away pirates.

Basic

1. ocean
2. police
3. depend
4. siren
5. defend
6. today
7. parent
8. become
9. below
10. relate
11. exit
12. polite
13. open
14. figure
15. event
16. belong
17. award
18. palace
19. delay
20. clever

Review

21. before
22. away
23. alive
24. begin
25. giraffe

Challenge

26. peril
27. marine
28. cadet
29. rival
30. alert

Write a Book List

Write a list of books that are your favorites or books you wish existed. Write a sentence about each one. Use five spelling words.

Proofreading Tip **Check that you capitalized and underlined book titles correctly.**

MY FAVORITE BOOKS

Proofreading Marks

¶ Indent
∧ Add
✎ Delete
≡ Capital letter
/ Small letter

Expanding Vocabulary

Spelling Word Link

relate

exclaimed
questioned
muttered
agreed
suggested
groaned

Thesaurus: Exact Words for *relate* *Relate* means "to tell something." Other words meaning "to tell something" also express *how* the words are spoken. What does *complained* tell you?

"I am late," Ed **related**.   "I am late," Ed **complained**.

Write the word from the box that best fits each speaker. Use the entry for *relate* in your Thesaurus to help you make your choices.

1. "Do you want to sail beyond the harbor?" _____ Rita.
2. "Aghhh!" _____ Mark, "I'm getting cold and wet."
3. "Rita, watch out for that rock!" _____ Pat.
4. "Perhaps we should turn back," _____ Ping.
5. "Yes, I think you are right," _____ Rita.
6. "I told you so," _____ Mark quietly.

Show You Know! Rewrite the comic strip into four sentences. Include a different word from the box in each sentence.

7–8.

9–10.

Vocabulary Enrichment

Real-World Connection

Careers: Coast Guard All the words in the box relate to the Coast Guard. Look up these words in your Spelling Dictionary. Then write the words to complete this story beginning.

> Frank stood on the deck of the Coast Guard __(1)__. He peered into the fog, searching for the lighthouse __(2)__. His life jacket and his blue __(3)__ were wet from the ocean spray. Ahead, a __(4)__ of fishing boats had crashed against the rocky coast. Frank knew these coastal __(5)__ well. As a student at the __(6)__, he had been on __(7)__ to guard these waters many times. He knew that the __(8)__ of these boats now would depend on his skill.

Spelling Word Link

ocean

rescue
fleet
patrol
borders
uniform
cutter
beacon
academy

Try This
CHALLENGE

Yes or No? Write *yes* if the underlined word is used correctly. Write *no* if it is not.

9. A <u>beacon</u> guided the sailor through the fog.
10. There was one boat in the <u>fleet</u>.
11. One of the fishing boats was a <u>cutter</u>.
12. A Coast Guard member wears a <u>uniform</u> on duty.

A	B	C	D	E	F
•—	—•••	—•—•	—••	•	••—•

G	H	I	J	K
——•	••••	••	•———	—•—

L	M	N	O	P
•—••	——	—•	———	•——•

Q	R	S	T	U
——•—	•—•	•••	—	••—

V	W	X	Y	Z
•••—	•——	—••—	—•——	——••

★ Fact File

The Morse code is a system of dots, dashes, and spaces used to send messages over wires. SOS is a famous distress signal sent by ships and boats that are in trouble.

VCCV and VCV Patterns

Read and Say

vc|cv
din|ner
vc|v
wag|on

Basic

READ the sentences. **SAY** each bold word.

1.	*wagon*	Horses are pulling a **wagon** of hay.
2.	*capture*	A picture can **capture** a special moment.
3.	*silver*	The shiny bowl is made of **silver**.
4.	*reward*	Will you offer a **reward** for the lost cat?
5.	*shelter*	The roof gave us **shelter** from the rain.
6.	*divide*	Jan will **divide** the pie into six pieces.
7.	*nature*	Bugs, flowers, and trees are part of **nature**.
8.	*alone*	I sat **alone** in a big waiting room.
9.	*office*	My mother works in an **office** downtown.
10.	*famous*	Everyone knows this **famous** movie star.
11.	*parade*	Marching bands led the **parade**.
12.	*narrow*	My feet hurt in these **narrow** shoes.
13.	*corner*	I hit my leg on the **corner** of the table.
14.	*bacon*	Breakfast will be eggs, toast, and **bacon**.
15.	*amaze*	This wonderful rainbow will **amaze** you.
16.	*diner*	Our family ate lunch in a **diner**.
17.	*dinner*	We eat **dinner** every night at six.
18.	*eager*	I was **eager** to leave the party.
19.	*minute*	Your bus will be here in just a **minute**.
20.	*fancy*	The gift box had a very **fancy** ribbon.

Think and Write

Divide each of these VCCV or VCV words into syllables. Look for patterns that you have learned, and spell each word by syllables.

VC | CV : **din | ner**   VC | V : **wag | on**   V | CV : **di | vide**

Where is a VCCV word divided into syllables? Where do you divide a VCV word if it has the short vowel pattern in the first syllable? if its first syllable ends with a vowel sound?

Write each Basic Word under its pattern.

VCCV	VCV

Review		Challenge	
Review	23. market	**Challenge**	28. prairie
21. again	24. pencil	26. frontier	29. stampede
22. enough	25. balloon	27. sheriff	30. corral

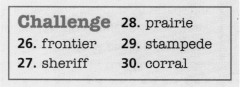

Independent Practice

Spelling Strategy

To help you spell a word with more than one syllable, divide the word into syllables. Remember to look for patterns you have learned, and spell the word by syllables.

Word Analysis/Phonics Complete the exercises with Basic Words.

1–2. Write *diner*. Then add a letter to write another word.

3–4. Write the two words that begin or end with the |ē| sound.

5–6. Write two words that begin with the |ə| sound spelled *a*.

Vocabulary: Word Clues Write the Basic Word that fits each clue.

7. part of an hour
8. opposite of *wide*
9. a math operation
10. very well known
11. where two roads meet
12. has four wheels
13. a metal used for jewelry

Challenge Words Write the Challenge Word that fits each meaning. Use your Spelling Dictionary.

14. flat, open grassland
15. a pen for horses
16. the farthest point of settlement
17. a sudden rush of animals
18. a person in charge of enforcing the law

Spelling-Meaning Connection

Nature and *natural* are related in spelling and meaning even though the two words have different vowel sounds. **Think of this:** *Nature* provides us with many important *natural* resources.

nature
natural

19–20. Write *natural*. Then write the Basic Word that is related to *natural* in spelling and meaning.

Dictionary

Homographs **Homographs** are words that are spelled the same but have different meanings and may be pronounced differently. They are listed in the dictionary as separate entry words. Each homograph is followed by a number.

> **min·ute¹** |mĭn′ ĭt| *n., pl.* **minutes** A unit of time equal to sixty seconds.
> **mi·nute²** |mī nōōt′| or |mī nyōōt′| *adj.* Very, very small; tiny: *The wind blew a minute speck of dirt into her eye.*

Practice Write *minute¹* or *minute²* to tell how *minute* is used in each sentence. Use the dictionary entry above.

1. The jeweler found a <u>minute</u> crack in the stone.
2. The rules allow one <u>minute</u> for you to answer.
3. A <u>minute</u> crumb would be a feast for some insects.
4. The runner finished the race in exactly one <u>minute</u>.

Review: Spelling Spree

Code Breaker Some Basic and Review Words are written in the code below. Figure out each word, and write it correctly.

Example: 15-16-4-4-7-6   *dinner*

CODE:	1	2	3	4	5	6	7	8	9	10	11	12	13	14	15	16	17	18	19
LETTER:	p	b	o	n	a	r	e	w	l	m	f	k	c	t	d	i	g	s	u

5. 2-5-9-9-3-3-4
6. 10-5-6-12-7-14
7. 10-16-4-19-14-7
8. 15-16-4-7-6
9. 13-3-6-4-7-6
10. 11-5-10-3-19-18
11. 4-5-14-19-6-7
12. 5-17-5-16-4
13. 1-7-4-13-16-9

14. 4-5-6-6-3-8
15. 13-5-1-14-19-6-7
16. 3-11-11-16-13-7
17. 1-5-6-5-15-7
18. 2-5-13-3-4
19. 6-7-8-5-6-15
20. 7-5-17-7-6
21. 5-9-3-4-7
22. 8-5-17-3-4

☑ How Are You Doing?

Write each spelling word in a sentence. Practice any misspelled spelling words with a partner.

Proofreading and Writing

Proofread for Spelling Find seven misspelled Basic or Review Words in this story part. Write each one correctly.

Becky watched her father divid the bacon into narrow strips for diner. The stars shone overhead like sliver.

"It may not be fansy, but it will be enuff," he smiled. His good spirits would always amaz Becky. They had been traveling for weeks, with only a covered wagon for sheltor, on their way to a new life in the West.

Basic

1. wagon
2. capture
3. silver
4. reward
5. shelter
6. divide
7. nature
8. alone
9. office
10. famous
11. parade
12. narrow
13. corner
14. bacon
15. amaze
16. diner
17. dinner
18. eager
19. minute
20. fancy

Review

21. again
22. enough
23. market
24. pencil
25. balloon

Challenge

26. frontier
27. sheriff
28. prairie
29. stampede
30. corral

Write a Personal Story

Write a story about an outdoor experience that you have had. Where were you? How did you feel during your experience? Try to use five spelling words.

Proofreading Tip

Be sure that you check for words that have silent letters.

Proofreading Marks

¶ Indent
∧ Add
ᵧ Delete
≡ Capital letter
/ Small letter

Expanding Vocabulary

Spelling Word Link

famous

The Suffix *-ous* The suffix *-ous* adds the meaning "full of" or "having" to a base word. A **base word** is a word to which a beginning or an ending can be added. How does the spelling of the base word *fame* change when *-ous* is added?

fame + ous = fam**ous**   "having fame"

Write the correct words with the suffix *-ous* to complete the chart .

BASE WORD	SUFFIX	WORD	
marvel		1.	?
adventure		2.	?
nerve	+ ous	3.	?
humor		4.	?
joy		5.	?

Show You Know! Write a word from the chart to complete each sentence. Use your Spelling Dictionary.

6. The _____ puppy was not afraid of anything.
7. Jake was scared and _____ when he gave his speech.
8. We laughed at the _____ message on the board.
9. Kay took some _____ pictures of the mountains.
10. The holidays make me feel cheerful and _____.

Real-World Connection

Social Studies: The Wild West All the words in the box relate to the Wild West. Look up these words in your Spelling Dictionary. Then write the words to complete this story beginning.

Spelling Word Link

wagon

stagecoach
rodeo
buffalo
homestead
settle
pioneer
ranch
cactus

Jake, a true __(1)__, had been one of the first people to __(2)__ in the small Texas town. When the government granted a __(3)__ to anyone willing to claim the land and build a home, Jake had come west. He cleared his land of prickly __(4)__ and roaming __(5)__. Now his cattle __(6)__ was thriving. Jake decided to give his cowhands time off to see the riding and roping at the __(7)__. Many were coming by __(8)__ to see the event.

Try This CHALLENGE

Category Clue Write a word from the box that fits each category.

9. Prickly Things
10. Things with Wheels
11. Government Gifts
12. Events for Cowhands

★★★ Fact File

In 1848 gold was discovered in California. The next year 75,000 people rushed there to find gold. Because this gold rush took place in 1849, these fortune seekers were called forty-niners.

Three-Syllable Words

Read and Say

de|liv|er

Basic

READ the sentences. SAY each bold word.

1. deliver   Please **deliver** the mail to my new address.
2. department   My mother works for the fire **department**.
3. camera   Which **camera** will take the best picture?
4. yesterday   Today is a better day than **yesterday**.
5. tomorrow   Is your birthday today or **tomorrow**?
6. important   Listening is an **important** step in learning.
7. together   Pat and I went to the park **together**.
8. victory   Winning this game is a big **victory** for us.
9. remember   Do you **remember** how to lock this gate?
10. library   This book belongs to the **library**.
11. enemy   The battle was won by our **enemy**.
12. animal   A camel is a tall **animal**.
13. another   Would you like **another** glass of water?
14. however   I trust that you will finish on time, **however**.
15. banana   The yellow **banana** is the ripe one.
16. alphabet   How many letters are in the **alphabet**?
17. hospital   My friend is a nurse at this **hospital**.
18. hamburger   Please order me a **hamburger** with cheese.
19. carpenter   Her house was built by a **carpenter**.
20. several   Your jacket is missing **several** buttons.

Think and Write

One syllable in each word has more stress than the other two syllables. Pay close attention to the spelling of the unstressed syllables.

yes | ter | day |yĕs′ tər dā| **de | liv | er** |dĭ lĭv′ ər|

• Which syllables are stressed in the examples? Which syllables are unstressed? Why are the unstressed syllables so important?

Now write each Basic Word under its stressed syllable.

First Syllable Stressed	Second Syllable Stressed

Review   23. October
21. grandmother   24. November
22. grandfather   25. unhappy

Challenge   28. journalist
26. interview   29. edition
27. article   30. photograph

Independent Practice

Spelling Strategy To spell a three-syllable word, divide the word into syllables. Remember to look for familiar spelling patterns. Pay attention to the spelling of the unstressed syllables. Spell the word by syllables.

Word Analysis/Phonics Complete the exercises with Basic Words.

1. Write the word that has the |ī| sound.

2–5. Write the word that contains each word below.

    2. depart   **4.** day

    3. other   **5.** how

6–8. Write the three words with the final |əl| sounds spelled with the *al* pattern.

Vocabulary: Word Clues Write the Basic Word that fits each clue.

9. synonym for *recall*

10. A photographer uses one.

11. opposite of *friend*

12. the day after today

13. a fruit with yellow skin

Challenge Words Write the Challenge Word that fits each meaning. Use your Spelling Dictionary.

14. a short piece of writing

15. a reporter or an editor

16. a conversation with a reporter

17. an image on film

18. all copies of a book printed at one time

Spelling-Meaning Connection

How can you remember how to spell the |ə| sound in *victory*? Think of the |ôr| sounds in the related word *victorious*.

19–20. Write *victorious*. Then write the Basic Word that is related in spelling and meaning to *victorious*.

victory
victorious

Dictionary

Stressed Syllables Some words with more than one syllable may have two accent marks in the dictionary pronunciation.

ham·bur·ger |hăm′ bûr′ gər|

The syllable shown in dark print with a heavy accent mark has **primary stress**. It is pronounced with the most stress. The syllable with a light accent mark has **secondary stress**. It is pronounced with less stress.

Practice Write each word in syllables. Then underline the syllable that has primary stress. Circle the syllable with secondary stress. Use your Spelling Dictionary.

1. anything   **3.** afternoon   **5.** understand

2. alphabet   **4.** library   **6.** astronaut

Review: Spelling Spree

Syllable Scramble Rearrange the syllables in each item to form a Basic or Review Word. Write the words correctly. (One syllable in each item is extra.)

7. hap un ham py   **15.** fa grand ther al

8. grand er moth to   **16.** ger vem bur ham

9. er an oth ful   **17.** a ba em nan

10. car cam pen ter   **18.** tal tant pi hos

11. my e mal en   **19.** bo vic y tor

12. pen por tant im   **20.** day yes am ter

13. cam ar er a   **21.** part mem ment de

14. sev de er liv   **22.** mor row to lot

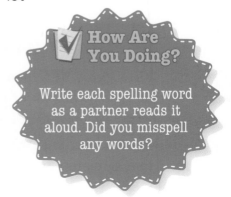

How Are You Doing?

Write each spelling word as a partner reads it aloud. Did you misspell any words?

Proofreading and Writing

Proofread for Spelling Find nine misspelled Basic or Review Words in this newspaper story. Write each one correctly.

Librarian Solves Mystery

Did you know that some mystery stories in a libary aren't in books? Just ask Mrs. White, the librarian.

"Last Octobor two people from the anamal hospital came in togather. They checked out sevral alfabet books," said Mrs. White.

"I rember thinking that was odd. It wasn't until Noveber, howevery, that I learned why they had checked out the books. They had been trying to teach a parrot to read!"

Basic

1. deliver
2. department
3. camera
4. yesterday
5. tomorrow
6. important
7. together
8. victory
9. remember
10. library
11. enemy
12. animal
13. another
14. however
15. banana
16. alphabet
17. hospital
18. hamburger
19. carpenter
20. several

Review

21. grandmother
22. grandfather
23. October
24. November
25. unhappy

Challenge

26. interview
27. article
28. journalist
29. edition
30. photograph

Write a News Story

Write a news story about an event in your school or neighborhood. Be sure to tell *who, what, when, where, why,* and *how*. Try to use five spelling words. You may also want to share your work.

Proofreading Tip **Check carefully for letters that have been left out of words.**

Proofreading Marks

¶ Indent
∧ Add
⌐ Delete
≡ Capital letter
/ Small letter

Expanding Vocabulary

graham cracker
bologna
cantaloupe
McIntosh apple
Swiss cheese

Words from Names Some foods are named for the places where they were first made or for the people who first made them. Where did the word *hamburger* come from?

History

Hamburger is named after *Hamburg,* a large city in northern Germany. Hamburgers were first made there.

Write the word from the box that matches each description.

1. a melon first grown in Cantalupo, Italy
2. a cheese first made in Switzerland
3. a fruit first grown by John McIntosh
4. a luncheon meat named for Bologna, Italy
5. a snack invented by Sylvester Graham

Work Together Each word in the box is pictured in the basket. With a partner write several sentences about the picture, using all the words in the box.

Fact File

The tangerine looks like an orange but is smaller and easier to peel. The name is taken from the city of Tangier, Morocco, where this yellowish-red fruit is grown.

Real-World Connection

Language Arts: Newspapers All the words in the box relate to newspapers. Look up these words in your Spelling Dictionary. Then write the words to complete this flow chart.

Spelling Word Link

journalist

newspaper
editor
press
headline
cartoon
deadline
reporter
caption

Many people work together to produce a story for a daily __(1)__ in time to meet the __(2)__.

First, a __(3)__ gathers the news and writes the story.

Another person gives the story a catchy __(5)__.

Next, the story goes to an __(4)__, who checks it for grammar.

For some stories an artist might draw a __(6)__ with a funny __(7)__ under it.

Then, before the paper goes to the printing __(8)__, someone decides on which page the story should appear.

Try This CHALLENGE

Clue Match Write a word from the box to match each clue.

9. If you meet it, you have done a job on time.
10. This person makes sure commas are used correctly.
11. This person questions people to get information.
12. It is usually set in big letters.

Silent Consonants

Read and Say

castle

Basic

READ the sentences. **SAY** each bold word.

1. knight — The king made the brave man a **knight**.
2. castle — The people inside the **castle** are safe from harm.
3. honor — A person of **honor** keeps every promise.
4. kneel — My legs hurt if I **kneel** too long.
5. climb — The child likes to **climb** trees.
6. wrinkle — My shirt has a **wrinkle** on the cuff.
7. limb — The strong wind broke the tree **limb**.
8. handsome — Your horse is such a **handsome** animal!
9. answer — Do you know the **answer** to my question?
10. calf — Every old cow was once a **calf**.
11. listen — My father always has time to **listen** to me.
12. calm — The ship is at rest in the **calm** waters.
13. knit — You need needles and yarn in order to **knit**.
14. often — The baby **often** falls asleep in the car.
15. palm — Which part of your hand is your **palm**?
16. thumb — I have green paint on my fingers and **thumb**.
17. wrist — Her watch is too small for her **wrist**.
18. lamb — The farmer cared for the **lamb** and the sheep.
19. knob — You can open the door by turning the **knob**.
20. honest — The judge is an **honest** woman you can trust.

Think and Write

Each word has a consonant that is not pronounced, or "silent."

kneel   clim**b**   calf   **w**rinkle   **h**onest

• Look at the twenty words on the list. Which letters are silent?

Now write each Basic Word under its silent consonant.

|n| Spelled kn	|r| Spelled wr	|ŏ| Spelled ho	Silent l
|m| Spelled mb		Silent t	Silent d or w

Review	23. wrong	Challenge	28. heir
21. talk	24. knock	26. reign	29. debt
22. knife	25. hour	27. knoll	30. wrestle

Independent Practice

Spelling Strategy Some words have silent consonants. The spellings of these words have to be remembered.

Word Analysis/Phonics Complete the exercises with Basic Words.

1–4. Write the word that rhymes with each word below.

    1. glisten   **3.** half

    2. numb   **4.** soften

5–6. Write the two words with the final |əl| sounds spelled *le*.

7–8. Write *palm*. Then change one letter to write another word.

Vocabulary: Analogies Write the Basic Word that completes each analogy.

    9. *Up* is to *down* as *stand* is to _____.

  10. *Cat* is to *kitten* as *sheep* is to _____.

  11. *Suitcase* is to *handle* as *door* is to _____.

  12. *Thread* is to *sew* as *yarn* is to _____.

  13. *Rough* is to *gentle* as *ugly* is to _____.

Challenge Words Write the Challenge Word that fits each meaning. Use your Spelling Dictionary.

  14. a small hill

  15. to rule over

  16. to struggle with

  17. something owed

  18. a person who has the right to property when someone dies

Spelling-Meaning Connection

How can you remember that *limb* ends with a *b*? Think of the related word *limber* in which the *b* is pronounced.

lim**b**
lim**b**er

19–20. Write *limb* and *limber*. Underline the letter that is silent in one word and pronounced in the other.

Review: Spelling Spree

Word Maze 1–11. Begin at the arrow and follow the Word Maze to find eleven Basic or Review Words. Write the words in order.

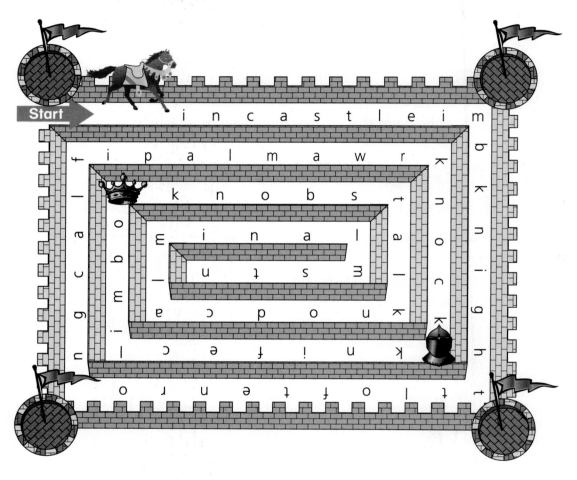

Words in Words Write the Basic or Review Word that appears in each word below.

12. hourglass
13. wristwatch
14. thumbtack
15. listener
16. handsomest
17. kneeling
18. wronged
19. lambskin
20. limber
21. honesty

22. knitting
23. wrinkled

24. honorable
25. answered

How Are You Doing?

List the spelling words that are hard for you. Practice them with a family member.

Proofreading and Writing

Proofread: Spelling and Using *I* and *me* Use *I* as the subject of a sentence. Use *me* after action verbs and words such as *to* and *with*. If you use *I* or *me* with another noun or pronoun, name yourself last.

> The **knight** and **I** met in the hall. He gave the ring to **me**.

Find four misspelled Basic or Review Words and two incorrect pronouns in this queen's note. Write the note correctly.

> The king and me are looking for the most honist knight in the kingdom. Come tak with the king and I for one hour. Whoever can anser our questions the most truthfully will be given a feast in his honer.

Basic

1. knight
2. castle
3. honor
4. kneel
5. climb
6. wrinkle
7. limb
8. handsome
9. answer
10. calf
11. listen
12. calm
13. knit
14. often
15. palm
16. thumb
17. wrist
18. lamb
19. knob
20. honest

Review
21. talk
22. knife
23. wrong
24. knock
25. hour

Challenge
26. reign
27. knoll
28. heir
29. debt
30. wrestle

Write a Proclamation

If you were a king or queen, what would you proclaim, or announce, to your subjects? Write a proclamation of your own. Try to use five spelling words.

Proofreading Tip

Check that you used *I* and *me* correctly in your sentences. Remember to name yourself last.

Proofreading Marks

¶ Indent
∧ Add
↘ Delete
≡ Capital letter
/ Small letter

213

Vocabulary Enrichment

Expanding Vocabulary

Spelling Word Link

thumb
palm
limb

Idioms If you are "all thumbs," are you made of thumbs? *All thumbs* means "having clumsy fingers." It is an **idiom**, an expression whose meaning differs from the meanings of its separate words.

Write the letter of the correct meaning for each underlined idiom. Use your Spelling Dictionary.

1. I <u>went out on a limb</u> when I corrected the teacher.
   a. climbed a tree   **b.** took a risk   **c.** fell down

2. The greedy thief had <u>an itchy palm</u>.
   a. a desire for money **b.** a rash   **c.** a large hand

3. I worked <u>around the clock</u> to finish the project.
   a. slowly   **b.** without stopping   **c.** next to a clock

4. Kate <u>threw in the towel</u> after she lost three times.
   a. cheered   **b.** put her towel away   **c.** gave up

5. The child <u>shed crocodile tears</u> when he saw the rain.
   a. pretended to cry   **b.** had a fear of crocodiles   **c.** cried loudly

Work Together With a partner choose three idioms, and use each one in a sentence. Then rewrite each sentence, replacing the idiom with words that show its meaning.

Example: Ira and José **hit it off** instantly.
Ira and José **liked each other** instantly.

 Fact File

Italian is another language rich with idioms. The expression *avere coda di paia*, for example, means "to be without courage." The literal translation is "to have a straw tail."

Real-World Connection

Social Studies: The Middle Ages All the words in the box relate to the Middle Ages. Look up these words in your Spelling Dictionary. Then write the words to complete the paragraph from a story.

Edgar shifted his body inside the heavy __(1)__. A crowd of poor __(2)__ lined the field. They had gathered to watch him compete in his first __(3)__. He was nervous, but he knew he could __(4)__ better than any of the other knights. He had received excellent training since coming to serve as a young __(5)__ in the large __(6)__ of his wealthy __(7)__ and lady. Edgar looked at the __(8)__ on his shield. He must do it honor by winning.

Spelling Word Link

knight

lord
manor
coat of arms
tournament
squire
peasants
armor
joust

Try This CHALLENGE

Write a Conversation Imagine that you have just discovered a time machine that takes you back to the Middle Ages. Write the conversation you have with the first person you meet. What do you talk about? What questions do you ask each other? Try to use words from the box.

Unusual Spellings

Read and Say

|ĕ|
health
|ē|
magazine

Basic

READ the sentences. **SAY** each bold word.

1. health   We nursed our sick cat back to **health**.
2. blood   The actor used red paint instead of **blood**.
3. type   I can **type** more words per minute than you.
4. against   Put your chair **against** the wall.
5. receive   Did you **receive** the card I mailed you?
6. flood   The rain caused a **flood** in the streets.
7. month   My birthday is the last day of this **month**.
8. magazine   Would you like to read a sports **magazine**?
9. guess   Take a **guess** at how many stairs we climbed.
10. women   These skirts and dresses are for short **women**.
11. guide   Our tour was led by a helpful **guide**.
12. style   Is a simple cotton shirt always in **style**?
13. wealth   The man with the big house has great **wealth**.
14. guilt   I feel no **guilt** if I have done nothing wrong.
15. says   My teacher **says** we need to study hard.
16. guard   The bank hires a **guard** to watch the safe.
17. wonder   The children **wonder** if the park will open.
18. guest   My aunt is bringing a **guest** to the party.
19. gasoline   Fill the tank of the car with **gasoline**.
20. either   The water is **either** too hot or too cold.

Think and Write

Each word has a sound with an unusual spelling pattern.

	ĕ	h**ea**lth, ag**ai**nst, s**ay**s		ē	rec**ei**ve, magaz**ine**
	ĭ	w**o**men		ī	t**y**pe (*y*-consonant-e)
	ŭ	bl**oo**d, m**o**nth		g	**gu**ess

- Look at the examples. What unusual spellings do you see?

Now write each Basic Word. Underline the unusual spellings.

Review
21. front
22. head
23. love
24. shoe
25. gym

Challenge
26. vaccine
27. quarantine
28. guarantee
29. threaten
30. rhyme

Independent Practice

Spelling Strategy Some words have sounds with unusual spellings. The spellings of these words have to be remembered.

Word Analysis/Phonics Complete the exercises with Basic Words.

1. Write the word that begins with the |ə| sound spelled *a*.

2–3. Write the two words that end with the |ər| sounds.

4–6. Write the word that rhymes with each word below.

    4. hard   **5.** ride   **6.** chest

Vocabulary: Definitions Write the Basic Word that fits each meaning.

7. adult females
8. four weeks
9. fuel for cars
10. a large amount of money
11. a large flow of water
12. liquid pumped by the heart
13. something published weekly or monthly

Challenge Words Write the Challenge Word that completes each sentence. Use your Spelling Dictionary.

14. Many diseases are curable and no longer _____ us.
15. Jonas Salk developed a _____ to protect against polio.
16. Sick people stay in _____ to keep germs from spreading.
17. My mom read me a nursery _____ whenever I was sick.
18. Eating properly cannot _____ good health, but it can help.

Spelling-Meaning Connection

Can you see *heal* in *health*? These words are related in spelling and meaning, though they have different vowel sounds.

Think of this: When you *heal*, you regain your *health*.

19–20. Write *heal* and the Basic Word that is related to *heal*.

Review: Spelling Spree

Hidden Words Write the Basic or Review Word that you find in each row of letters. Don't let the other words fool you!

Example: e i t h e a l t h e n   *health*

1. r e g y m u n t h
2. s e e f r o n t y p
3. g e s g u a r d e
4. f i e i t h e r y l e
5. m a g a s a y s h o
6. w e a g u i d e i t
7. b a g a i n s t i n g
8. h a p r e c e i v e r
9. f l o d b l o o d e d
10. w o m o n t h e a f

11. g u e s h o e a d
12. f e w o n d e r e s t
13. w o n w o m e n d e r
14. g a s t y l e a n
15. s w e a l t h y p e
16. g i m a g a z i n e x t
17. f r u n t y p e n
18. b e g a s o l i n e a r

Find a Rhyme Write the Basic or Review Word that rhymes with each underlined word and makes sense in the sentence.

Example: The tour _____ will be giving us a <u>ride</u>.   *guide*

19. Can you _____ who made this <u>mess</u>?
20. The man at the _____ of the table wants <u>bread</u>.
21. I would rather have good _____ than fame or <u>wealth</u>.
22. The <u>dove</u> is the symbol of _____.
23. I admit my _____. I let the flowers <u>wilt</u>.
24. We asked our _____ if she wanted to <u>rest</u>.
25. Please donate <u>blood</u> to help victims of the _____.

How Are You Doing?

Write your spelling words in ABC order. Practice any misspelled words with a family member.

Red Cross Volunteers Wanted

Proofreading and Writing

Basic

Proofread: Spelling and Contractions A **contraction** is formed by combining a verb and *not* or by combining a pronoun and a verb. Use an apostrophe to replace the letters that are dropped. (See page 250 in your Student's Handbook for more examples.)

I **have not** given blood before.   I **will** take your pulse.
I **haven't** given blood before.   **I'll** take your pulse.

Find four misspelled Basic or Review Words and two missing apostrophes in these instructions. Write the instructions correctly.

To give blood, see one of the woman at the frunt of the room. She'll record your blood tipe and make sure youre in good helth. Also, you'll receive some forms to fill out.

Basic
1. health
2. blood
3. type
4. against
5. receive
6. flood
7. month
8. magazine
9. guess
10. women
11. guide
12. style
13. wealth
14. guilt
15. says
16. guard
17. wonder
18. guest
19. gasoline
20. either

Review
21. front
22. head
23. love
24. shoe
25. gym

Challenge
26. vaccine
27. quarantine
28. guarantee
29. threaten
30. rhyme

Write a Personal Story

The Red Cross helps people in need. How have you helped someone? Write a personal story describing what you did. Perhaps you helped a classmate in school or helped out at home. Try to use five spelling words.

Helping Hands

Proofreading Tip

Be careful to check that you have used apostrophes correctly in contractions.

Proofreading Marks

¶ Indent
∧ Add
ꝰ Delete
≡ Capital letter
/ Small letter

Expanding Vocabulary

Spelling Word Link

gasoline

gym
exam
phone
sub
math

Shortened Forms Many long words have shortened forms. Read this example. How was *gasoline* shortened?

GASOLINE STATION ⟶ **GAS** STATION

Write a word from the box to make the short form of each underlined word.

1. The <u>telephone</u> rang two times before I answered it.
2. We have a history <u>examination</u> after every unit.
3. I wore my sneakers in the <u>gymnasium</u>.
4. The <u>submarine</u> moved slowly under the water.
5. Gloriann's favorite subject is <u>mathematics</u>.

Work Together Write the shortened form of the label for each picture. Use your Spelling Dictionary. Then, with a partner, write a sentence for each shortened form.

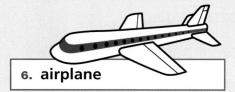

6. airplane

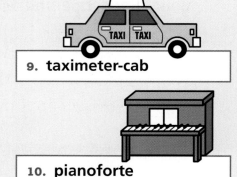

9. taximeter-cab

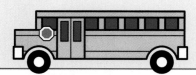

7. omnibus

10. pianoforte

8. automobile

Fact File

Good-bye comes from an old English farewell, "God be with you." First, it was shortened to "God be wi'ye." Next, it changed to "God bw' ye," then to "God bwye," and finally to "Good-bye." Now we often simply say "Bye!"

BUS

Real-World Connection

Health: The Red Cross All the words in the box relate to the Red Cross. Look up these words in your Spelling Dictionary. Then write the words to complete this poster.

Spelling Word Link

health

nurse
volunteer
disaster
accident
donor
victims
supplies
assist

Join Our Blood Drive!

Please __(1)__ to give to your local blood bank. We need you! Blood __(2)__ for every blood type are at an all-time low. Many people, such as the __(3)__ of an earthquake or other __(4)__ and people who have been in a car __(5)__, need your help. A registered __(6)__ in a white uniform will __(7)__ you in every way. Someday you may need a blood __(8)__ to save your own life!

AMBULANCE

Try This CHALLENGE

Yes or No? Write *yes* if the underlined word is used correctly. Write *no* if it is not.

9. I plan to <u>volunteer</u> at the clinic to earn some money.
10. The <u>victims</u> of the flood needed food and shelter.
11. If you need blood, please sign up to be a <u>donor</u>.
12. No one could prevent the <u>accident</u>.

36 Review: Units 31–35

v|cv
si|ren

Unit 31 VCV Pattern pages 192–197

| depend | ocean | police | parent | today |
| palace | event | exit | belong | award |

Spelling Strategy

| VC \| V | V \| CV |
| par \| ent | de \| pend |

Write a spelling word by adding the missing syllable.

1. ___ | long
2. ___ | vent
3. ___ | lice
4. ___ | ward
5. pal | ___
6. ___ | pend

Write the word that completes each sentence.

7. Are we going on a field trip _____ or tomorrow?
8. In case of fire, walk quickly to the nearest _____.
9. I swim in the _____ almost every day during the summer.
10. Children will not be admitted to the show without a _____.

Unit 32 VCCV and VCV Patterns pages 198–203

vc|cv
din|ner
vc|v
wag|on

| famous | reward | alone | wagon | divide |
| narrow | fancy | eager | parade | amaze |

Spelling Strategy

| VC \| CV | V \| CV | VC \| V |
| nar \| row | di \| vide | wag \| on |

Write a spelling word by adding the missing syllable.

11. ea | ___
12. fa | ___
13. ___ | rade
14. ___ | ward
15. ___ | maze
16. ___ | lone

Write the word that completes each analogy.

17. *Tall* is to *short* as *wide* is to _____.
18. *Runners* are to *sled* as *wheels* are to _____.
19. *Dull* is to *sharp* as *plain* is to _____.
20. *Add* is to *subtract* as *multiply* is to _____.

Unit 33 Three-Syllable Words pages 204–209

tomorrow	deliver	remember	department	yesterday
another	animal	several	hamburger	carpenter

de|liv|er

Spelling Strategy To spell a three-syllable word, divide the word into syllables. Remember to look for familiar spelling patterns, and spell the word by syllables.

Write the word that fits each meaning.

21. the day before today

22. a living creature

23. part of a company

24. the day after today

25. a second one

26. to take to someone

Write the word that belongs in each group.

27. bun, ketchup, _____

28. few, some, _____

29. plumber, mechanic, _____

30. forget, think, _____

Unit 34 Silent Consonants pages 210–215

climb	honor	knight	handsome	castle
wrist	knob	listen	thumb	calm

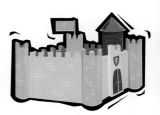

castle

Spelling Strategy Some words have silent consonants. The spellings of these words have to be remembered.

Write the word that completes each phrase.

31. a _____ in shining armor

32. the stone walls of the _____

33. truth, love, and _____

34. finger and _____

35. stop, look, and _____

36. peaceful and _____

Write the word that fits each clue.

37. You turn it to open a door.

38. It's how you go up a ladder.

39. It joins your arm and hand.

40. It describes someone who is good-looking.

|ĕ|
health
|ē|
magazine

receive	against	flood	health	women
guide	wonder	says	style	gasoline

Spelling Strategy   Some words have sounds with unusual spellings. The spellings of these words have to be remembered.

Write the word that rhymes with each word below.

41. hide   **42.** wealth   **43.** blood

Write the word that completes each sentence.

44. A car runs on _____.
45. Did you _____ a gift?
46. Many _____ are mothers.
47. Don't lean _____ the door.
48. Simon _____, "Sit down."
49. This suit is in _____ now.
50. I _____ what went wrong.

Challenge Words   **Units 31–35**   **pages 192–221**

quarantine	journalist	frontier	wrestle	reign
photograph	guarantee	stampede	marine	peril

Write the word that belongs in each group.

51. fight, struggle, _____
52. danger, threat, _____
53. reporter, writer, _____
54. painting, drawing, _____
55. promise, vow, _____

Write the word that completes each sentence.

56. Dr. Pym put Jill in _____ so that we wouldn't get sick.
57. In the sea there are many kinds of _____ animals.
58. Cattle might _____ if they are frightened.
59. Queen Elizabeth I of England had a long _____.
60. Life was often hard on the western _____.

Spelling-Meaning Strategy

Consonant Changes: The Sound of *t*

You have learned that some words in a word family often have the same spellings for different sounds. Read this paragraph.

> Casey needed time to **locate** her lost slippers. She finally found them in an odd **location**. They were in the wastebasket!

**locate
location**

Think

- What does *locate* mean? What does *location* mean? How are they related in meaning?
- What sound does the letter *t* spell in each word?

Here are more related words in which the spelling remains the same even though the sound of the *t* changes.

operate	decorate	punctuate
operation	decoration	punctuation

Apply and Extend

Complete these activities on a separate sheet of paper.

1. Use your Spelling Dictionary to look up the words in the box above. Write six sentences, using each word.

2. With a partner, list as many words as you can that are related to *locate*, *operate*, *decorate*, and *punctuate*. Then look at the section "Consonant Changes: The Sound of *t*" beginning on page 272 of your Spelling-Meaning Index. Add to your list any other words that you find in these families.

Summing Up

Knowing that words are related may help you spell them. In many words the sound of a final *t* may change when the ending *-ion* is added, but the spelling stays the same.

Literature and Writing

from

"The Adobe Way"

Adobes are buildings made of sun-dried bricks formed from a mixture of special soil, straw, and water. What kind of modern buildings were early Pueblo adobes like?

About two thousand years ago, the Pueblo Indians began building with adobe. If you visit the southwestern part of the United States today, you can still see very old Pueblo adobes, as well as new, modern ones.

The apartment-like buildings of the early Pueblos stood three to four stories high. Each level was built on top of the other in tiers, which were like giant steps. The flat roof of the ground floor made a front porch for the families living on the second floor, and so on up to the top.

The Pueblo adobes were simple but pleasant. The living spaces inside the apartments were small, and each family lived in one room. Narrow, T-shaped doors connected the rooms on each apartment level. The walls were painted with a fresh whitewash made from a chalk found in the desert. The whitewash gave the room a clean, fresh look and reflected firelight.

Think and Discuss

1 Early Pueblo adobes were similar to what kind of modern building? Why?

2 What facts do you learn about adobes in the first paragraph?

3 What is the topic sentence of the last paragraph? What supporting details are given in the other sentences?

The Writing Process
Research Report

What topic would you like to learn about? Choose one to research, and write a short report. Use the guidelines, and follow the Writing Process.

1 Prewriting
- Write five questions to answer about your topic.
- Research the answers and take notes.
- Organize your notes into an outline.

2 Draft
- Follow your outline.

3 Revise
- Highlight each topic sentence. Add ones that are missing.
- Use your Thesaurus to find exact words.
- Have a writing conference.

4 Proofread
- Did you spell each word correctly?
- Did you use capital letters and punctuation marks correctly?

5 Publish
- Add a title to a neat final copy.
- Make a Big Book with pictures that show facts in your report.

Guidelines for Writing a Research Report

✔ Write topic sentences that state the main ideas.
✔ Support each main idea with facts and details.
✔ Put all the paragraphs in an order that makes sense.
✔ Include an introduction and a conclusion.

Composition Words

today
important
event
tomorrow
amaze
honest
famous
wonder

My Cactus Report

Student's Handbook

Extra Practice and Review   Cycle 1

blade	gain	safe	drag	drain
plant	sale	shall	jail	glass

|ă|
plant

Spelling Strategy   Remember that the |ă| sound is usually spelled **a** followed by a consonant sound. When you hear the |ā| sound, think of the patterns **a-consonant-e**, **ai**, and **ay**.

Write the word that rhymes with each word below.

1. flag
2. ant
3. pass
4. shade

Write the word that fits each clue.

5. It means the opposite of *lose*.
6. You can keep valuables in it.
7. It takes place at a store.
8. Its rooms are cells.
9. Water goes down it.
10. It often means *will*.

|ā|
skate

free	feast	cream	fresh	peach
real	speed	dream	desk	east

|ĕ| |ē|
fresh   **peach**

Spelling Strategy   Remember that the |ĕ| sound is usually spelled **e** followed by a consonant sound. When you hear the |ē| sound, think of the patterns **ea** and **ee**.

Write the word that belongs in each group.

11. milk, butter, _____
12. chair, table, _____
13. new, clean, _____
14. west, north, _____

Write the word that rhymes with each underlined word.

15. The <u>beast</u> ate the _____.
16. Did I <u>scream</u> in my _____?
17. I tried to <u>reach</u> the _____.
18. Do the <u>deed</u> with _____!
19. Please _____ the <u>bee</u>.
20. Is that a _____ <u>seal</u>?

|ĭ|
brick

|ī|
shine

Unit 3　　Spelling |ĭ| and |ī|　　pages 24–29

brick	lift	skill	pride	crime
sting	inch	wind	ripe	sigh

Spelling Strategy　　Remember that the |ĭ| sound is often spelled **i** followed by a consonant sound. When you hear the |ī| sound, think of the patterns **i**-consonant-**e**, **igh**, and **i**.

Write the word that appears in each word below.

21. prideful　　　**24.** skillful
22. ripen　　　　**25.** inching
23. sighed　　　 **26.** lifted

Write the word that completes each phrase.

27. a bee _____
28. the cold, blowing _____
29. to commit a _____
30. a _____ wall

|ŏ|
block

|ō|
gold

Unit 4　　Spelling |ŏ| and |ō|　　pages 30–35

globe	goal	spoke	snow	odd
chose	folk	shock	bowl	host

Spelling Strategy　　Remember that the |ŏ| sound is usually spelled **o** followed by a consonant sound. When you hear the |ō| sound, think of the patterns **o**-consonant-**e**, **oa**, **ow**, and **o**.

Write the word that means the same as each word below.

31. picked　　　**34.** aim
32. strange　　 **35.** said
33. surprise　　**36.** people

Write the word that belongs in each group.

37. party, guest, _____　　**39.** map, chart, _____
38. cup, plate, _____　　　**40.** rain, sleet, _____

Unit 5   Homophones   pages 36–41

lead	peak	beet	creek	deer
led	peek	beat	creak	dear

ring

Spelling Strategy

Homophones are words that sound alike but have different meanings and spellings. When you write a homophone, be sure to spell the word that has the meaning you want.

wring

Write the word that fits each clue.

41. This metal is very heavy.
42. This plant is tasty.
43. A mountaintop has one.

44. An old door might do this.
45. This animal is very swift.
46. This person is much loved.

Write a word to replace the underlined word or words in each phrase below.

47. to win against another team
48. to be guided through a cave

49. a quick look at a baby
50. to wade in a brook

Challenge Words   Units 1–5   pages 12–41

recognize	relay	vane	restaurant	advice
longitude	rigid	vain	activity	motion
accomplish	yeast	vein	champion	menu

Write the word that rhymes with the word in parentheses to complete each phrase.

51. _____ for bread (least)
52. a _____ attempt (pain)
53. a weather _____ (cane)

54. to _____ the news (delay)
55. a swift _____ (lotion)
56. _____ planks of wood (frigid)

Write the word that fits each clue.

57. may help you solve a problem
58. to succeed in doing something
59. to remember someone's face
60. something you do to keep busy
61. something that lists sandwiches
62. where waiters work

63. opposite of latitude
64. a blood vessel
65. the one who finished the race first

|oo|	|ŭ|
tube	**brush**

Unit 7   Spelling |ŭ|, |yōō|, and |ōō| pages 48–53

brush	few	true	crumb	juice
pump	sum	dull	blew	due

Spelling Strategy

|ŭ| → **u** followed by a consonant sound

|yōō| or |ōō| → **u**-consonant-**e, ew, ue, ui**

Write the word that fits each meaning.

1. liquid from fruit
2. sent a stream of air
3. total
4. owed
5. not interesting
6. a small number

Write the word that completes each analogy.

7. *Wrong* is to *right* as *false* is to _____.
8. *Wood* is to *chip* as *bread* is to _____.
9. *Water* is to *faucet* as *gasoline* is to _____.
10. *Pen* is to *pencil* as *comb* is to _____.

|ŏŏ|	|ōō|
wood	**stool**

Unit 8   Spelling |ōō| and |ŏŏ| pages 54–59

brook	wool	roof	put	full
stood	bush	fool	shoot	smooth

Spelling Strategy

|ōō| → **oo**

|ŏŏ| → **oo** or **u** followed by a consonant sound

Write the word that rhymes with each word below.

11. push
12. wood
13. boot
14. pool
15. cook
16. proof

Write the word that fits each clue.

17. You can make mittens from it.
18. It could describe the feeling of silk.
19. It means the opposite of *empty*.
20. It can mean "to place."

Cycle 2

Unit 9   Spelling |ou| and |ô| pages 60–65

| bounce | shout | aloud | south | jaw |
| drawn | proud | scout | mount | gown |

|ou|
pound
howl

Spelling Strategy

|ou| → **ou, ow** |ô| → **aw, au, a** before **l**

Write the word that means the same as each word below.

21. dress   **24.** explore

22. sketched   **25.** climb

23. yell

Write the word that completes each sentence.

26. The weather grows warmer as you travel _____.

27. Sarah felt _____ to be a member of the winning team.

28. Emilio had a funny thought, but he did not say it _____.

29. The baby watched the ball _____ down the steps.

30. Charlie has a toothache in his lower _____.

Unit 10   Spelling |îr|, |är|, and |âr| pages 66–71

| gear | spear | sharp | stare | hairy |
| year | scarf | starve | charge | stairs |

|îr| |âr|
gear   **stare**

Spelling Strategy

|îr| → **ear, eer** |är| → **ar** |âr| → **are, air**

Write the word by adding the missing letters.

31. ch _ _ ge   **33.** st _ _ _   **35.** sh _ _ p

32. sp _ _ _   **34.** st _ _ ve   **36.** y _ _ _

Write the word that belongs in each group.

37. supplies, equipment, _____

38. elevator, escalator, _____

39. belt, tie, _____

40. feather, woolly, _____

|ôr| |ûr|

worn shirt

Unit 11 Spelling |ôr|, |ûr|, and |yŏŏr| pages 72–77

chore	firm	dirty	world	pure
worn	earn	curl	burn	shirt

Spelling Strategy

|ôr| → **or, ore** |ûr| → **ur, ear, ir, or** |yŏŏr| → **ure**

Write the word that rhymes with the word in parentheses to complete each phrase.

41. to button a _____ (flirt)

42. _____ from much use (born)

43. a _____ white horse (cure)

44. a tiring _____ (store)

45. to _____ a living (learn)

46. _____ laundry (thirty)

Write the word that fits each clue.

47. where all humans live

48. to set on fire

49. solid or fixed in place

50. a ring of hair

Challenge Words Units 7–11 pages 48–77

earnest	cocoon	weary	attitude	marvel
startle	superb	doubt	foreign	soot
slumber	hurdle	prowl	tissue	gnaw

Write the word that is a synonym for each word below.

51. strange

52. magnificent

53. tired

54. dirt

55. distrust

56. frighten

57. doze

58. truthful

59. chew

Write a word to replace the underlined word or words in each phrase below.

60. to move secretly in the dark

61. a moth leaving its shell

62. to gaze with wonder at

63. wrapped in thin paper

64. to jump over a fence

65. a happy state of mind

Unit 13   Compound Words   pages 84–89

railroad	airport	understand	ninety-nine	homesick
whenever	all right	everything	fireplace	afternoon

railroad

Spelling Strategy   A **compound word** is made up of two or more smaller words. To spell a compound word correctly, you must know if it is written as one word, as two words joined by a hyphen, or as two separate words.

Write the compound word that contains each underlined word.

1. <u>sick</u>ly   **2.** <u>noth</u>ing   **3.** re<u>place</u>   **4.** <u>stand</u>ing   **5.** <u>air</u>y

Write the compound word that fits each clue.

6. It is the last number before one hundred.

7. This time of day is neither morning nor night.

8. It means "good enough."

9. It has tracks that go all over the country.

10. It means "at whatever time."

Unit 14   Final |ər| pages 90–95

enter	labor	ladder	suffer	weather
favor	bitter	shower	temper	proper

|ər|
sailor

Spelling Strategy   When you hear the final |ər| sounds in a two-syllable word, think of the patterns **er, or,** and **ar.**

Write the word that rhymes with each underlined word.

11. Nothing looked <u>sadder</u> than the old, broken _____.

12. Please _____ through the door in the <u>center</u>.

13. Fish is the <u>flavor</u> that most kittens _____.

14. If you were a <u>flower</u>, you would like a spring _____.

Write the word by adding the missing syllable.

15. weath | ___   **17.** bit | ___   **19.** tem | ___

16. prop | ___   **18.** la | ___   **20.** suf | ___

Unit 15　　　　Final |l| or |əl|　　　　pages 96–101

| nickel | metal | total | middle | bottle |
| handle | title | uncle | simple | battle |

Spelling Strategy　　When you hear the final |l| or |əl| sounds in a two-syllable word, think of the patterns **el, al,** and **le.**

|l|　　　|əl|
medal　**eag**le

Write the word that is a synonym for each word below.

21. center　**23.** fight　**25.** complete

22. easy　**24.** name

Write the word that belongs in each group.

26. wood, plastic, _____

27. strap, knob, _____

28. cousin, nephew, _____

29. can, jar, _____

30. penny, dime, _____

Unit 16　　　Words with *-ed* and *-ing*　　pages 102–107

| dancing | hiking | flipped | landed | dared |
| wasting | dimmed | tanning | traced | smelling |

Spelling Strategy

land + **ed** = land**ed**　　　dare − e + **ed** = dar**ed**

ta**n** + n + **ing** = tan**ning**

Write the word that rhymes with each word below.

31. cared　**33.** tasting　**35.** prancing

32. tripped　**34.** placed

Write the word that fits each clue.

36. the opposite of *brightened*　**39.** climbing mountains

37. happening from the sun　**40.** past tense of *land*

38. sniffing an odor

Cycle 3

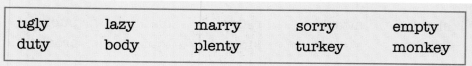

Unit 17   Final |ē| pages 108–113

ugly	lazy	marry	sorry	empty
duty	body	plenty	turkey	monkey

|ē|
hungry
turkey
empty

Spelling Strategy

final |ē| → **y, ey**

Write the word that means the opposite of each word below.

41. glad   **43.** few   **45.** pretty

42. full   **44.** active

Write the word that completes each sentence.

46. The Pacific Ocean is the largest _____ of water.

47. The _____ leaped from tree to tree.

48. A doctor's _____ is to help the sick.

49. Uncle Lenny roasted a big _____ for Thanksgiving.

50. The princess agreed to _____ the prince.

Challenge Words   Units 13–17   pages 84–113

motorcycle	anchor	lunar	breathing	landmark
postscript	cancel	mercy	scarred	solar
industrial	urged	fiery	decimal	envy

Write the word that fits each meaning.

51. fraction   **54.** longing   **57.** ablaze

52. sympathy   **55.** to end   **58.** begged

53. damaged   **56.** inhaling

Write the word that completes each analogy.

59. *Pedals* are to *bicycle* as *engine* is to _____.

60. *Tree* is to *roots* as *boat* is to _____.

61. *Book* is to *bookmark* as *land* is to _____.

62. *Pole* is to *polar* as *sun* is to _____.

63. *Star* is to *moon* as *stellar* is to _____.

64. *Dr.* is to *doctor* as *P.S.* is to _____.

65. *Finance* is to *financial* as *industry* is to _____.

|k|
shark

Unit 19   Spelling |k|, |ng|, and |kw| pages 120–125

shark	attack	risk	blank	public
drink	struck	junk	topic	crooked

Spelling Strategy

|k| → **k, ck, c** |ng| → **n** before **k** |kw| → **qu**

Write the word that rhymes with the word in parentheses to complete each phrase.

1. a box full of _____ (chunk)
2. a _____ in the water (park)
3. _____ out the batter (luck)
4. a cool _____ (think)
5. a dangerous _____ (disk)
6. a _____ page (crank)

Write the word that fits each meaning.

7. subject
8. not straight
9. open to all people
10. to make a sudden, violent move against

|ĭj| **cott**age
|j| **bri**dge
|s| **fen**ce

Unit 20   Final |j| and |s| pages 126–131

cottage	fence	chance	cage	village
cabbage	ridge	manage	dodge	marriage

Spelling Strategy

|j| → **dge, ge** (one-syllable words) |s| → **ce**
|ĭj| → **age** (two-syllable words)

Write the word by adding the missing letters.

11. r i _ _ _
12. man _ _ _
13. fen _ _
14. do _ _ _
15. chan _ _
16. vill _ _ _

Write the word that completes each analogy.

17. *Fruit* is to *apple* as *vegetable* is to _____.
18. *Carry* is to *carriage* as *marry* is to _____.
19. *Fish* is to *bowl* as *bird* is to _____.
20. *Big* is to *little* as *castle* is to _____.

Unit 21   Words with Prefixes   pages 132–137

| refill | discolor | untidy | rewind | redo |
| reheat | distrust | unpaid | unpack | reread |

Spelling Strategy   A **prefix** is a word part added to the beginning of a base word. It adds meaning to the word. **Un-, re-,** and **dis-** are prefixes.

Write the word that contains each underlined base word below.

21. pack<u>age</u>   **23.** <u>fill</u>ed   **25.** un<u>wind</u>

22. mis<u>trust</u>   **24.** <u>color</u>less   **26.** <u>do</u>ing

Write the word that completes each sentence.

27. We will _____ the leftovers in the oven.

28. A room with an unmade bed always looks _____.

29. Have you written a check for your _____ bill?

30. I liked the book so much that I am going to _____ it.

Unit 22   VCCV Pattern   pages 138–143

| attend | number | support | person | offer |
| helmet | tender | suppose | fellow | harvest |

vc|cv
hel|met
pic|ture

Spelling Strategy   To spell a word with the VCCV syllable pattern, divide the word between the consonants.

Write the word by adding the missing syllable.

31. ___ | son   **34.** ___ | pose

32. fel | ___   **35.** of | ___

33. ___ | port   **36.** har | ___

Write a word to replace the underlined word or words in each phrase below.

37. to <u>go to a wedding</u>   **39.** <u>gentle, loving care</u>

38. an even <u>numeral</u>   **40.** a football <u>head covering</u>

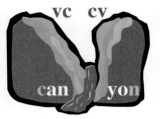

vc   cv
can   yon

Unit 23   VCCV Pattern   pages 144–149

| bottom | hollow | member | current | plastic |
| pillow | master | thirty | lumber | engine |

Spelling Strategy   To spell a word with the VCCV syllable pattern, divide the word between the consonants. Look for patterns you have learned, and spell the word by syllables.

Write the word that rhymes with each word below.

41. faster   **43.** dirty   **45.** elastic
42. number   **44.** ember

Write the word that belongs in each group.

46. top, middle, _____
47. sheet, blanket, _____
48. wave, tide, _____
49. tires, steering wheel, _____
50. empty, vacant, _____

Challenge Words   Units 19–23   pages 120–149

aquatic	fleece	filter	discontinue	peculiar
venture	vessel	rascal	fragrance	squid
unusual	candid	fringe	rearrange	eddy

Write the word that is a synonym for each word below.

51. reorganize   **54.** risk   **57.** edge
52. scoundrel   **55.** smell   **58.** stop
53. ship   **56.** unposed

Write the word that completes each sentence.

59. The ability to breathe underwater is _____ to fish.
60. An octopus has eight arms, but a _____ has ten!
61. Blue is an _____ color for a rose.
62. The _____ was caused by a change in the water's direction.
63. The swimmers practiced diving and other _____ skills.
64. Those fluffy white clouds remind me of a sheep's _____.
65. My sunglasses have a _____ that blocks out harmful rays.

Unit 25 — Changing Final *y* to *i* — pages 156–161

sunnier	noisier	cloudier	windier	heaviest
funnier	hobbies	crazier	copied	emptied

cloud *y* → *ier*

Spelling Strategy If a word ends with a consonant and **y**, change the **y** to **i** when adding **-es, -ed, -er,** or **-est.**

Write the word by adding the missing letters.

1. hobb _ _ _
2. cloud _ _ _
3. wind _ _ _
4. cop _ _ _
5. craz _ _ _
6. sunn _ _ _

Write the word that completes each analogy.

7. *Smallest* is to *largest* as *lightest* is to _____.
8. *Softer* is to *quieter* as *louder* is to _____.
9. *Added* is to *subtracted* as *filled* is to _____.
10. *Silly* is to *sillier* as *funny* is to _____.

Unit 26 — VCV Pattern — pages 162–167

navy	silent	human	music	pilot
tuna	stolen	basic	fever	moment

Spelling Strategy When the first vowel sound in a VCV word is long, divide the word into syllables before the consonant. Remember to look for patterns you have learned, and spell the word by syllables.

v|cv
pi|lot

Write the word that belongs in each group.

11. cough, sore throat, _____
12. aqua, blue, _____
13. driver, conductor, _____
14. cod, salmon, _____
15. art, dance, _____

Write the word that fits each meaning.

16. taken without right
17. forming the main part
18. a person
19. quiet
20. an instant

Unit 27   VCV Pattern   pages 168–173

| planet | visit | salad | magic | seven |
| talent | limit | never | habit | punish |

**vc|v
rob|in
cab|in**

Spelling Strategy

When the first syllable of a VCV word has a short vowel sound followed by a consonant sound, divide the word into syllables after the consonant. Remember to look for patterns you have learned, and spell the word by syllables.

Write the word by adding the missing syllable.

21. vis | ___   **23.** plan | ___   **25.** nev | ___

22. ___ | ic   **24.** ___ | ish

Write the word that fits each clue.

26. It is an action you repeat.   **29.** It comes after six.

27. You need it to be an artist.   **30.** It stops you.

28. It often includes lettuce.

Unit 28   Words with Suffixes   pages 174–179

| sickness | colorful | painful | fearful | endless |
| darkness | restless | kindness | statement | hopeless |

**ill   ness
sick   ness**

Spelling Strategy

color + **ful** = color**ful**   hope + **less** = hope**less**

Write the word that means the opposite of each word below.

31. limited   **33.** cruelty   **35.** health

32. still   **34.** brightness   **36.** brave

Write the word that completes each sentence.

37. The speaker answered the question with a brief _____.

38. The _____ bouquet of flowers cheered me up.

39. Cool water can relieve a _____ burn.

40. With no chance of winning, the team felt _____.

Cycle 5

Unit 29	VCCV Pattern		pages 180–185

machine	secret	gather	other	asleep
bucket	apron	pocket	ticket	rather

vcc|v
chick|en
rock|et

Spelling Strategy   If the consonants in a VCCV word are different and form a cluster or spell one sound, divide the word before or after the two consonants. Look for patterns you have learned, and spell the word by syllables.

Write the word that completes each phrase.

41. on the _____ hand
42. a hole in your shirt _____
43. a _____ that needs oil
44. a free _____ to a game

Write the word that fits each clue.

45. to come together
46. something hidden
47. to a certain extent
48. worn for cooking
49. not awake
50. holds water

Challenge Words	Units 25–29		pages 156–185

ailment	abrupt	vivid	reflect	cleanliness
jealous	diesel	waver	hazard	qualities
vibrate	hazier	radar	iciest	numbness

Write the word that contains each word below.

51. clean   **52.** numb   **53.** ail

Write the word that fits each clue.

54. It uses radio waves to locate objects.
55. If you sway back and forth about a decision, you do this.

Write a word to replace each underlined word or phrase.

56. sudden changes in the weather
57. the most frozen, slippery road
58. piano strings that quiver
59. a less clear sky than yesterday's
60. resentful of another's fortune
61. to mirror
62. clear, bright colors
63. a fire danger
64. oil-burning engines
65. positive features

v|cv
si|ren

Unit 31   VCV Pattern   pages 192–197

defend	become	below	relate	siren
polite	figure	delay	clever	open

Spelling Strategy

VC | V   V | CV

fig | ure   si | ren

Write the word by adding the missing syllable.

1. ___ | fend   3. fig | ___   5. ___ | late
2. o | ___   4. ___ | come   6. si | ___

Write the word that completes each rhyme.

7. On the lake people <u>row</u> while the fish swim _____.
8. After farmers cut the <u>hay</u>, they gather it without _____.
9. Dogs that <u>bite</u> are not _____.
10. My teacher has <u>never</u> had students so _____!

vc|cv
din|ner
vc|v
wag|on

Unit 32   VCCV and VCV Patterns   pages 198–203

silver	nature	office	capture	shelter
corner	dinner	minute	bacon	diner

Spelling Strategy

VC | CV   V | CV   VC | V

din | ner   ba | con   min | ute

Write the word that belongs in each group.

11. ham, pork, _____   14. second, hour, _____
12. breakfast, lunch, _____ 15. copper, tin, _____
13. cafeteria, restaurant, _____

Write the word that fits each clue.

16. It is a synonym for *catch*.   19. A circle never has one.
17. It keeps you warm and dry.   20. It is a place to work.
18. The outdoors is part of it.

Cycle 6

Unit 33   Three-Syllable Words   pages 204–209

camera	victory	library	important	together
banana	however	alphabet	hospital	enemy

de|liv|er

Spelling Strategy   To spell a three-syllable word, divide the word into syllables. Remember to look for familiar spelling patterns, and spell the word by syllables.

Write the word that contains each underlined syllable.

21. vic̲tim   **23.** l̲icense   **25.** some̲how̲
22. digit̲al   **24.** a̲lbum   **26.** por̲tion

Write the word that completes each analogy.

27. *Painter* is to *paintbrush* as *photographer* is to _____.
28. *Love* is to *hate* as *friend* is to _____.
29. *Red* is to *tomato* as *yellow* is to _____.
30. *Divided* is to *whole* as *apart* is to _____.

Unit 34   Silent Consonants   pages 210–215

kneel	limb	calf	wrinkle	answer
often	lamb	knit	honest	palm

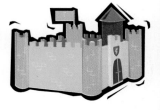

castle

Spelling Strategy   Some words have silent consonants. The spellings of these words have to be remembered.

Write the word by adding the missing letter.

31. lim _   **34.** pa _ m
32. _ nit   **35.** ca _ f
33. _ rinkle   **36.** lam _

Write the word that completes each sentence.

37. Chandra raised her hand to _____ the question.
38. We trust Caleb because he is always _____.
39. I wish Aunt Grace would visit us more _____.
40. I had to _____ to get a closer look at the tiny flower.

245

|ĕ|
health
|ē|
magazine

Unit 35   Unusual Spellings   pages 216–221

blood	guess	month	type	magazine
guest	guilt	guard	wealth	either

Spelling Strategy   Some words have sounds with unusual spellings. The spellings of these words have to be remembered.

Write the word that fits each clue.

41. rhymes with *neither*

42. someone who keeps watch

43. opposite of *host*

44. a bad feeling from doing something wrong

Write the word that belongs in each group.

45. fame, fortune, _____

46. heart, veins, _____

47. book, newspaper, _____

48. day, week, _____

49. write, print, _____

50. assume, suppose, _____

Challenge Words   Units 31–35   pages 192–221

rhyme	vaccine	cadet	alert	interview
sheriff	prairie	rival	heir	threaten
edition	article	knoll	debt	corral

Write the word that completes each phrase.

51. a polio _____

52. an owed _____

53. _____ to the throne

54. horses in a _____

55. a _____ wearing a badge

56. a _____ in training to be an officer

Write the word that belongs in each group.

57. field, meadow, _____

58. conversation, meeting, _____

59. enemy, opponent, _____

60. copy, version, _____

61. endanger, bother, _____

62. awake, aware, _____

63. hill, rise, _____

64. poem, verse, _____

65. story, report, _____

Writer's Resources

Capitalization and Punctuation Guide

Abbreviations

	Abbreviations are shortened forms of words. Most abbreviations begin with a capital letter and end with a period.
Titles	Mr. *(Mister)* Mr. Juan Albano Sr. *(Senior)* John Helt, Sr. Mrs. *(Mistress)* Mrs. Frances Wong Jr. *(Junior)* John Helt, Jr. Ms. Leslie Clark Dr. *(Doctor)* Dr. Janice Dodd Note: *Miss* is not an abbreviation and does not end with a period.
Words used in addresses	St. *(Street)* Blvd. *(Boulevard)* Rd. *(Road)* Ave. *(Avenue)*
Days of the week	Sun. *(Sunday)* Wed. *(Wednesday)* Fri. *(Friday)* Mon. *(Monday)* Thurs. *(Thursday)* Sat. *(Saturday)* Tues. *(Tuesday)*
Months of the year	Jan. *(January)* Apr. *(April)* Oct. *(October)* Feb. *(February)* Aug. *(August))* Nov. *(November)* Mar. *(March)* Sept. *(September)* Dec. *(December)* Note: *May, June,* and *July* are not abbreviated.
States	**The United States Postal Service uses two capital letters and no period in each of its state abbreviations.**

AL	*(Alabama)*	IN	*(Indiana)*	NE	*(Nebraska)*
AK	*(Alaska)*	IA	*(Iowa)*	NV	*(Nevada)*
AZ	*(Arizona)*	KS	*(Kansas)*	NH	*(New Hampshire)*
AR	*(Arkansas)*	KY	*(Kentucky)*	NJ	*(New Jersey)*
CA	*(California)*	LA	*(Louisiana)*	NM	*(New Mexico)*
CO	*(Colorado)*	ME	*(Maine)*	NY	*(New York)*
CT	*(Connecticut)*	MD	*(Maryland)*	NC	*(North Carolina)*
DE	*(Delaware)*	MA	*(Massachusetts)*	ND	*(North Dakota)*
FL	*(Florida)*	MI	*(Michigan)*	OH	*(Ohio)*
GA	*(Georgia)*	MN	*(Minnesota)*	OK	*(Oklahoma)*
HI	*(Hawaii)*	MS	*(Mississippi)*	OR	*(Oregon)*
ID	*(Idaho)*	MO	*(Missouri)*	PA	*(Pennsylvania)*
IL	*(Illinois)*	MT	*(Montana)*	RI	*(Rhode Island)*

(continued)

States (continued)	SC *(South Carolina)*	UT *(Utah)*	WV *(West Virginia)*
	SD *(South Dakota)*	VT *(Vermont)*	WI *(Wisconsin)*
	TN *(Tennessee)*	VA *(Virginia)*	WY *(Wyoming)*
	TX *(Texas)*	WA *(Washington)*	

Titles

Underlining	**Titles of books, newspapers, magazines, and TV series are underlined. The important words and the first and last words are capitalized.**
	Life on the Mississippi Newsweek Nova
Quotation marks	**Put quotation marks (" ") around the titles of short stories, articles, songs, poems, and book chapters.**
	"The Necklace" *(short story)* "Home on the Range" *(song)*

Quotations

Quotation marks	**A direct quotation tells a speaker's exact words. Use quotation marks (" ") to set off a direct quotation from the rest of the sentence.**
	"Please put away your books now," said Mr. Emory.
	Begin a quotation with a capital letter. When a quotation comes at the end of a sentence, use a comma to separate the quotation from the words that tell who is speaking. Put end marks inside the last quotation marks.
	The driver announced, "This is the Summer Street bus."
Writing a conversation	**Begin a new paragraph each time a new person begins speaking.**
	"Are your seats behind home plate or along the first-base line?" asked the voice on the phone. "I haven't bought any tickets yet," said Mr. Williams. "I was hoping that you would reserve three seats for me now."

Capitalization

Rules for capitalization

Capitalize the first word of every sentence.

What an unusual color the roses are!

Capitalize the pronoun *I*.

What should I do next?

Capitalize every important word in the names of particular people, pets, places, and things (proper nouns).

Rover   District of Columbia   Elm Street   Lincoln Memorial

Capitalize titles and initials that are parts of names.

Governor Bradford   Emily G. Hesse   Senator Smith

Capitalize family titles when they are used as names or as parts of names.

We visited Uncle Harry.   May we play now, Grandma?

Capitalize the names of months and days.

My birthday is on the last Monday in March.

Capitalize the names of groups.

Sutton Bicycle Club   National League

Capitalize the names of holidays.

Memorial Day   Fourth of July   Veterans Day

Capitalize the first and last words and all important words in the titles of books and newspapers.

From Earth to the Moon   The New York Times

Capitalize the first word in the greeting and the closing of a letter.

Dear Marcia,   Yours truly,

Rules for capitalization *(continued)*

In an outline, each Roman numeral and capital letter is followed by a period. Capitalize the first word of each main topic and subtopic.

I. Types of libraries
   A. Large public library
   B. Bookmobile

Punctuation

End marks

There are three end marks. A period (.) ends a statement or a command. A question mark (?) follows a question. An exclamation point (!) follows an exclamation.

The scissors are on my desk. *(statement)*
Look up the spelling of that word. *(command)*
How is the word spelled? *(question)*
This is your best poem so far! *(exclamation)*

Apostrophe

To form the possessive of a singular noun, add an apostrophe and *s* (*'s*).

baby's   Russ's   grandmother's   family's

For a plural noun ending in *s*, add only an apostrophe (').

sisters'   families'   Smiths'   hound dogs'

For a plural noun that does not end in *s*, add an apostrophe and *s* (*'s*).

women's   mice's   children's

Use an apostrophe in contractions in place of dropped letters.

isn't *(is not)*   it's *(it is)*
can't *(cannot)*   I'm *(I am)*
won't *(will not)*   you'll *(you will)*
wasn't *(was not)*   they've *(they have)*
you're *(you are)*

Comma

A comma (,) tells the reader to pause between the words that it separates.

Use commas to separate items in a series. Put a comma after each item in the series except the last one.

Clyde asked if we had any apples, peaches, or grapes.

You can combine two short, related sentences to make one compound sentence. Use a comma and the connecting word *and, but,* or *or.*

Some students were at lunch, but others were studying.

Use commas to set off the words *yes, no,* and *well* when they are at the beginning of a sentence.

Well, it's just too cold out.   No, it isn't six yet.

Use a comma or commas to set off the names of people who are spoken to directly.

Jean, help me fix this tire.   How was your trip, Grandpa?

Use a comma to separate the month and the day from the year.

Our nation was born on July 4, 1776.

Use a comma between the names of a city and a state.

Chicago, Illinois   Miami, Florida

Use a comma after the greeting in a friendly letter.

Dear Deena,   Dear Uncle Rudolph,

Use a comma after the closing in a letter.

Your nephew,   Sincerely yours,

Writer's Resources

Letter Model
Friendly Letter

Use correct letter form, capitalization, and punctuation when you write a friendly letter. Remember that a friendly letter has **five** parts.

1 The **heading** gives your complete address and the date.

2 The **greeting** usually includes the word *Dear* and the name of the person to whom you are writing.

3 The **body** is the main part of the letter. It includes all the information that you want to tell your reader.

4 The **closing** says "good-bye." Use closings such as *Your friend* or *Love*.

5 The **signature** is your name. Sign your first name below the closing.

Study this model.

Heading ⟶
483 Mill Road
Durham, NH 03824
September 15, 1998

Greeting ⟶ Dear Uncle Pete,

Body ⟶
I saw a hawk today. Dad says that all the hawks will fly south soon. Will you see them when they stop in North Carolina?

It is too cold to go swimming here. I'm sorry I can't fly down and go to the beach with you right now!

Let me know how many hawks you see. Maybe one will be mine!

Closing ⟶ Love,

Tonya ⟵ **Signature**

Using the Thesaurus

Why Use a Thesaurus?

A **thesaurus** is a reference that can help you make your writing clearer and more interesting. Use it to find a word to replace an overused word or to find an exact word to say what you mean.

How to Use This Thesaurus

Understanding a Main Entry This thesaurus includes main entries for words you often use. The **main entry words** appear in blue and are in alphabetical order. The main entry for *important* is shown below. Each main entry includes

- the **part of speech,** a **definition**, and a **sample sentence** for the main entry word;

- several **subentry words** that could be used in place of the main entry word, with a definition and a sample sentence for each one;

- **antonyms**, or opposites, for the main entry word.

For example   **How would you decide which subentry to use to replace *important* in this sentence?**

*July 4 is an **important** date in history.*

1 Find each subentry word given for *important*. They are *major* and *significant*.

2 Read the definition and the sample sentence for each subentry. Decide which subentry fits the meaning of the sentence most closely.

*July 4 is a **significant** date in history.*

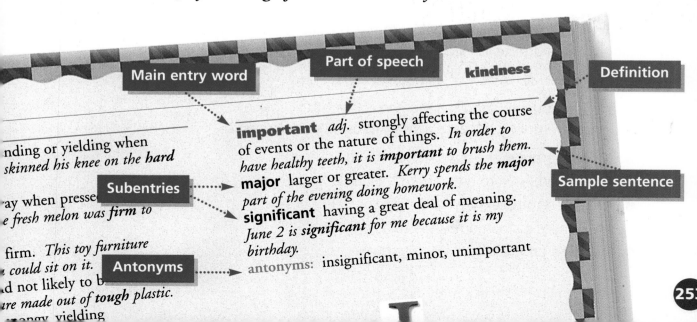

Main entry word   **Part of speech**   *kindness*   **Definition**

nding or yielding when
skinned his knee on the **hard**

ay when presse
e fresh melon was **firm** to

Subentries

firm. *This toy furniture*
could sit on it.   **Antonyms**

d not likely to b
re made out of **tough** plastic.
ongy, yielding

important *adj.* strongly affecting the course of events or the nature of things. *In order to have healthy teeth, it is **important** to brush them.*

major larger or greater. *Kerry spends the **major** part of the evening doing homework.*

significant having a great deal of meaning. *June 2 is **significant** for me because it is my birthday.*

antonyms: insignificant, minor, unimportant

Sample sentence

253

Using the Thesaurus Index

The Thesaurus Index will help you find a word in this Thesaurus. The Thesaurus Index lists **all** of the main entry words, the subentries, and any antonyms included in the Thesaurus. The words in the Thesaurus Index are in alphabetical order.

When you look in the Thesaurus Index, you will see that words are shown in three ways.

Main entry words are shown in blue. For example, the word *important* is a main entry word.

Subentries are shown in dark print. For example, *inquiry* is a subentry.

Antonyms are shown in regular print. For example, *insignificant* is an antonym.

I

important *adj.*
incident **event** *n.*
incorrect **true** *adj.*
infer **guess** *v.*
inquiry **question** *n.*
insecure **safe** *adj.*
insignificant **important** *adj.*
instant **minute** *n.*
intelligent **sharp** *adj.*
interrogation **question** *n.*

Practice Look up each word below in the Thesaurus Index. Write the main entry word for each word.

1. fitness   **2.** messy   **3.** keen   **4.** lowly   **5.** silence

Use the Thesaurus to choose a more exact word to replace each underlined word. Rewrite each sentence, using the new word.

6. My father drove the tractor over the <u>rough</u> field.

7. Cam's clothes were <u>dirty</u> after he planted the seeds.

8. Kate tried to break the hard, <u>cold</u> soil with her hoe.

9. My father's instructions were <u>easy</u> to follow.

10. Everyone on the farm helped to <u>gather</u> the crops.

Thesaurus Index

A

ability **skill** *n.*
accomplish **do** *v.*
achieve **do** *v.*
acid **sharp** *adj.*
acrid **sharp** *adj.*
acute **sharp** *adj.*
admire **dislike** *v.*
adore **dislike** *v.*
adult **grown** *adj.*
after **before** *adv.*
agree *v.*
agree **relate** *v.*
ailment **sickness** *n.*
alarm **fright** *n.*
allow **let** *v.*
alone **lonely** *adj.*
always *adv.*
amaze **surprise** *v.*
amber **yellow** *adj.*
amusing **funny** *adj.*
animosity **kindness** *n.*
answer **question** *n.*
antique **modern** *adj.*
anxious **upset** *adj.*
appalling **awful** *adj.*
approve **agree** *v.*
aptitude **skill** *n.*
assemble **gather** *v.*
astound **surprise** *v.*
at the end **last** *adv.*
attractive **pretty** *adj.*
award *n.*
awful *adj.*

B

barbed **sharp** *adj.*
bare **empty** *adj.*
beautiful **pretty** *adj.*
before *adv.*
begin **start** *v.*
behold **look** *v.*
bellow **shout** *v.*
big **small** *adj.*
bite **burn** *v.*
biting **sharp** *adj.*
bitter **sharp** *adj.*
blank **empty** *adj.*
blare **noise** *n.*
board **wood** *n.*
boiling **cold** *adj.*
bounce **jump** *v.*
bound **jump** *v.*
break *v.*
bright **dark** *adj.*
bright **sharp** *adj.*
bumpy **rough** *adj.*
burn *v.*
burning **cold** *adj.*

C

calm **upset** *adj.*
capture **throw** *v.*
care for **dislike** *v.*
careful **careless** *adj.*
careful **safe** *adj.*
careless *adj.*
careless **safe** *adj.*
carry out **do** *v.*
cast **throw** *v.*
catch **throw** *v.*
cause **reason** *n.*
cautious **careless** *adj.*
challenging **easy** *adj.*
charity **kindness** *n.*
charming **pretty** *adj.*

chartreuse **green** *adj.*
cheer **shout** *v.*
chief **main** *adj.*
childish **grown** *adj.*
chilly **cold** *adj.*
clang **noise** *n.*
clean **dirty** *adj.*
clear **dark** *adj.*
close **start** *v.*
cloudy **dark** *adj.*
clever **sharp** *adj.*
coarse **rough** *adj.*
coil **wind** *v.*
cold *adj.*
collect **gather** *v.*
comical **funny** *adj.*
commence **start** *v.*
common **strange** *adj.*
complain **relate** *v.*
comply **agree** *v.*
conceal **show** *v.*
conclude **start** *v.*
consent **agree** *v.*
consent **let** *v.*
contemplate **look** *v.*
contemporary **modern** *adj.*
continually **always** *adv.*
cool **cold** *adj.*
counterfeit **true** *adj.*
countless **many** *adj.*
count on **depend** *v.*
cover *n.*
crack **break** *v.*
cruel **sharp** *adj.*
curl **wind** *v.*
current **modern** *adj.*
curve **wind** *v.*

D

danger *n.*
dangerous **safe** *adj.*

Thesaurus Index

dark *adj.*
dash **run** *v.*
dawdle **run** *v.*
delay **wait** *v.*
demonstrate **show** *v.*
deny **agree** *v.*
depart **wait** *v.*
depend *v.*
deplorable **awful** *adj.*
deserve **earn** *v.*
despise **dislike** *v.*
detest **dislike** *v.*
difficult **easy** *adj.*
dim **dark** *adj.*
dirty *adj.*
discover **learn** *v.*
disease **sickness** *n.*
disgusting **awful** *adj.*
disheveled **dirty** *adj.*
dislike *v.*
disperse **gather** *v.*
display **show** *v.*
disregard **look** *v.*
distrust **depend** *v.*
do *v.*
doubt **depend** *v.*
drag **pull** *v.*
dreadful **awful** *adj.*

E

earlier **before** *adv.*
earn *v.*
easy *adj.*
easygoing **upset** *adj.*
edged **sharp** *adj.*
effortless **easy** *adj.*
embark **start** *v.*
empty *adj.*
end **start** *v.*
endlessly **always** *adv.*
endure **live** *v.*

escape **wait** *v.*
estimate **guess** *v.*
eternally **always** *adv.*
event *n.*
examination **question** *n.*
excellent **awful** *adj.*
exclaim **relate** *v.*
exit **wait** *v.*
experience **event** *n.*
explanation **reason** *n.*
exposed **safe** *adj.*
exposure **cover** *n.*
exquisite **awful** *adj.*
eye **look** *v.*

F

factual **true** *adj.*
faculty **skill** *n.*
familiar **strange** *adj.*
famished **hungry** *adj.*
fancy **dislike** *v.*
fast **quick** *adj.*
fear **fright** *n.*
fearful **awful** *adj.*
fever **sickness** *n.*
few **many** *adj.*
filthy **dirty** *adj.*
finally **last** *adv.*
find out **learn** *v.*
fine **awful** *adj.*
finish **start** *v.*
firm **hard** *adj.*
first **last** *adv.*
fitness **sickness** *n.*
forever **always** *adv.*
foul **dirty** *adj.*
friendless **lonely** *adj.*
friendliness **kindness** *n.*
fright *n.*
frightful **awful** *adj.*

frozen **cold** *adj.*
full **empty** *adj.*
full **hungry** *adj.*
funny *adj.*

G

gain **earn** *v.*
gape **look** *v.*
gather *v.*
gawk **look** *v.*
gaze **look** *v.*
generosity **kindness** *n.*
ghastly **awful** *adj.*
glance **look** *v.*
glower **look** *v.*
gold **yellow** *adj.*
grab **throw** *v.*
great **small** *adj.*
green *adj.*
grimy **dirty** *adj.*
groan **relate** *v.*
grounds **reason** *n.*
group **gather** *v.*
grown *adj.*
grubby **dirty** *adj.*
guess *v.*
guide **show** *v.*

H

handsome **pretty** *adj.*
harbor **cover** *n.*
hard *adj.*
hard **easy** *adj.*
hard **sharp** *adj.*
harvest **gather** *v.*
hasty **quick** *adj.*
hate **dislike** *v.*
hatred **kindness** *n.*
hazard **danger** *n.*
health **sickness** *n.*
heartiness **sickness** *n.*
helpfulness **kindness** *n.*

hide **show** v.
hinder **let** v.
homely **pretty** adj.
homesick lonely adj.
honed sharp adj.
honorable true adj.
horrendous awful adj.
horrible awful adj.
hostility **kindness** n.
hot **cold** adj.
howl shout v.
huge **small** adj.
humorous funny adj.
hungry adj.
hurl throw v.
hush noise n.
hushed silent adj.

I

ignore **look** v.
illness sickness n.
immaculate **dirty** adj.
immature **grown** adj.
important adj.
incident event n.
infer guess v.
inquiry question n.
insecure **safe** adj.
insignificant **important** adj.
instant minute n.
intelligent sharp adj.
interrogation question n.

J

jiffy minute n.
jump v.

K

keen sharp adj.
kindling wood n.
kindness n.
knifelike sharp adj.

L

large **small** adj.
last adv.
later **before** adv.
laughable funny adj.
lavender purple adj.
leap jump v.
learn v.
leave **wait** v.
lemon yellow adj.
let v.
light **dark** adj.
like **dislike** v.
linger wait v.
little small adj.
live v.
loathe dislike v.
lonely adj.
look v.
lose **earn** v.
loud **silent** adj.
love **dislike** v.
lovely pretty adj.
lowly **main** adj.
lumber wood n.

M

main adj.
major important adj.
many adj.
master learn v.
mature grown adj.
meager **many** adj.

medal award n.
melody music n.
menace danger n.
mend **break** v.
merit earn v.
messy dirty adj.
mindful **careless** adj.
miniature small adj.
minor **important** adj.
minute n.
minute small adj.
miss **look** v.
modern adj.
moment minute n.
muddy dirty adj.
murky dark adj.
murmur **shout** v.
music n.

N

nasty **awful** adj.
nasty dirty adj.
neat **dirty** adj.
negligent careless adj.
nervous upset adj.
nice **awful** adj.
nip burn v.
noise n.
noisy **silent** adj.
notice look v.
numerous many adj.

O

obnoxious awful adj.
observe look v.
occasion event n.
odd strange adj.
old **modern** adj.
old-fashioned **modern** adj.
old-time **modern** adj.

Thesaurus Index

olive **green** *adj.*
once **before** *adv.*
openness **cover** *n.*
orange *adj.*
ordinary **strange** *adj.*
outdated **modern** *adj.*
overfed **hungry** *adj.*
overlook **look** *v.*

P

packed **empty** *adj.*
pass throw *v.*
past **modern** *adj.*
patch **break** *v.*
patter noise *n.*
peculiar **strange** *adj.*
peek look *v.*
peep look *v.*
perform do *v.*
peril danger *n.*
permit let *v.*
persist live *v.*
piercing sharp *adj.*
pitch throw *v.*
plain **pretty** *adj.*
pleasing **awful** *adj.*
point minute *n.*
pointed sharp *adj.*
polished **rough** *adj.*
present modern *adj.*
presume guess *v.*
pretty *adj.*
prevent **let** *v.*
previously before *adv.*
primary main *adj.*
principal main *adj.*
prize award *n.*
protected safe *adj.*
protection cover *n.*
pull *v.*

pungent sharp *adj.*
purple *adj.*
push **pull** *v.*

Q

question *n.*
question relate *v.*
quick *adj.*
quick sharp *adj.*
quiet **noise** *n.*
quiet **silent** *adj.*
quiz question *n.*

R

race **run** *v.*
racket noise *n.*
rapid quick *adj.*
rash careless *adj.*
ravenous hungry *adj.*
reason *n.*
reckless careless *adj.*
red *adj.*
reek smell *v.*
refuge cover *n.*
refuse **agree** *v.*
regard look *v.*
relate *v.*
relaxed **upset** *adj.*
rely depend *v.*
remain wait *v.*
repair **break** *v.*
reply **question** *n.*
repulsive awful *adj.*
response **question** *n.*
reveal show *v.*
revolting awful *adj.*
reward award *n.*
ripe grown *adj.*
risk danger *n.*
roar noise *n.*

rotten awful *adj.*
rough *adj.*
rough sharp *adj.*
run *v.*
rush run *v.*

S

safe *adj.*
safety **danger** *n.*
scan look *v.*
scant **many** *adj.*
scarlet red *adj.*
scatter **gather** *v.*
scorching cold *adj.*
scream shout *v.*
secure safe *adj.*
security **danger** *n.*
seize throw *v.*
serious **funny** *adj.*
several many *adj.*
shabby dirty *adj.*
shady dark *adj.*
sharp *adj.*
shatter break *v.*
shelter cover *n.*
shock surprise *v.*
shocking awful *adj.*
shoot throw *v.*
shout *v.*
shove **pull** *v.*
show *v.*
shrewd sharp *adj.*
sickness *n.*
sigh **shout** *v.*
significant important *adj.*
silence **noise** *n.*
silent *adj.*
simple easy *adj.*
skill *n.*
sloppy dirty *adj.*
slow **quick** *adj.*
small *adj.*
smart burn *v.*

smart sharp *adj.*
smell *v.*
smooth **rough** *adj.*
soft **hard** *adj.*
soiled dirty *adj.*
solemn **funny** *adj.*
solid hard *adj.*
solitary lonely *adj.*
song music *n.*
speedy quick *adj.*
spiked sharp *adj.*
spiral **wind** *v.*
splendid **awful** *adj.*
spongy **hard** *adj.*
spot look *v.*
spotless **dirty** *adj.*
spread **gather** *v.*
spring jump *v.*
squalid dirty *adj.*
stabbing sharp *adj.*
stained dirty *adj.*
stare look *v.*
start *v.*
stay wait *v.*
starving hungry *adj.*
still silent *adj.*
sting burn *v.*
stinging sharp *adj.*
stink smell *v.*
stop **let** *v.*
straighten **wind** *v.*
strange *adj.*
stroll **run** *v.*
study learn *v.*
study look *v.*
stuffed **empty** *adj.*
suggest relate *v.*
sunny **dark** *adj.*
superb **awful** *adj.*
suppose guess *v.*
surprise *v.*
survey look *v.*
survive live *v.*

T

talent skill *n.*
tangerine orange *adj.*
tart sharp *adj.*
terror fright *n.*
thoughtless careless *adj.*
throw *v.*
tidy **dirty** *adj.*
timber wood *n.*
tiny small *adj.*
torrid **cold** *adj.*
toss throw *v.*
tough hard *adj.*
tow pull *v.*
trophy award *n.*
troubled upset *adj.*
trust depend *v.*
tune music *n.*
turquoise green *adj.*
twist wind *v.*

U

ugly **pretty** *adj.*
unattractive **pretty** *adj.*
uncomplicated easy *adj.*
uncurl **wind** *v.*
uneven rough *adj.*
unhurried **quick** *adj.*
unimportant **important** *adj.*
unimportant **main** *adj.*
unsoiled **dirty** *adj.*
untidy dirty *adj.*
untrue **true** *adj.*
untwist **wind** *v.*
unusual strange *adj.*
upset *adj.*
up-to-date modern *adj.*

V

vacant empty *adj.*
view look *v.*
vile awful *adj.*

W

wait *v.*
walk **run** *v.*
warm cold *adj.*
watch look *v.*
weather live *v.*
weird strange *adj.*
well-being **sickness** *n.*
whisper **shout** *v.*
win earn *v.*
wind *v.*
wonderful **awful** *adj.*
wood *n.*
worried upset *adj.*

Y

yell shout *v.*
yellow *adj.*
yielding **hard** *adj.*
young **grown** *adj.*
youthful **grown** *adj.*

Thesaurus

A

agree *v.* to express one's willingness or approval. *My parents agreed to get a dog for my brother and me.*
approve to say officially that something is correct or should be done. *The principal approved the plan for the field trip.*
comply to follow a request or a rule. *Please comply with the rules when you visit the museum.*
consent to say yes. *Did Judy consent to the plan?*
antonyms: deny, refuse

always *adv.* for as long as one can imagine. *Tina and Laurie will always be best friends.*
continually for a long time without a break or a pause. *My little sister continually bothers me when I am doing my homework.*
endlessly constantly, incessantly. *The highway seemed to stretch forward endlessly.*
eternally in a manner that seems to last forever. *I will be eternally grateful to the firefighters who saved my dog.*
forever for all time. *The character Peter Pan wanted to be young forever.*

award *n.* something given for outstanding performance or quality. *Jon received an award for perfect attendance.*
medal a small, flat, often circular piece of metal with a design, often awarded to honor a person, an action, an accomplishment, or an event. *The officer won a medal for bravery.*
prize something offered or won in a competition. *Ed won a prize for the best story.*
reward something that is offered, given, or received in return for a worthy act, service, or accomplishment. *Sue received a reward for returning the lost wallet.*
trophy a prize given or received as a symbol of victory or achievement. *The team won a trophy for winning the championship.*

Word Bank

awful *adj.* very bad; horrible.

appalling	ghastly	repulsive
deplorable	horrendous	revolting
disgusting	horrible	rotten
dreadful	nasty	shocking
fearful	obnoxious	vile
frightful		

antonyms: excellent, exquisite, fine, nice, pleasing, splendid, superb, wonderful

B

before *adv.* in the past. *He was excited because he had never been to Texas before.*
earlier coming or happening before the usual or expected time. *Since the game ended earlier than usual, we had time to spare.*
once at a time in the past. *Once we lived in a big city, but now we live in the country.*
previously taking place in the past. *Previously she wore her hair long, but now it is short.*
antonyms: after *adv.*, later *adv.*

break *v.* to separate into pieces as the result of force or strain. *A branch broke under the weight of the snow.*
crack to come apart with a sudden sharp sound. *Dale hit the ball hard enough to crack the bat.*
shatter to come apart suddenly into many pieces. *The delicate cup shattered against the floor.*
antonyms: mend, patch *v.*, repair *v.*

burn *v.* to feel or cause to feel a burning sensation. *The fire's heat made my face burn.*
bite to cause to sting. *The icy water bit my cheeks when I splashed it on my face.*

nip to sting or chill. *The cold wind nipped my nose and ears.*

smart to cause to feel a stinging pain. *I clapped so hard that my hands smarted.*

sting to feel or cause to feel a sharp, burning pain. *After a few minutes in the smoky room, my eyes began to sting.*

C

careless *adj.* not taking the necessary care.
I made a careless mistake on my math test.

negligent not acting with proper care or concern. *The negligent boy left his jacket out in the rain.*

rash too hasty; reckless. *Wanda regretted her rash statement about David.*

reckless not careful or cautious. *The reckless driver sped through the red light.*

thoughtless not thinking; careless. *It was thoughtless of Jenny to forget her bus fare.*

antonyms: careful, cautious, mindful

cold *adj.* having or being at a lower temperature than normal. *The water in the lake is cold in early spring.*

chilly cold enough to cause or feel unpleasant coldness. *My light clothes did not protect me from the damp, chilly air.*

cool somewhat cold. *We were relieved to find a cool, shady place to rest after our long hike.*

frozen uncomfortably cold. *After a day of skating, my feet were frozen.*

antonyms: boiling *adj.*, burning *adj.*, hot, scorching *adj.*, torrid, warm

cover *n.* a shelter or protection. *When it began to rain, we ran to find cover.*

harbor a shelter; refuge. *The large rock served as a harbor for rattlesnakes.*

protection something that guards against harm, attack, or injury. *Special glasses provide protection for the workers' eyes.*

refuge a place of protection. *Hunting is not allowed in the wildlife refuge.*

shelter something that protects or covers. *The hikers found shelter for the night.*

antonyms: exposure, openness

D

danger *n.* the chance of harm or destruction. *The sailor knew the dangers of sailing at night.*

hazard something that may cause injury or harm. *Firefighters face many hazards.*

menace a threat or danger. *The damaged electrical lines were a menace to public safety.*

peril the condition of being in danger. *We had put our lives in peril by going out in the blizzard.*

risk the possibility of suffering harm or loss. *Cross that broken bridge at your own risk.*

antonyms: safety, security

dark *adj.* without light or with very little light. *We used a flashlight to find our way through the dark house.*

cloudy full of or covered with clouds. *The sky looks so cloudy that I am sure it will rain.*

dim somewhat dark. *I could barely see the stack of boxes in the dim basement.*

murky very dark or gloomy. *The river was so murky that we could not see the bottom.*

shady blocked off from the light. *Our porch is shady because a large tree shelters it from the sun.*

antonyms: bright, clear, light, sunny

depend *v.* to have trust. *Mrs. Li knew that she could depend on Al to feed the dog.*

count on to rely on for help or support. *We can count on the parents to help us with the fair.*

rely to have confidence. *You can rely on us to be on time for the play.*

trust to have or put confidence in. *Sumi trusted her best friend to keep her secret.*

antonyms: distrust *v.*, doubt *v.*

Shades of Meaning

dirty *adj.* full of or covered with dirt.

1. somewhat dirty:

   disheveled   **shabby**   **untidy**
   messy   **sloppy**

2. quite dirty:

   grimy   **muddy**   **stained**
   grubby   **soiled**

3. extremely dirty:

   filthy   **nasty**
   foul   **squalid**

antonyms: **1.** neat, tidy **2.** clean, unsoiled **3.** immaculate, spotless

dislike *v.* to have a feeling of not liking. *I dislike scary movies.*
despise to regard with great dislike. *The spy despised the enemy agents.*
detest to dislike very much. *Rich detests liver and onions.*
hate to feel strong dislike for. *I hate to shop.*
loathe to feel great dislike for. *Katherine loathes being called Kate.*
antonyms: admire, adore, care for, fancy *v.*, like, love *v.*

do *v.* to carry out an act or action. *Nate does his homework right after school.*
accomplish to perform a task. *We can accomplish the job in an hour.*
achieve to succeed in doing or accomplishing. *Emily achieved good grades.*
carry out to put into practice. *My dog carried out my command to sit.*
perform to carry out; do. *Mrs. Hudson performed the science experiment in class.*

E

earn *v.* to gain by working or by supplying service. *Lisa earns her allowance.*
deserve to be worthy of or have a right to. *Alex deserves credit for his hard work.*

gain to get or obtain by effort. *Jill has gained the respect of her classmates.*
merit to be worthy of. *This problem merits our close attention.*
win to get by hard work. *George won the right to hold the flag in the parade.*
antonym: lose

easy *adj.* needing very little effort or thought. *I finished the book quickly because it was easy to read.*
effortless easily done. *The excellent players made winning the game look effortless.*
simple not complicated. *The game is so simple that a young child can play it.*
uncomplicated not hard to understand or deal with. *A cat's life is uncomplicated.*
antonyms: challenging, difficult, hard

empty *adj.* containing nothing. *Please put the papers in the empty box on the porch.*
bare without the usual furniture or supplies. *The shelves of the refrigerator were bare.*
blank free of marks or decoration. *The teacher told us to get out a blank piece of paper.*
vacant not occupied or rented. *Our steps echoed as we walked through the vacant rooms of the new house.*
antonyms: full, packed *adj.*, stuffed *adj.*

event *n.* something that happens. *Roberto's wedding was a happy event.*
experience a happening that one has lived through. *My trip was a good experience.*
incident a brief or unimportant happening. *There was a funny incident at school.*
occasion a very important event. *Grandma's birthday was a great occasion.*

F

fright *n.* sudden, strong fear. *A sudden movement in the bushes gave us a fright.*

alarm sudden fear caused by a feeling that danger is near. *The chance of a flood always causes **alarm** in my town.*
fear a feeling caused by a sense of danger. *Toni has a **fear** of high places.*
terror very great fear. *The monsters in the movie made the children scream in **terror**.*

---

funny *adj.* causing amusement or laughter. *My uncle told a **funny** joke.*
amusing pleasantly entertaining. *The playful kittens were **amusing**.*
comical producing laughter; silly. *A clown is supposed to be **comical**.*
humorous being funny. *Kim told a **humorous** story about camping with her family.*
laughable causing laughter. *Putting my shirt on backwards was a **laughable** mistake.*
antonyms: serious, solemn

G

gather *v.* to bring or come together into one place. *I **gathered** all the library books.*
assemble to bring together to make a group. *Bev **assembled** the broken pieces.*
collect to bring or come together in a group. *Tad **collects** baseball cards.*
group to arrange or gather in a group. *Our teacher always **groups** us in alphabetical order.*
harvest to gather a crop. *Farmers **harvest** wheat at this time of year.*
antonyms: disperse, scatter, spread *v.*

---

green *adj.* having the color of growing grass. *The plant's **green** leaves turned brown.*
chartreuse light yellowish green. *Cora's **chartreuse** scarf looks almost yellow in this light.*
olive dull yellowish green. *Ted's **olive** jacket blended in with the leaves on the bushes.*
turquoise light bluish green. *White sea gulls dove into the **turquoise** ocean water.*

---

grown *adj.* having reached an adult age. *When I am **grown**, I want to be a pilot.*

adult fully developed and mature. ***Adult** turtles do not stay with their young.*
mature fully grown or developed. *Dad wanted a **mature** dog rather than a puppy.*
ripe fully grown and developed. *Those apples will be bright red when they are **ripe**.*
antonyms: childish, immature, young, youthful

---

guess *v.* to form an opinion without enough information to be sure of it. *I correctly **guessed** the answers to the math quiz.*
estimate to guess about; calculate roughly. *Can you **estimate** the distance to Dallas?*
infer to conclude from evidence. *We **inferred** from the dark house that no one was home.*
presume to suppose to be true. *If you are watching TV, I **presume** that you have already done your homework.*
suppose to be inclined to think; assume. *I **suppose** that Sylvia will be late as usual.*

H

hard *adj.* not bending or yielding when pushed. *The child fell on **hard** cement steps.*
firm not giving way when pressed or pushed; solid. *The fresh melon was **firm** to the touch.*
solid strong and firm. *This toy furniture is so **solid** that you could sit on it.*
tough strong and not likely to break or tear. *Football helmets are made out of **tough** plastic.*
antonyms: soft, spongy, yielding

---

hungry *adj.* wanting food. *Ellen was **hungry** and tired after her walk.*
famished extremely hungry. *We missed lunch and were **famished** by dinnertime.*
ravenous greedily eager for food. *The **ravenous** puppy gobbled down the bowl of food.*
starving suffering or dying from lack of food. *The stray kitten looks **starving** and weak.*
antonyms: full, overfed

I

important *adj.* strongly affecting the course of events or the nature of things. *In order to have healthy teeth, it is **important** to brush them.*

major larger or greater. *Kerry spends the **major** part of the evening doing homework.*

significant having a great deal of meaning. *June 2 is **significant** for me because it is my birthday.*

antonyms: insignificant, minor, unimportant

J

jump *v.* to rise up and move through the air by using the legs. *How high can you **jump**?*

bounce to come back or up after hitting a surface. *I **bounced** on the trampoline.*

bound to leap upward and forward. *The dog **bounded** after the frightened rabbit.*

leap to jump quickly or suddenly. *Vera **leaped** up to catch the ball.*

spring to move upward in one quick motion. *The diver **sprang** off the high diving board.*

K

kindness *n.* the quality or condition of being helpful or considerate; generosity. *Grandpa is known for his **kindness** to animals.*

charity good will or love toward others. *Keith's volunteer work is an act of **charity**.*

friendliness the quality of showing or encouraging friendship. *Our host's **friendliness** made us feel right at home.*

generosity willingness to give or share. *Letting others use your favorite toys shows great **generosity**.*

helpfulness usefulness, assistance. *My parents appreciated Roy's **helpfulness**.*

antonyms: animosity, hatred, hostility

L

last *adv.* after all the others. *Add the ice **last** so that it does not melt.*

at the end at the conclusion. *Karen gave a good speech, but she stumbled **at the end**.*

finally after a long while. *After we had waited two hours, the train **finally** arrived.*

antonym: first *adv.*

learn *v.* to get knowledge of or skill in through study or instruction. *I finally **learned** my times tables.*

discover to find out. *Rick **discovered** that the strange rock was a mineral.*

find out to get information about. *Did you **find out** what time our train leaves?*

master to become skilled in. *Chris **mastered** skating in just three lessons.*

study to try to learn. *I will **study** my spelling words before the test on Friday.*

let *v.* to give permission to. *Dave took the leash off his dog and **let** her run free.*

allow to let do or happen. *Please **allow** me to go to Jenny's party.*

consent to agree to let do. *My parents finally **consented** to my request.*

permit to give permission or the opportunity to. *The state law **permits** sixteen-year-olds to drive cars.*

antonyms: hinder, prevent, stop *v.*

live *v.* to be alive; exist. *Insects can **live** in almost every part of the world.*

endure to continue to exist; last. *Many trees can **endure** for hundreds of years.*

persist to continue to happen or exist. *Jay's bad mood **persisted** for several days.*

survive to stay alive or in existence. *The lost man **survived** in the woods by eating berries.*

weather to pass through safely. *The rabbits **weathered** the harsh winter by burrowing deep in the snow.*

---

lonely *adj.* sad at being alone. *Phil was **lonely** when his best friend moved away.*

alone without anyone or anything else. *Grandmother enjoys living **alone** in the apartment above ours.*

friendless without friends. *The **friendless** boy ate lunch by himself.*

homesick unhappy and longing for home and family. *I was **homesick** during the first week of camp.*

solitary being or living alone. *A lighthouse keeper lives a **solitary** life.*

Word Bank

look *v.* to use the eyes to see.

behold	glower	spot
contemplate	notice	stare
eye	observe	study
gape	peek	survey
gawk	peep	view
gaze	regard	watch
glance	scan	

antonyms: disregard, ignore, miss, overlook

M

main *adj.* most important or primary. *The **main** street in our town is called Main Street!*

chief most important. *Wheat is the **chief** product of the state.*

---

primary first in importance, degree, or quality. *Mr. Chang's **primary** goal is to learn English.*

principal first in rank or importance. *Safety is my **principal** concern.*

antonyms: lowly *adj.*, unimportant

---

many *adj.* adding up to a great number. *Many people bought tickets to the show.*

countless too many to count. *Countless fans were disappointed by the canceled game.*

numerous made up of a large number. *Colds and other illnesses are more **numerous** in the winter.*

several more than two but not many. *Kathy walks **several** blocks to school.*

antonyms: few *adj.*, meager, scant

---

minute *n.* a short time. *Dinner will be ready in a **minute**.*

instant a very brief period of time. *She recognized me in an **instant**.*

jiffy a moment; no time at all. *I will be ready to go in a **jiffy**.*

moment a very short period of time. *A **moment** later, the doorbell rang.*

point an instant of time. *At that **point**, the bell rang.*

---

modern *adj.* of or relating to the present or recent past. *Modern transportation is fast and clean.*

contemporary living or occurring during the present time. *We heard the recordings of some **contemporary** musicians.*

current belonging to the present time. *We read about **current** events in the daily newspaper.*

present being or happening now. *At the **present** time, there is no cure for that disease.*

up-to-date showing or using the latest improvements or style. *Sonia's clothes are always **up-to-date**.*

antonyms: antique, old, old-fashioned, old-time, outdated, past *adj.*

music *n.* vocal or instrumental sounds that have rhythm, melody, and harmony. *Beautiful* **music** *filled the auditorium.*

melody a pleasing series of musical tones. *The* **melody** *you are humming sounds familiar to me.*

song a usually short musical piece that is meant to be sung. *The class learned a* **song** *about civil rights.*

tune a melody, especially one that is simple and easy to remember. *Can you remember the name of this* **tune**?

N

noise *n.* a loud or unpleasant sound. *We closed the windows to block out the* **noise**.

blare a loud, harsh noise, as of a horn. *The* **blare** *of the car's horn made Eric jump.*

clang a loud, ringing, metallic sound. *I listened to the* **clang** *of the lighthouse bell.*

patter quick, light sounds. *I love to hear the* **patter** *of rain on the roof.*

racket a loud, unpleasant noise. *The hens in the barnyard make a* **racket** *whenever they see a dog or a cat.*

roar a loud, deep noise or cry, as that made by a lion. *The* **roar** *of the jet engines was so loud that we could not hear the captain's words.*
antonyms: hush *n.*, quiet *n.*, silence *n.*

O

orange *adj.* reddish yellow. *Alice placed a large,* **orange** *pumpkin on the front porch.*

tangerine deep reddish orange. *Dick used a* **tangerine** *crayon to color in the sunset.*

P

pretty *adj.* pleasing, attractive, or appealing to the eye or ear. *Betty thought that the dress was* **pretty**, *but Jane did not like it.*

attractive appealing or charming. *The color green looks* **attractive** *on a redhead.*

beautiful being very pleasing to the senses or the mind. *The audience fell silent as* **beautiful** *music filled the hall.*

charming very pleasing; delightful. *The* **charming** *hostess made us feel at home.*

handsome pleasing in appearance; good-looking. *The two ice skaters made a* **handsome** *couple.*

lovely having pleasant qualities. *The clear sky and warm breeze made it a* **lovely** *night.*
antonyms: homely, plain *adj.*, ugly, unattractive

pull *v.* to apply force to in order to draw someone or something in the direction of the force. *I* **pulled** *the door toward me as hard as I could.*

drag to draw along the ground by force. *Jim* **dragged** *the trash barrel across the lawn.*

tow to drag along behind with a chain or a rope. *With a strong rope, the motor boat* **towed** *our kayak into the harbor.*
antonyms: push, shove

purple *adj.* having the color between red and blue. *The* **purple** *grape juice stained the tablecloth.*

lavender pale purple. *Greg picked a bunch of* **lavender** *and white flowers to take to the hospital.*

Q

question *n.* something that is asked. *I do not know the answer to that question.*

examination a set of questions designed to test knowledge. *Edward has to take an examination to become a lawyer.*

inquiry a request for information. *The governor responded to Ms. Pitt's inquiry about safety regulations.*

interrogation the act of questioning closely. *During the interrogation, the thief confessed to the crime.*

quiz a short test. *Mrs. Garcia gave us a surprise math quiz.*

antonyms: answer *n.*, reply *n.*, response

---

quick *adj.* very fast; rapid. *With a quick leap, the basketball player caught the ball.*

fast moving, acting, or done quickly. *Fast cars should stay in the left lane.*

hasty acting or done fast. *Glenn made a hasty sketch of the building.*

rapid marked by speed. *The river became more rapid as we floated downstream.*

speedy moving quickly; swift. *Joe is a speedy runner and wins almost every race.*

antonyms: slow *adj.*, unhurried

R

reason *n.* an explanation for an act or belief. *The reason we took no pictures is that I forgot my camera!*

cause someone or something that makes something happen. *Was lightning the cause of the fire?*

explanation something that reveals why something else is so. *There is an explanation for why iron is heavier than wood.*

grounds the reason for a belief, action, or thought. *What grounds do you have for being angry?*

---

red *adj.* having the color of blood or of a ruby. *All cars must stop for a red traffic light.*

maroon a dark purplish red. *If you mix red and brown, you will create a rusty maroon color.*

scarlet bright red. *Rick wore a scarlet scarf so that he could be seen in the woods.*

---

relate *v.* to tell or narrate. *Suki related the tale of the hidden treasure.*

agree to express one's willingness or approval; consent. *I agreed that the movie was scary.*

complain to express unhappiness or discontent. *Lee always complains about having too much homework.*

exclaim to cry out or speak suddenly. *"Surprise!" exclaimed the guests.*

groan to make a deep sound that expresses pain, grief, or annoyance. *The class groaned when Mr. Price announced the test.*

mutter to speak in a low voice with lips barely moving; to complain or grumble. *People are muttering about the high price of food.*

question to ask questions of. *The police questioned us about the accident.*

suggest to offer for consideration. *Hal suggested having a car wash to earn money.*

---

rough *adj.* full of bumps and ridges. *The carpenter sanded the rough wood until it was smooth.*

bumpy covered with lumps. *Riding on the bumpy road made us bounce in our seats.*

coarse not polished or fine. *Sandpaper has a coarse surface.*

uneven not level, smooth, or straight. *Because the floor was uneven, the bookcase would not sit straight.*

antonyms: smooth *adj.*, polished *adj.*

---

run *v.* to move quickly on foot. *Please do not run in the halls.*

dash to move with sudden speed. *We dashed out the door when the alarm sounded.*
race to rush at top speed. *Leon raced to catch the bus.*
rush to hurry. *I had to rush to get to school on time this morning.*
antonyms: dawdle, stroll *v.*, walk *v.*

S

safe *adj.* free from danger, risk, or harm. *This old bridge is not safe.*
careful taking the necessary caution. *My father is a careful driver.*
protected covered or guarded from harm. *Wild animals are protected in this park.*
secure safe against danger or risk of loss. *The shed is a secure place to keep your bicycle.*
antonyms: careless, dangerous, exposed, insecure

Shades of Meaning

sharp *adj.*

1. having a thin edge that cuts or a fine point that pierces:

barbed	keen	pointed
edged	knifelike	spiked
honed		

2. harsh; severe:

acute	piercing	stabbing
cruel	rough	stinging
hard		

3. acting strongly on the senses:

acid	biting	pungent
acrid	bitter	tart

4. alert in noticing or thinking:

bright	intelligent	shrewd
clever	quick	smart

shout *v.* to cry out or say loudly. *Sally shouted a good-bye as her bus left the station.*
bellow to give a load roar. *The army officer bellowed his commands in a deep voice.*
cheer to shout in happiness, approval, encouragement, or enthusiasm. *People cheered wildly as the astronauts in the parade passed by.*
howl to cry or scream, as in pain. *Jordan howled when he caught his hand in the door.*
scream to make a long, loud, piercing cry. *Joseph screamed when Sid jumped out of the bushes.*
yell to cry out loudly. *Jenny yelled at her puppy when it wandered into the busy street.*
antonyms: murmur *v.*, sigh *v.*, whisper *v.*

show *v.* to cause or allow to be seen. *Mother showed us pictures of her grandparents.*
demonstrate to show with the help of examples or explanation. *Ana demonstrated how to make paper.*
display to put on view; exhibit. *Ms. Wong displayed our work on the bulletin board.*
guide to show the way to; direct. *Mr. Rodriguez will guide us through the museum exhibits.*
reveal to make known. *This map reveals where the treasure is hidden.*
antonyms: conceal, hide *v.*

sickness *n.* the condition of being sick. *Brett missed the school play because of sickness.*
ailment an illness or disease. *The doctor talked with Uncle Edgar about his ailment.*
disease a condition that keeps the body from functioning normally. *This disease affects the heart and lungs.*
fever a body temperature that is higher than normal. *Mr. Sims used an ice pack to bring down his fever.*
illness a sickness or disease. *Many people have caught the same illness this winter.*
antonyms: fitness, health, heartiness, well-being

silent *adj.* making or having no sound; quiet. *The students were absolutely **silent** during the fire drill.*
hushed becoming quiet or still. *The librarian spoke to us in a **hushed** voice.*
quiet marked by little or no noise. *We could scarcely hear the **quiet** breathing of the sleeping baby.*
still without noise; silent. *The class remained **still** while the principal was speaking.*
antonyms: loud, noisy

skill *n.* the ability to do something well. *Eduardo has **skill** in carpentry.*
ability the quality of being able to do something. *I wish I had the **ability** to take good photographs.*
aptitude a natural ability or talent. *Hilda seems to have an **aptitude** for math.*
faculty an ability for doing something. *This story shows Tony's **faculty** for creative writing.*
talent a natural ability to do something well. *Pat's musical **talent** was apparent at the concert.*

small *adj.* little in size, amount, or extent. *I would like a **small** piece of meat, please.*
little small in size or quantity. *These **little** chairs must be for very young children.*
miniature much smaller than the usual size. *The dollhouse even had a **miniature** stove in the kitchen.*
minute very, very small; tiny. *You need a magnifying glass to read that **minute** print.*
tiny extremely small. *Grandma made **tiny** clothes for each of our dolls.*
antonyms: big, great, huge, large

smell *v.* to give off an odor. *The air **smells** like burning leaves.*
reek to give off an unpleasant odor. *Our tent **reeked** of campfire smoke.*
stink to give off a strong, bad smell. *Old garbage in the kitchen made the house **stink**.*

start *v.* to begin to move, go, or act. *The racers **started** to run at the sound of the whistle.*
begin to start to do. *Mr. Stone **began to** read as soon as the class was quiet.*

commence to perform the first part of an action. *The concert will **commence** at noon.*
embark to set out on an activity or task. *Fred **embarked** on a new project right after he completed his model train.*
antonyms: close *v.*, conclude, end *v.*, finish *v.*

strange *adj.* not known before; unfamiliar. *We turned down a **strange** street and realized that we were lost.*
odd not ordinary or usual. *I read a story about an **odd** animal that had three humps!*
peculiar hard to understand or explain. *The cat's **peculiar** behavior was a mystery.*
unusual rare or different from what might be expected. *Her **unusual** name was easy to remember.*
weird strange, odd, or unusual. *A **weird** noise in the empty house frightened the children.*
antonyms: common, familiar, ordinary

surprise *v.* to cause to feel astonishment. *Rico **surprised** his grandfather with a birthday party.*
amaze to fill with surprise or wonder. *The magician's tricks **amazed** the young children.*
astound to strike with sudden wonder. *The winless team's first victory **astounded** the fans.*
shock to surprise or upset greatly. *The news of the fire **shocked** us all.*

T

throw *v.* to send through the air with a fast motion of the arm. *Matt **threw** a rock into the pond.*
cast to throw or fling. *Dora **cast** the net over the side of the boat.*
hurl to throw with great force. *The prisoner **hurled** himself over the fence and escaped.*
pass to hand or throw to another person. *Tina quickly **passed** the basketball to her teammate.*
pitch to throw or toss, as in baseball or horseshoes. *Tim **pitched** six strikes in a row.*

shoot to throw toward a target. *Kate shot the ball toward the basket.*

toss to throw with a quick, easy movement. *Chuck tossed his hat into the closet.*
antonyms: capture, catch, grab, seize

U

upset *adj.* sad or unsettled. *I was upset when I heard the bad news.*

anxious unsettled about something that is uncertain. *The anxious riders were not quite sure where they were going.*

nervous shaken and jittery because of fear or challenge. *Dean was very nervous when he gave a speech in front of the class.*

troubled upset and worried. *Brad was troubled by his sister's bad mood.*

worried uneasy. *Janet was worried about getting lost in the big city.*
antonyms: calm *adj.*, easygoing, relaxed *adj.*

W

wait *v.* to do nothing or stay in a place until something expected happens. *Please wait here until I return.*

delay to slow, stop, or prevent for a time. *We delayed our departure.*

linger to stay in a place longer than usual. *The children lingered on the playground after school.*

remain to stay in the same place. *We remained in our seats after the bell rang.*

stay to remain in one place or condition. *It's wise to stay indoors when the temperature is below zero.*
antonyms: depart, escape *v.*, exit *v.*, leave

wind *v.* to wrap or be wrapped around something. *This road winds around the mountainside.*

coil to wind into a ring or a series of rings. *Please coil the garden hose after you finish watering the flowers.*

curl to twist into or form ringlets. *Long ago, women used rags to curl their hair.*

curve to move in or take the shape of a curve. *The path curves gently along the seashore.*

spiral to make a curve that gradually widens as it winds around. *A staircase spiraled up to the top of the tower.*

twist to wind together to form a single strand. *A spinning wheel twists wool into yarn.*
antonyms: straighten, uncurl, untwist

wood *n.* the hard material beneath the bark of trees and shrubs that makes up the trunk and branches. *The saw made a deep cut in the hard wood.*

board a piece of sawed lumber that has more length and width than thickness. *Wanda used a board to make a shelf in her room.*

kindling dry sticks of wood used for building a fire. *Please collect some kindling for the campfire.*

lumber timber that is sawed into boards and planks. *The hardware store delivered a truckload of lumber to our house.*

timber wood for building. *The pioneers used timber to build their houses.*

Y

yellow *adj.* having the color of ripe lemons or dandelions. *Yellow sunflowers dotted the field.*

amber brownish yellow. *The cat in the painting had large amber eyes.*

gold having a deep yellow color. *Wheat turns gold when it is ripe.*

lemon having a bright yellow color named for the fruit. *The lemon walls seemed to fill the room with sunshine.*

Spelling-Meaning Index

This Spelling-Meaning Index contains pairs of words related in spelling and in meaning. The letters in dark print in these words show that the spelling stays the same even though the sound may change. This Index also includes other words in the same family as the related word pairs. The words in each part of this Index are in alphabetical order.

Consonant Changes

Word pairs are listed under the heading for the kind of consonant change that fits the word pairs.

Consonant Changes:
Silent to Sounded

Sometimes you can remember how to spell a word with a silent consonant by thinking of a related word in which the letter is pronounced.

bomb-bombard

bombarded, bombarder, bombardier, bombarding, bombardment, bombards, bombed, bomber, bombing, bombs

column-columnist

columned, columnists, columns

crumb-crumble

crumbled, crumbles, crumbliness, crumbling, crumbly, crumbs, crumby

fasten-fast

fastened, fastener, fastening, fastens, faster, fastest, fastness, unfasten

hasten-haste

hastened, hastening, hastens, hastily, hastiness, hasty

heir-inherit

disinherit, heiress, heirless, heirs, hereditary, heredity, heritage, inheritable, inheritance, inherited, inheriting, inheritor, inherits

limb-limber

limbered, limbering, limberly, limberness, limbers, limbs

moisten-moist

moistened, moistener, moistening, moistens, moister, moistest, moistly, moistness, moisture, moisturize, moisturizer

muscle-muscular

muscled, muscles, muscling, muscularity, muscularly, musculature

receipt-reception

receipts, receivable, receive, receiver, receptacle, receptionist, receptions, receptive, receptor, recipient

sign-signal

signaled, signaler, signaling, signals, signature, signed, signer, signet, significance, significant, significantly, signifier, signify, signing, signs, unsigned

soften-soft

softened, softener, softening, softens, softer, softest, softly, softness

Spelling-Meaning Index

Consonant Changes:
The Sound of *c*

The |k| sound of *c* may change to |s| or |sh| in some words. Thinking of a related word can help you remember that the sound is spelled *c*.

electric-electrician

electrical, electrically, electricians, electricity, electrify, electrocute, electrocution, electrode, electron, electronic

magic-magician

magical, magically, magicians

mathematics-mathematician

mathematic, mathematical, mathematically, mathematicians, nonmathematical

music-musician

musical, musicale, musically, musicians, musicianship, musicologist, musicology, unmusical

practical-practice

impractical, impracticality, impracticalness, impractically, practicable, practically, practicalness, practiced, practicer, practices, practicing, practitioner, unpracticed

Consonant Changes:
The Sound of *t*

The sound of a final *t* may change when an ending or suffix is added. Thinking of a related word can help you remember that the sound is spelled *t*.

create-creature

created, creates, creating, creation, creative, creatively, creativeness, creativity, creator, creaturely, creatures, noncreative, re-create

decorate-decoration

decor, decorated, decorates, decorating, decorations, decorative, decoratively, decorativeness, decorator, decorum, redecorate, redecoration, undecorated

depart-departure

departed, departing, departs, departures, undeparted

fact-factual

factitious, factitiously, factitiousness, factor, facts, factually, nonfactual

habit-habitual

habits, habitualize, habitually, habitualness, habitat

invent-invention

invented, inventing, inventions, inventive, inventively, inventiveness, inventor, invents

locate-location

dislocate, dislocated, dislocation, local, locatable, located, locator, locates, locating, locational, locations, nonlocal, relocate, relocation

moist-moisture

moisten, moistener, moister, moistest, moistly, moistness, moisturize, moisturizer

object-objection

objected, objecting, objectionable, objectionably, objector, objects

operate-operation

cooperate, cooperation, cooperative, cooperatively, cooperativeness, operated, operates, operating, operational, operationally, operations, operative, operatively, operator, nonoperating, nonoperative

punctuate-punctuation

punctual, punctuality, punctuated, punctuates, punctuating, punctuator

regulate-regulation

deregulate, deregulation, irregular, irregularity, irregularly, regular, regularity, regularize, regularly, regulated, regulates, regulating, regulations, regulator, regulatory, unregulated

relate-relation

relatable, related, relatedness, relater, relates, relating, relations, relationship, relative, relatively, relativeness, relativity, unrelated, unrelatedness

Vowel Changes
Word pairs are listed under the heading for the kind of vowel change that fits the word pairs.

Vowel Changes:
Long to Short Vowel Sound
Words that are related in meaning are often related in spelling, even though one word has a long vowel sound and the other word has a short vowel sound.

breathe-breath

breathable, breathed, breather, breathes, breathily, breathiness, breathing, breathless, breathlessly, breathlessness, breaths, breathtaking, breathy

cave-cavity

caved, cavern, cavernous, cavernously, caves, caving, cavities

clean-cleanse

cleanable, cleaned, cleaner, cleanest, cleaning, cleanliness, cleanly, cleanness, cleans, cleansed, cleanser, cleanses, cleansing, unclean, uncleanable, uncleanliness, uncleanly

compete-competition

competed, competes, competing, competitions, competitive, competitively, competitiveness, competitor, noncompeting, noncompetitive, noncompetitively, noncompetitiveness

crime-criminal

crimes, criminality, criminalize, criminally, criminals, criminologist, criminology, decriminalize, incriminate, incrimination, incriminatory

cycle-bicycle

bicycled, bicycles, bicycling, bicyclist, cycled, cycler, cycles, cycling, cyclist, tricycle, unicycle, unicyclist

deal-dealt

dealer, dealership, dealing, deals

dream-dreamt

dreamed, dreamer, dreamily, dreaminess, dreaming, dreamless, dreamlike, dreams, dreamy

273

Spelling-Meaning Index

heal-health

healable, healed, healer, healing, heals, healthful, healthfully, healthfulness, healthily, healthiness, healthy, unhealthful, unhealthily, unhealthiness, unhealthy

mean-meant

meaning, meaningful, meaningfully, meaningfulness, meaningless, meaninglessly, meaninglessness, means, unmeant

minus-minimum

minimal, minimalization, minimally, minimize, minimizer, minor, minimums, minuscule

nation-national

international, internationalism, internationalist, internationalize, internationally, nationalism, nationalist, nationalistic, nationality, nationalization, nationalize, nationalizer, nationally, nationals, nationhood, nationwide, native, natively, nativeness

nature-natural

naturalism, naturalist, naturalistic, naturalistically, naturalization, naturalize, naturally, naturalness, natures, supernatural, unnatural, unnaturally, unnaturalness

page-paginate

paged, pages, paginated, paginates, paginating, pagination, paging

pale-pallid

paled, paleness, paler, pales, palest, paling, pallidly, pallidness, pallor

please-pleasant

displease, displeasing, displeasure, plea, plead, pleasantly, pleasantness, pleasantry, pleased, pleases, pleasing, pleasingly, pleasingness, pleasurable, pleasurableness, pleasurably, pleasure, pleasureless, unpleasant, unpleasantly, unpleasantness

sole-solitary

solely, soliloquy, solitude, solo, soloist

steal-stealth

stealer, stealing, steals, stealthily, stealthiness, stealthy

wise-wisdom

wisely, wiser, wisest, unwise, unwisely

Vowel Changes:
Schwa to Long Vowel Sound

You can remember how to spell the schwa sound in some words by thinking of a related word with a long vowel sound spelled the same way.

ability-able

abilities, abler, ablest, ably, disability, disable, disabled, inability, unable

admiration-admire

admirable, admirableness, admirably, admired, admirer, admires, admiring, admiringly

composition-compose

component, composed, composedly, composedness, composer, composes, composing, composite, compositor, compost, composure, decomposable, decompose, recompose, recomposition

definition-define

definability, definable, definably, defined, definer, defines, defining, definite, definitely, definiteness, definitions, definitive, definitively, definitiveness, indefinable, indefinableness, indefinably, indefinite, indefinitely, indefiniteness

proposition-propose

proposal, proposed, proposer, proposes, proposing, propositional, propositionally, propositions

relative-relate

related, relatedness, relater, relates, relating, relation, relations, relationship, relative, relatively, relativeness, relatives, relativism, relativist, relativity, unrelated, unrelatedness

supposition-suppose

supposed, supposedly, supposes, supposing, suppositional, suppositionally, suppositions

Vowel Changes:
Schwa to Short Vowel Sound

You can remember how to spell the schwa sound in some words by thinking of a related word with a short vowel sound spelled the same way.

democratic-democracy

democracies, democrat, democratically, democratization, democratize, undemocratic, undemocratically

final-finality

finale, finalist, finalities, finalization, finalize, finally, finals

formal-formality

form, formalism, formalities, formalization, formalize, formally, format, formula, informal, informality, informally, nonformal, reform, transform, unformed

general-generality

generalities, generalization, generalize, generally, generalness, generic, generically, genre

history-historical

historian, historic, historically, historicalness, histories, prehistoric, prehistorical, prehistorically, prehistory

human-humanity

humane, humanely, humaneness, humanitarian, humanities, humanization, humanize, humanizer, humankind, humanlike, humanly, humanness, humanoid, humans, inhuman, inhumane, inhumanely, inhumanity, inhumanly

individual-individuality

individualism, individualist, individualistic, individualistically, individualities, individualization, individualize, individually, individuals

legal-legality

illegal, illegality, illegally, legalism, legalistic, legalistically, legalities, legalization, legalize, legally

local-locality

locale, localities, locally, locate, locus, nonlocal, relocate, relocation

major-majority

majorities

Spelling-Meaning Index

medal-medallion

medalist, medallions, medals

mental-mentality

demented, mentalities, mentally

metal-metallic

metallically, metallurgy, metals, nonmetal, nonmetallic

method-methodical

methodic, methodically, methodicalness, methodology, methods, unmethodical, unmethodically

mortal-mortality

immortal, immortality, immortalize, immortally, immortals, mortalities, mortally, mortals

normal-normality

abnormal, abnormality, abnormally, norm, normalcy, normalization, normalize, normalizer, normally, subnormal, supernormal

perfect-perfection

imperfect, imperfection, imperfectly, imperfectness, perfected, perfectibility, perfectible, perfecting, perfectionism, perfectionist, perfections, perfectly, perfectness, perfects

personal-personality

depersonalize, impersonal, impersonally, impersonalize, impersonate, impersonation, impersonator, person, persona, personable, personalities, personalization, personalize, personally, personification, personify, personnel

poem-poetic

poems, poet, poetical, poetically, poetry, nonpoetic, unpoetic, unpoetical

regular-regularity

irregular, irregularity, irregularly, regularities, regularization, regularize, regularly, regulate, regulation, regulatory, unregulated

reside-resident

nonresident, nonresidential, resided, residence, residency, residential, residentially, resider, resides, residing

similar-similarity

dissimilar, dissimilarity, dissimilarly, similarities, similarly, simile

total-totality

totaled, totaling, totalities, totalization, totalize, totalizer, totally, totals

victory-victorious

victor, victories, victoriously, victoriousness

Spelling Dictionary

Spelling Table

This Spelling Table shows many of the letter combinations that spell the same sounds in different words. Use this table for help in looking up words that you do not know how to spell.

Sounds	Spellings	Sample Words	Sounds	Spellings	Sample Words
|ă|	a, au	bat, have, laugh	|îr|	ear, eer, eir, ier	near, deer, weird, pier
|ā|	a, ai, ay, ea	made, later, rain, play, great	|j|	dge, g, ge, j	judge, gem, range, jet
|âr|	air, ar, are, eir, ere	fair, scarce, care, their, where	|k|	c, ch, ck, k	picnic, school, tick, key
|ä|	a, al	father, calm	|kw|	qu	quick
|är|	ar, ear	art, heart	|l|	l, ll	last, all
|b|	b, bb	bus, rabbit	|m|	m, mb, mm, mn	mop, bomb, summer, column
|ch|	ch, tch, tu	chin, match, culture	|n|	gn, kn, n, nn	sign, knee, no, inn
|d|	d, dd	dark, sudden	|ng|	n, ng	think, ring
|ĕ|	a, ai, ay, e, ea, ie	any, said, says, went, head, friend	|ŏ|	a, ho, o	was, honor, pond
|ē|	e, ea, ee, ei, ey, i, ie, y	these, we, beast, fleet, receive, honey, ski, magazine, chief, bumpy	|ō|	o, oa, ough, ow	most, hope, float, though, row
|f|	f, ff, gh	funny, off, enough	|ô|	a, al, au, aw, o, ough	wall, talk, haunt, lawn, soft, brought
|g|	g, gg, gu	get, egg, guide	|ôr|	oar, oor, or, ore, our	roar, door, storm, store, court
|h|	h, wh	hat, who			
|hw|	wh	when	|oi|	oi, oy	join, toy
|ĭ|	a, e, ee, i, ia, u, ui, y	cottage, before, been, mix, give, carriage, busy, build, gym	|ou|	ou, ough, ow	loud, bough, now
|ī|	ei, i, ie, igh, y	height, time, mind, pie, fight, try, type	|o͝o|	oo, ou, u	good, could, put

(continued)

Sounds	Spellings	Sample Words
|o͞o|	ew, o, oe, oo, ou, u, ue, ui	flew, do, lose, shoe, spoon, you, truth, blue, juice
|p|	p, pp	paint, happen
|r|	r, rh, rr, wr	rub, rhyme, borrow, write
|s|	c, ce, ps, s, sc, ss	city, fence, psychology, same, scent, lesson
|sh|	ce, ch, ci, s, sh, ss, ti	ocean, machine, special, sure, sheep, mission, nation
|t|	ed, t, tt	stopped, talk, little
|th|	th	they, other
|th|	th	thin, teeth

Sounds	Spellings	Sample Words
|ŭ|	o, oe, oo, ou, u	front, come, does, flood, tough, sun
|yo͞o|	eau, ew, iew, u, ue	beauty, few, view, use, fuel, cue
|ûr|	ear, er, ir, or, ur	learn, herd, girl, word, turn
|v|	f, v	of, very
|w|	o, w	one, way
|y|	i, y	million, yes
|z|	s, z, zz	rise, zoo, fizz
|zh|	ge, s	garage, usual
|ə|	a, ai, e, eo, i, o, ou, u	about, captain, silent, surgeon, pencil, lemon, famous, circus

How to Use a Dictionary

Finding an Entry Word

Guide Words

The word you want to find in a dictionary is listed in alphabetical order. To find it quickly, turn to the part of the dictionary that has words with the same first letter. Use the guide words at the top of each page. Guide words name the first and last entries on the page.

Base Words

To find a word ending in **-ed** or **-ing**, you usually must look up its base word. To find **cooked** or **cooking**, for example, look up the base word **cook**.

Homographs

Homographs have separate, numbered entries. For example, **minute** meaning "sixty seconds" is listed as **minute**[1]. **Minute** meaning "very, very small" is listed as **minute**[2].

Reading an Entry

Read the dictionary entry below. Note the purpose of each part.

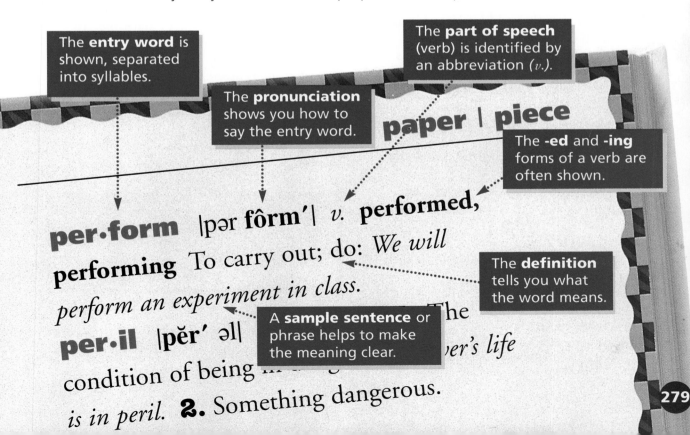

The **entry word** is shown, separated into syllables.

The **pronunciation** shows you how to say the entry word.

The **part of speech** (verb) is identified by an abbreviation (*v.*).

The **-ed** and **-ing** forms of a verb are often shown.

The **definition** tells you what the word means.

A **sample sentence** or phrase helps to make the meaning clear.

paper | piece

per·form |pər fôrm′| *v.* **performed, performing** To carry out; do: *We will perform an experiment in class.*

per·il |pĕr′ əl| ... The ...er's life ...condition of being in ... is in peril. **2.** Something dangerous.

Spelling Dictionary

a·ble |**ā′** bəl| *adj.* **abler, ablest** Having what is necessary to do something: *I will be able to see you tomorrow.*

-able A suffix that forms adjectives and means: **1.** Capable of; able to: *refillable.* **2.** Worthy of; deserving: *lovable.*

a·brupt |ə **brŭpt′**| *adj.* Taking place without warning: *I made an abrupt turn.*

a·cad·e·my |ə **kăd′** ə mē| *n., pl.* **academies** A school where a special field of study is taught: *I went to a police academy.*

ac·cent |**ăk′** sĕnt′| *n., pl.* **accents** A mark showing the stress given to one or more syllables in pronouncing a word.

ac·ci·dent |**ăk′** sĭ dənt| *n., pl.* **accidents** An unexpected and undesirable event: *An accident held up traffic for miles.*

ac·com·plish |ə **kŏm′** plĭsh| *v.* **accomplished, accomplishing** To carry out or achieve: *We accomplished the job quickly.*

ache |āk| *v.* **ached, aching** To feel a dull, steady pain: *I ache all over. n., pl.* **aches** A steady pain: *I have an ache in my back.*

a·chieve |ə **chēv′**| *v.* **achieved, achieving** To succeed in doing or accomplishing.

ac·tiv·i·ty |ăk **tĭv′** ĭ tē| *n., pl.* **activities** **1.** Energetic movement or action: *The store was a scene of great activity.* **2.** Something done for fun: *Stamp collecting is my favorite activity.*

ad·mi·ra·tion |ăd′ mə **rā′** shən| *n.* Great pleasure and delight.

ad·mire |ăd **mīr′**| *v.* **admired, admiring** To regard with great pleasure and delight.

ad·ven·tur·ous |əd **vĕn′** chər əs| *adj.* Willing to risk danger in order to have exciting adventures.

ad·vice |əd **vīs′**| *n.* An idea or suggestion about how to solve a problem: *My father gave me some advice on how to pitch.*

a·fraid |ə **frād′**| *adj.* Filled with fear; scared.

af·ter·noon |ăf′ tər **nōōn′**| *n., pl.* **afternoons** The part of the day from noon until sunset.

a·gain |ə **gĕn′**| *adv.* Once more: *If you don't win, try again.*

a·gainst |ə **gĕnst′**| *prep.* In or into contact with: *I leaned against a tree to rest.*

a·gree |ə **grē′**| *v.* **agreed, agreeing** To have or share the same opinion; concur: *I agree with you that it's too hot to work.*

aid |ād| *v.* **aided, aiding** To give help to; assist: *Glasses aid my sight. A map aids us in finding our way. n., pl.* **aids** **1.** Help or assistance given. **2.** Someone or something that helps or is helpful.

ail·ment |**āl′** mənt| *n., pl.* **ailments** An illness or disease.

air |âr| *n., pl.* **airs** The colorless, odorless, tasteless mixture of gases that surrounds the earth. The two main gases in air are nitrogen and oxygen.

air·plane |**âr′** plān′| *n., pl.* **airplanes** A vehicle with fixed wings that is heavier than air but can fly through it; plane.

air·port |**âr′** pôrt′| *n., pl.* **airports** A place with marked, open spaces where aircraft can take off and land.

-al A suffix that forms adjectives and means "having to do with": *coastal.*

a·larm |ə **lärm′**| *n., pl.* **alarms** A bell, light, or other signal that warns people of possible danger. *v.* **alarmed, alarming** To fill with sudden fear; frighten.

a·lert |ə **lûrt′**| *adj.* Quick to notice or act: *The alert child caught the falling dish.*

a·live |ə **līv′**| *adj.* Having life; living: *My grandfather is dead, but my grandmother is still alive.*

al·ley |**ăl′** ē| *n., pl.* **alleys** A narrow street or passageway between buildings.

History

Alley comes from the Old French word *alée,* meaning "a walk."

---

al·li·ga·tor |**ăl′** ĭ gā′ tər| *n., pl.* **alligators** A large reptile with sharp teeth and long, powerful jaws.

al·low |ə **lou′**| *v.* **allowed, allowing**
To let do or happen; permit: *No ball playing
is allowed! Please allow me to finish.*

all right |ôl rīt| *adj.* and *adv.* Satisfactory
but not excellent; good enough: *These peaches
are all right, but they could be fresher.*

a·lone |ə **lōn′**| *adj.* Without anyone or
anything else: *The person next door is alone all
day. adv.* Without help.

a·loud |ə **loud′**| *adv.* Not in a whisper or
to oneself; out loud: *I read the story aloud.*

al·pha·bet |ăl′ fə bĕt′| *n., pl.* **alphabets**
The letters used to represent the different
sounds in a language, arranged in a set order.

al·read·y |ôl rĕd′ ē| *adv.* By this time:
I ran to the station, but the bus had already left.

a·lu·mi·num |ə lōo′ mə nəm| *n.* A
lightweight, silver-white metal that is one of
the elements. It is used to make pots and pans,
tools, airplanes, parts of buildings, and many
other things.

al·ways |ôl′ wāz| or |ôl′ wĭz| *adv.* **1.** At
all times; every single time: *I always leave at
six o'clock.* **2.** For as long as one can imagine;
forever: *They will always be friends.*

a·maze |ə **māz′**| *v.* **amazed, amazing**
To fill with surprise or wonder; astonish: *The
idea of water carving a deep canyon out of solid
rock amazes me.*

a·nal·o·gy |ə **năl′** ə jē′| *n., pl.* **analogies**
An explanation of something by comparing it
with something similar: *The author uses the
analogy of a beehive when describing the city.*

an·chor |ăng′ kər| *n., pl.* **anchors** A heavy
metal device that is attached to a ship by a
cable. An anchor is dropped overboard and
keeps the ship in place by its weight or by
catching on the sea bottom.

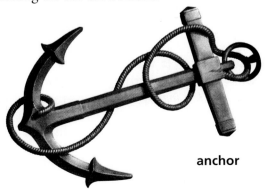

anchor

Pronunciation Key

ă	pat	ō	go	th	**thin**
ā	pay	ô	**paw, for**	hw	**which**
â	care	oi	**oil**	zh	usual
ä	father	ŏŏ	book	ə	ago,
ĕ	pet	ōō	boot		item,
ē	be	yōō	cute		pencil,
ĭ	pit	ou	**out**		atom,
ī	ice	ŭ	cut		circus
î	near	û	fur	ər	butter
ŏ	pot	*th*	**the**		

Abbreviation Key

n.	noun	*prep.*	preposition
v.	verb	*interj.*	interjection
adj.	adjective	*sing.*	singular
adv.	adverb	*pl.*	plural
pron.	pronoun	*p.*	past
conj.	conjunction	*p. part.*	past participle

an·gry |ăng′ grē| *adj.* **angrier, angriest**
Feeling or showing strong displeasure with
someone or something: *You say you aren't angry,
but your face looks angry.*

an·i·mal |ăn′ ə məl| *n., pl.* **animals** A
living being that is not a plant. Unlike plants,
most animals move from place to place, have
sense organs, and eat food rather than make it.
Human beings, horses, fish, and ants are all
animals.

an·oth·er |ə **nŭth′** ər| *adj.* Being a second
or an additional one: *I'd love another helping.*

an·swer |ăn′ sər| *v.* **answered, answering**
To say, write, or do something in reply or in
reply to.

an·to·nym |ăn′ tə nĭm′| *n., pl.* **antonyms**
A word meaning the opposite of another word.
For example, **dirty** is an antonym of **clean.**

an·y |ĕn′ ē| *adj.* **1.** One or some, no matter
which, out of three or more: *Take any books
you want.* **2.** Every: *Any student in my class can
come to the party.*

an·y·bod·y |ĕn′ ē bŏd′ ē| *pron.* Any
person at all; anyone.

Spelling Dictionary

an·y·place |ĕn′ ē plās′| *adv.* To, in, or at any place; anywhere: *Move the chair anyplace you like.*

an·y·thing |ĕn′ ē thĭng′| *pron.* Any thing whatever: *Is there anything left in the box?*

ap·ple |ăp′ əl| *n., pl.* **apples** A firm, rounded, often red-skinned fruit that can be eaten.

ap·point·ment |ə **point′** mənt| *n., pl.* **appointments** An arrangement to meet at a particular time or place.

ap·proach |ə **prōch′**| *v.* **approached, approaching** To come toward; to come near or nearer: *The car approached the garage.*

a·pron |ā′ prən| *n., pl.* **aprons** A garment worn over the front of the body to protect the clothes.

a·quat·ic |ə **kwăt′** ĭk| *adj.* Of, living in, or growing in water: *The water lily is an aquatic plant.*

ar·mor |är′ mər| *n.* A heavy covering, especially of metal, worn to protect the body in battle.

ar·my |är′ mē| *n., pl.* **armies** A large body of men and women organized and trained for land warfare.

ar·row |ăr′ ō| *n., pl.* **arrows** A straight, thin shaft that is shot from a bow. An arrow has a pointed head at one end and feathers at the other.

ar·ti·cle |är′ tĭ kəl| *n., pl.* **articles** A short piece of writing that forms an independent part of a newspaper, magazine, or book: *Write an article about your hobbies.*

a·sleep |ə **slēp′**| *adj.* Not awake; sleeping.

as·sist |ə **sĭst′**| *v.* **assisted, assisting** To give help; aid.

as·tro·naut |ăs′ trə nôt′| *n., pl.* **astronauts** A person trained to travel in a spacecraft.

ath·lete |ath′ lēt′| *n., pl.* **athletes** A person who is trained in or is good at physical exercises, games, or sports.

ath·let·ic |ăth **lĕt′** ĭk| *adj.* **1.** Of or for athletics or athletes. **1.** Good at sports.

at·tack |ə **tăk′**| *v.* **attacked, attacking** To make a sudden violent move against; assault. *n., pl.* **attacks** The act of attacking.

at·tend |ə **tĕnd′**| *v.* **attended, attending** To be present at: *Everyone attended the party.*

at·ten·dance |ə **tĕn′** dəns| *n.* **1.** The act or practice of attending: *My attendance at school is excellent.* **2.** The number of persons present: *Attendance was large at the play.*

at·ten·dant |ə **tĕn′** dənt| *n., pl.* **attendants** A person who is present at a specific place, such as a parking lot, in order to wait on those using the facilities.

at·ten·tion |ə **tĕn′** shən| *n., pl.* **attentions** **1.** The ability to concentrate: *The story held our attention for more than an hour.* **2.** The act of noticing or giving careful thought: *Your letter has come to our attention.* **3.** Thoughtful care and kindness: *They gave their aging parents much attention.*

at·ten·tive |ə **tĕn′** tĭv| *adj.* **1.** Giving attention to something; alert. **2.** Considerate and polite.

at·ti·tude |ăt′ ĭ tōōd′| or |ăt′ ĭ tyōōd′| *n., pl.* **attitudes** A state of mind; point of view: *Take a positive attitude toward studying.*

Au·gus·ta |ô **gŭs′** tə| The capital of Maine.

Aus·tin |ô′ stən| The capital of Texas.

au·to·mo·bile |ô′ tə mō **bēl′**| *n., pl.* **automobiles** A usually four-wheeled vehicle that is powered by a gasoline engine and that can carry passengers; auto; car.

av·er·age |ăv′ ər ĭj| *adj.* Typical, usual, or ordinary: *The average two-year-old loves teddy bears.*

a·vi·a·tion |ā′ vē ā′ shən| *n.* The operation of aircraft. Airplane pilots receive special training in aviation.

a·wake |ə **wāk′**| *v.* **awoke** or **awaked, awaked** or **awoken, awaking** To wake up: *The alarm clock awoke me at seven. I always awake at dawn. adj.* Not asleep.

a·ward |ə **wôrd′**| *n., pl.* **awards** Something given for outstanding performance or quality.

a·ware·ness |ə **wâr′** nĭs| *n.* **1.** Knowledge of something: *to have an awareness of the news.* **2.** Alertness; watchfulness.

a·way |ə **wā′**| *adv.* At or to a distance: *The lake is two miles away.*

aw·ful |ô′ fəl| *adj.* Very bad; terrible; horrible: *That movie was awful.*

B

ba·by |bā′ bē| *n., pl.* **babies** A very young child; infant.

back·ground |băk′ ground′| *n., pl.* **backgrounds** The part of a picture, scene, or view that appears far away.

back·pack |băk′ păk′| *n., pl.* **backpacks** A bag worn on the back to carry camping supplies. It is sometimes mounted on a light metal frame.

backpack

ba·con |bā′ kən| *n.* Salted and smoked meat from the back and sides of a pig.

bal·ance |băl′ əns| *n., pl.* **balances** A steady or stable position: *I lost my balance on ice skates and fell.*

bal·loon |bə lōōn′| *n., pl.* **balloons** A large bag filled with hot air or some other gas that is lighter than normal air; hot-air balloon.

ba·nan·a |bə năn′ ə| *n., pl.* **bananas** A curved fruit with sweet, soft flesh and yellow or reddish skin that peels off easily. Bananas grow in bunches on large tropical plants.

bank |băngk| *n., pl.* **banks** A place of business where money is kept and loans are made.

ban·quet |băng′ kwĭt| *n., pl.* **banquets** A large elaborate meal; a feast.

bar·be·cue |bär′ bĭ kyōō′| *v.* **barbecued, barbecuing** To cook over a grill, pit, or fireplace.

bar·ber |bär′ bər| *n., pl.* **barbers** A person whose work is cutting hair and shaving or trimming beards.

bar·na·cle |bär′ nə kəl| *n., pl.* **barnacles** A small, hard-shelled sea animal that attaches itself to the bottoms of ships and to underwater rocks.

bar·ra·cu·da |băr′ ə kōō′ də| *n., pl.* **barracudas** A sea fish with a long, narrow body

Pronunciation Key

ă	pat	ō	go	th	**th**in
ā	pay	ô	paw, for	hw	**wh**ich
â	care	oi	**oi**l	zh	u**s**ual
ä	father	ōō	b**oo**k	ə	**a**go,
ĕ	pet	ōō	b**oo**t		it**e**m,
ē	be	yōō	c**u**te		penc**i**l,
ĭ	pit	ou	**ou**t		at**o**m,
ī	ice	ŭ	c**u**t		circ**u**s
î	near	û	f**u**r	ər	butt**er**
ŏ	pot	th	**th**e		

and very sharp teeth, found mostly in tropical waters.

base·ball |bās′ bôl′| *n., pl.* **baseballs** A game played with a bat and ball by two teams of nine players each. Baseball is played on a field with four bases laid out in a diamond pattern. A run is scored when a player is able to touch all the bases while his or her team is at bat.

base word |bās wôrd| *n., pl.* **base words** A word to which other word parts may be added. For example, in *filled, refill,* and *filling, fill* is the base word.

ba·sic |bā′ sĭk| *adj.* Forming the base or main part of something: *The ability to read is basic to an education.*

bas·set |băs′ ĭt| *n.* Also **basset hound.** A dog with a long, heavily built body, short legs, and long, drooping ears.

ba·tik |bə tēk′| or |băt′ ĭk| *n.* A method of dyeing a design on cloth by putting wax over the areas not meant to be dyed.

bat·tle |băt′ l| *n., pl.* **battles** A fight between two armed forces, usually in a war.

bea·con |bē′ kən| *n., pl.* **beacons** A light or fire used as a warning or guide.

beard |bîrd| *n., pl.* **beards** The hair on the chin and cheeks of a man.

beat |bēt| *v.* **beat, beaten** or **beat, beating** To win against: *We beat their team.*
♦ *These sound alike* **beat, beet.**

beau·ti·ful |byōō′ tə fəl| *adj.* Being very pleasing to the senses or mind: *Beautiful music filled the air.*

beau·ty |byōō′ tē| *n., pl.* **beauties** A quality that pleases the senses or the mind: *We were charmed by the beauty of the singer's voice. There is great beauty in the poetry.*

be·come |bĭ **kŭm′**| *v.* **became** |bĭ **kām′**|, **become, becoming** To grow or come to be: *The children became restless.*

beet |bēt| *n., pl.* **beets** A leafy plant with a thick, round, dark-red root eaten as a vegetable.
♦ *These sound alike* **beet, beat.**

be·fore |bĭ **fôr′**| *adv.* In the past: *I've heard that before.* *prep.* Ahead of; earlier than: *The dog got home before me.*

beg·gar |**bĕg′** ər| *n., pl.* **beggars** A person who begs for a living.

be·gin |bĭ **gĭn′**| *v.* **began** |bĭ **găn′**|, **begun** |bĭ **gŭn′**|, **beginning** To start to do: *I began taking piano lessons last year.*

bel·low |**bĕl′** ō| *v.* **bellowed, bellowing** To shout in a deep, loud voice.

be·long |bĭ **lông′**| *v.* **belonged, belonging** To have a proper place.

be·low |bĭ **lō′**| *adv.* In or to a lower place or position: *Look at the valley below.*

be·tween |bĭ **twēn′**| *prep.* In the position separating: *A few trees stand between the house and the road.*

bird |bûrd| *n., pl.* **birds** A warm-blooded animal that lays eggs and that has wings and a body covered with feathers.

birth·day |**bûrth′** dā| *n., pl.* **birthdays** The day of a person's birth.

bit·ter |**bĭt′** ər| *adj.* **bitterer, bitterest** Sharp and unpleasant: *The fruit is bitter. We nearly froze in the bitter cold.*

blade |blād| *n., pl.* **blades** **1.** The flat, sharp-edged part of a cutting instrument, such as a knife, saw, razor, or sword. **2.** A wide, flat part, as of an oar, fan, or propeller. **3.** A thin, narrow leaf of grass. **4.** The metal runner of an ice skate.

blank |blăngk| *adj.* **blanker, blankest** **1.** Free of marks or decoration: *Give me a blank piece of paper.* **2.** Having empty spaces to be filled in: *Fill in this blank form.*

blank·et |**blăng′** kĭt| *n., pl.* **blankets** A covering for beds, used to keep a sleeper warm.

blew |blōo| *v.* Past tense of **blow:** *A gust of wind blew the door shut.*

blind |blīnd| *adj.* **blinder, blindest** Unable to see; sightless.

bliz·zard |**blĭz′** ərd| *n., pl.* **blizzards** A very long, heavy snowstorm with strong winds.

block |blŏk| *n., pl.* **blocks** A solid piece of a material, such as wood or stone, that has one or more flat sides.

blood |blŭd| *n.* The fluid circulated by the heart through the arteries, veins, and capillaries of persons and animals.

blue |blōo| *n., pl.* **blues** The color of a clear sky. *adj.* **bluer, bluest** **1.** Of the color blue. **2.** Sad and gloomy.

board |bôrd| *n., pl.* **boards** **1.** A piece of sawed lumber that has more length and width than thickness; plank. **2.** A flat piece of hard material that has a special use: *Here's a notice for your bulletin board.*
♦ *These sound alike* **board, bored.**

bod·y |**bŏd′** ē| *n., pl.* **bodies** **1.** The whole physical structure of a living person or animal. **2.** A separate mass of matter: *The Pacific Ocean is a vast body of water.*

bon·y |**bō′** nē| *adj.* **bonier, boniest** **1.** Of or like bone. **2.** Full of bones: *The fish we caught were too bony to eat.* **3.** Having bones that stick out or show through; thin.

book·let |**book′** lĭt| *n., pl.* **booklets** A small book or pamphlet.

boost·er |**boo′** stər| *n., pl.* **boosters** A device used to help launch a vehicle such as a spacecraft.

bor·der |**bôr′** dər| *n., pl.* **borders** The line where an area, as a country, ends and another area begins.

bore |bôr| *v.* **bored, boring** To cause to feel that one has had enough, as by seeming dull or uninteresting: *The movie bored us.*
♦ *These sound alike* **bored, board.**

bor·row |**bŏr′** ō| *v.* **borrowed, borrowing** To get from someone else with the understanding that what is gotten will be returned or replaced: *The book I borrowed from the library is due today.*

both·er |**bŏth′** ər| *v.* **bothered, bothering** **1.** To disturb or irritate: *That constant little noise bothers me.* **2.** To concern, worry, or trouble: *High places bother me.*

bot·tle |**bŏt′** l| *n., pl.* **bottles** A container, usually made of glass or plastic, with a narrow neck and mouth and no handle.

bot·tom |**bŏt′** əm| *n., pl.* **bottoms** The lowest part of something.

bounce |bouns| *v.* **bounced, bouncing**
To come back or up after hitting a surface.
n., pl. **bounces** A sudden spring or leap.

bowl |bōl| *n., pl.* **bowls** A round, hollow
container or dish.

break |brāk| *v.* **broke** |brōk|, **broken,
breaking** To separate into two or more pieces as
the result of force or strain; crack or split: *The
rock broke the window. We pulled until the rope
broke.*

break·fast |brĕk′ fəst| *n., pl.* **breakfasts**
The first meal of the day. *v.* **breakfasted,
breakfasting** To eat breakfast.

breath |brĕth| *n., pl.* **breaths** The air taken
into the lungs and forced out when a person
breathes.

breathe |brēth| *v.* **breathed, breathing**
To inhale and exhale: *All mammals breathe air.
Quiet! Don't even breathe.*

breez·y |brē′ zē| *adj.* **breezier, breeziest**
Exposed to breezes; windy. *adv.* **breezily**

brick |brĭk| *n., pl.* **bricks** An oblong block of
clay, baked by the sun or in an oven until hard.
Bricks are used for building and paving.

bridge |brĭj| *n., pl.* **bridges** A structure built
over a river, railroad, or other obstacle so that
people or vehicles can cross from one side to the
other.

bri·dle |brīd′ l| *n., pl.* **bridles** The
straps, bit, and reins that are placed over a
horse's head and used to control the animal.
v. **bridled, bridling** To put a bridle on:
I saddled and bridled my favorite horse.

bril·liant |brĭl′ yənt| *adj.* Very vivid in
color: *The lilies in the field were a brilliant yellow.*

broke |brōk| *v.* Past tense of **break:** *When I
fell I broke my wristwatch.*

bronze |brŏnz| *n.* **1.** A yellowish brown
metal that is a mixture of copper and tin and
sometimes other elements. Bronze is used for
statues, bells, machine parts, and other things.
2. A yellowish brown color.

brook |brŏŏk| *n., pl.* **brooks** A small, natural
stream.

brush |brŭsh| *n., pl.* **brushes** A device for
scrubbing, grooming the hair, or applying
liquids. A brush is made of bristles, hairs, or wire
fastened to a hard back or a short handle.

Pronunciation Key

ă	pat	ō	go	th	thin
ā	pay	ô	paw, for	hw	which
â	care	oi	oil	zh	usual
ä	father	ŏŏ	book	ə	ago,
ĕ	pet	ōō	boot		item,
ē	be	yōō	cute		pencil,
ĭ	pit	ou	out		atom,
ī	ice	ŭ	cut		circus
î	near	û	fur	ər	butter
ŏ	pot	*th*	**the**		

buck·et |bŭk′ ĭt| *n., pl.* **buckets** A round,
open container with a curved handle, used for
carrying things such as water, coal, and sand; pail.

buf·fa·lo |bŭf′ ə lō′| *n., pl.* **buffaloes** or
buffalos *or* **buffalo** A large animal of western
North America that has a shaggy, dark-brown
mane and short, curved horns; the bison.

buffalo

build |bĭld| *v.* **built, building** To make or
form by putting together materials or parts;
construct: *Engineers build bridges.*

built |bĭlt| *v.* Past tense and past participle of
build: *We built a birdhouse for a wren.*

bul·le·tin |bŏŏl′ ĭ tn| *n., pl.* **bulletins**
A short announcement on a matter of public
interest, as in a newspaper or on radio.

bu·reau |byŏŏr′ ō| *n., pl.* **bureaus** A chest
of drawers, especially one with a mirror: *Please
put your clothes away in your bureau.*

burn |bûrn| *v.* **burned** or **burnt, burning** To
undergo or cause to undergo damage,
destruction, or injury by fire or heat; scorch.

bur·ro |bûr′ ō| *n., pl.* **burros** A small
donkey, usually used for riding or carrying loads.

bush |bŏosh| *n., pl.* **bushes** An often low woody plant with many branches; shrub.

bush·y |bŏosh′ ē| *adj.* **bushier, bushiest 1.** Overgrown with bushes. **2.** Thick and shaggy.

bus·y |bĭz′ ē| *adj.* **busier, busiest** Engaged in work or activity: *I am busy studying.*

C

cab·bage |kăb′ ĭj| *n., pl.* **cabbages** A plant with a rounded head of tightly overlapping leaves. It is eaten as a vegetable.

cab·in |kăb′ ĭn| *n., pl.* **cabins** A small, simply built house; a cottage or hut.

cac·tus |kăk′ təs| *n., pl.* **cacti** |kăk′ tī| *or* **cactuses** One of many kinds of plants that have thick, often spiny stems without leaves and that grow in hot, dry places.

ca·det |kə dĕt′| *n., pl.* **cadets** A student at a military school who is training to be an officer.

cage |kāj| *n., pl.* **cages** An enclosure that has openings covered with wire mesh or bars and is used for confining birds or animals.

cal·ci·um |kăl′ sē əm| *n.* A silvery, moderately hard metallic chemical element that is found in substances such as milk, bone, and shells.

calf |kăf| *n., pl.* **calves** |kăvz| The young of cattle; a young cow or bull.

calm |käm| *adj.* **calmer, calmest** Peaceful; quiet: *a calm summer night.* *v.* **calmed, calming** To become or make calm: *I calmed down after the argument.*

cam·er·a |kăm′ ər ə| *n., pl.* **cameras** A device for taking photographs or motion pictures. Most cameras consist of a box that has a lens through which an image is recorded on film.

camp·site |kămp′ sīt| *n., pl.* **campsites** An area used for camping.

can·cel |kăn′ səl| *v.* **canceled, canceling 1.** To give up; call off: *I canceled my dentist appointment.* **2.** To invalidate or end: *cancel a magazine subscription.*

can·did |kăn′ dĭd| *adj.* Not posed or rehearsed: *a candid photograph.*

can·dle |kăn′ dl| *n., pl.* **candles** A solid stick of wax or tallow with a wick inside that is lit and burned to give light.

can·teen |kăn tēn′| *n., pl.* **canteens** A container for carrying liquid, as drinking water.

can·yon |kăn′ yən| *n., pl.* **canyons** A deep valley with steep walls on both sides that was formed by running water; gorge.

cap·sule |kăp′ səl| *n., pl.* **capsules** A compartment in a spacecraft, especially one that carries the crew.

cap·tain |kăp′ tən| *n., pl.* **captains** The person in command of a ship.

cap·tion |kăp′ shən| *n., pl.* **captions** A title or explanation that goes with an illustration or photograph.

cap·ture |kăp′ chər| *v.* **captured, capturing** To seize and hold, as by force or skill; catch: *The play captured my imagination.*

care |kâr| *v.* **cared, caring** To be concerned or interested: *Who cares what happens?*

care·ful |kâr′ fəl| *adj.* Done or made with attention, effort, or caution: *The doctor gave the patient a careful examination.*

care·less |kâr′ lĭs| *adj.* Done or made without attention, effort, or caution: *Careless work merits a low grade.*

car·pen·ter |kär′ pən tər| *n., pl.* **carpenters** A person who builds or repairs wooden objects and structures.

car·pet |kär′ pĭt| *n., pl.* **carpets** A heavy woven fabric used as a covering for a floor.

car·riage |kăr′ ĭj| *n., pl.* **carriages** A vehicle that has wheels and is used for carrying passengers.

car·ry |kăr′ ē| *v.* **carried, carrying** To take from one place to another: *Please carry my groceries into the house.*

car·toon |kär tōōn′| *n., pl.* **cartoons** A sketch or drawing, often with a caption, that is meant to be funny.

cas·tle |kăs′ əl| *n., pl.* **castles** A large fort or building with high, thick walls, towers, and other defenses against attack.

cat·e·go·ry |kăt′ ə gôr′ ē| *n., pl.* **categories** A division or group within a system; class: *The strings are one category of musical instruments.*

cat·er·pil·lar |kăt′ ər pĭl′ ər| *n., pl.*
caterpillars The wormlike larva of a moth or butterfly that has just hatched from its egg. A caterpillar has a long body that is often covered with hair or bristles.

cat·tle |kăt′ l| *pl. n.* Large, heavy animals, as cows, bulls, or oxen, that have hoofs, grow horns, and are raised for milk, meat, or hides.

History

Cattle comes from the Old French word *catel,* meaning "wealth or property."

cause |kôz| *n., pl.* **causes 1.** Someone or something that makes something happen: *What was the cause of the fire?* **2.** An ideal or goal that many people believe in and support: *World peace is a cause we should all work for.* *v.* **caused, causing** To be the cause of; bring about.

cav·ern |kăv′ ərn| *n., pl.* **caverns** A very large cave. Many caverns have unusual formations of rock.

cavern

cel·lar |sĕl′ ər| *n., pl.* **cellars** A room or rooms under a building where things are stored.

cent |sĕnt| *n., pl.* **cents** A coin used in the United States and Canada. One hundred cents equals one dollar.

Pronunciation Key

ă	pat	ō	go		th	thin	
ā	pay	ô	paw, for		hw	which	
â	care	oi	oil		zh	usual	
ä	father	ōō	book		ə	ago,	
ĕ	pet	ōō	boot			item,	
ē	be	yōō	cute			pencil,	
ĭ	pit	ou	out			atom,	
ī	ice	ŭ	cut			circus	
î	near	û	fur		ər	butter	
ŏ	pot	th	the				

cen·ter |sĕn′ tər| *n., pl.* **centers** A point that is the same distance from every other point of a circle or a sphere.

ce·re·al |sîr′ ē əl| *n., pl.* **cereals** A food made from the seeds of such plants as wheat, oats, or corn.

chair |châr| *n., pl.* **chairs** A piece of furniture that is built for sitting on. A chair has a seat, a back, and usually four legs.

chal·lenge |chăl′ ənj| *n., pl.* **challenges 1.** A call to take part in a contest or fight to see who is better, faster, or stronger: *The Red Team will meet the challenge of the Blue Team.* **2.** Something that requires all of a person's efforts and skills: *That job will be a challenge.*

cham·pi·on |chăm′ pē ən| *n., pl.* **champions** The winner of a game or contest, accepted as the best of all.

chance |chăns| *n., pl.* **chances** The possibility or probability that something will happen: *We have a good chance of winning the game.*

change |chānj| *n., pl.* **changes 1.** The act or result of making or becoming different. **2.** The money returned when the amount given in paying for something is more than what is owed. **3.** Coins. *v.* **changed, changing** To make or become different.

chap·ter |chăp′ tər| *n., pl.* **chapters** A main division of a book. A chapter may have a number or a title or both.

charge |chärj| *v.* **charged, charging** To ask as payment; set a price: *How much will you charge me for repairing my bike? n., pl.* **charges** An amount asked as payment; cost: *There is no charge for this service.*

charm |chärm| *n., pl.* **charms** The power or ability to please or delight; appeal: *the charm of the peaceful countryside.*

cheap |chēp| *adj.* **cheaper, cheapest** Low in price; inexpensive: *Tomatoes are cheap in August.*

check |chĕk| *n., pl.* **checks 1.** Something that restrains or controls. **2.** Examination to be sure that something is as it should be. **3.** A mark made to show that something has been noted. **4.** A restaurant bill. *v.* **checked, checking** To test, examine, or compare to find out if something is correct or in good condition: *Check your answers after doing the arithmetic.*

cheer |chîr| *v.* **cheered, cheering** To shout in happiness, approval, encouragement, or enthusiasm: *The audience cheered and clapped. n., pl.* **cheers 1.** A shout of happiness, approval, encouragement, or enthusiasm. **2.** Good spirits; happiness.

cheer·ful |chîr′ fəl| *adj.* In good spirits; happy.

cheer·less |chîr′ lĭs| *adj.* Lacking cheer; gloomy and depressing.

cheer·y |chîr′ ē| *adj.* **cheerier, cheeriest** Bright and cheerful.

cheese·bur·ger |chēz′ bûr′ gər| *n., pl.* **cheeseburgers** A hamburger topped with melted cheese.

chef |shĕf| *n., pl.* **chefs** A cook, especially the chief cook of a restaurant.

chew |chōō| *v.* **chewed, chewing** To bite and grind with the teeth. *n., pl.* **chews** The act of chewing.

chick·en |chĭk′ ən| *n., pl.* **chickens** The common domestic fowl; hen or rooster.

chief |chēf| *adj.* Highest in rank: *My cousin was appointed chief engineer of the project.*

chip·munk |chĭp′ mŭngk′| *n., pl.* **chipmunks** An animal that resembles a squirrel but is smaller and has a striped back.

chipmunk

chore |chôr| *n., pl.* **chores** A small job, usually done on a regular schedule.

chose |chōz| *v.* Past tense of **choose.** Picked: *Each captain chose ten players for their team.*

cho·sen |chō′ zən| *v.* Past participle of **choose:** *We have chosen you to be class president.*

cir·cle |sûr′ kəl| *n., pl.* **circles** A curved line made up of points that are all at the same distance from an inside point called the center.

cit·y |sĭt′ ē| *n., pl.* **cities** A place where many people live close to one another. Cities are larger than towns and are usually centers of business activity.

clam |klăm| *n., pl.* **clams** A shellfish that has a shell with two parts hinged together. Clams burrow into sand where they live. The soft body of the clam can be eaten.

clamp |klămp| *n., pl.* **clamps** A device for gripping or fastening two things together.

clay |klā| *n., pl.* **clays** A firm kind of earth made up of small particles. Clay is soft when wet and can be shaped. After heating, clay hardens. It is used to make bricks and pottery.

clean |klēn| *adj.* **cleaner, cleanest** Free from dirt, stains, or clutter: *Put on a clean shirt.*

clean·li·ness |klĕn′ lē nĭs| *n.* Condition of being free from dirt: *the cleanliness of the house.*

clean·ly |klĕn′ lē| *adj.* **cleanlier, cleanliest** Habitually and carefully neat and clean: *A cat is a very cleanly animal.* |klēn′ lē| *adv.* In a clean manner: *The fruit had been severed cleanly by a knife.*

clev·er |klĕv′ ər| *adj.* **cleverer, cleverest** Having or showing a quick mind; smart: *I tried to be as clever as I could and think what to do before it was too late.*

climb |klīm| *v.* **climbed, climbing** To go in various directions, such as up, down, or over, often by use of the hands and feet: *I climbed up the ladder.*

clin·ic |klĭn′ ĭk| *n., pl.* **clinics** A place that gives medical treatment to patients who do not have to stay in a hospital.

clock |klŏk| *n., pl.* **clocks** An instrument for measuring and indicating time, often having a numbered dial with moving hands.

◊ *Idiom* **around the clock** Nonstop; night and day.

cloud·y |klou′ dē| *adj.* **cloudier, cloudiest** Full of or covered with clouds: *The sky was cloudy, so I took my umbrella.*

clown |kloun| *n., pl.* **clowns** A performer, often in a circus, who does funny tricks.

coal |kōl| *n., pl.* **coals** A black natural solid substance that is formed from partly decayed plant matter, consists mainly of carbon, and is widely used as a fuel.

coarse |kôrs| *adj.* **coarser, coarsest** Not smooth; rough.

◆ *These sound alike* **coarse, course.**

coast |kōst| *n., pl.* **coasts** The land next to or near the sea; seashore.

coast·al |kō′ stəl| *adj.* On, along, or near a coast: *We swam in coastal water.*

coast·line |kōst′ līn′| *n., pl.* **coastlines** The shape or outline of a seacoast.

coat of arms |kōt ŭv ärmz| *n., pl.* **coats of arms** A design, as on a shield, that serves as the emblem of a nation or group.

coat of arms

cob·ble·stone |kŏb′ əl stōn′| *n., pl.* **cobblestones** A round stone formerly used for paving streets.

co·coon |kə kōōn′| *n., pl.* **cocoons** The silky covering spun by a caterpillar to protect itself until it turns into a fully developed moth or butterfly.

cold |kōld| *adj.* **colder, coldest** Feeling a lack of warmth; chilly.

col·lage |kə läzh′| *n., pl.* **collages** A picture made by pasting various materials or objects on a surface.

col·lar |kŏl′ ər| *n., pl.* **collars** The part of a garment that fits around the neck.

Pronunciation Key

ă	pat	ō	go	th	thin
ā	pay	ô	paw, for	hw	which
â	care	oi	oil	zh	usual
ä	father	ōō	book	ə	ago,
ĕ	pet	ōō	boot		item,
ē	be	yōō	cute		pencil,
ĭ	pit	ou	out		atom,
ī	ice	ŭ	cut		circus
î	near	û	fur	ər	butter
ŏ	pot	*th*	*the*		

col·lie |kŏl′ ē| *n., pl.* **collies** A large dog with long hair and a narrow snout, often used to herd sheep.

col·or·ful |kŭl′ ər fəl| *adj.* Full of color, especially having several vivid colors: *Many butterflies have colorful wings.*

colt |kōlt| *n., pl.* **colts** A young horse, especially a male.

Co·lum·bi·a |kə lŭm′ bē ə| The capital of South Carolina.

comb |kōm| *n., pl.* **combs** A strip of hard material that has teeth and is used to arrange the hair. *v.* **combed, combing** To smooth or arrange with a comb.

com·mon |kŏm′ ən| *adj.* **commoner, commonest** Often seen; ordinary: *Windy weather is common in March.*

com·mute |kə myōōt′| *v.* **commuted, commuting** To travel regularly between home and work or school.

com·pass |kŭm′ pəs| *n., pl.* **compasses** An instrument with a magnetic needle that is used to show directions. The needle always points to the north.

com·pose |kəm pōz′| *v.* **composed, composing** To make or create by putting parts or elements together: *An artist composes a picture by arranging forms and colors.*

com·po·si·tion |kŏm′ pə zĭsh′ ən| *n., pl.* **compositions** A work that has been composed, especially a musical work.

com·pound word |kŏm′ pound′ wôrd| *n., pl.* **compound words** A word made up of two or more smaller words. A compound word may be written as one word, as two words joined by a hyphen, or as two separate words.

Spelling Dictionary

con·ti·nent |kŏn′ tə nənt| *n., pl.*
continents One of the main land masses of
the earth, including Africa, Antarctica, Asia,
Australia, Europe, North America, and South
America.

con·trac·tion |kən trăk′ shən| *n., pl.*
contractions The shortened form of one
or more words. An apostrophe replaces the
missing letter or letters. For example, *isn't* is
a contraction of *is not.*

con·trol tow·er |kən trōl′ tou′ ər| *n., pl.*
control towers A tower at an airport from
which the takeoffs and landings are controlled by
radio and radar.

cook |kŏŏk| *v.* **cooked, cooking** To
prepare food for eating by using heat.

cop·per |kŏp′ ər| *n.* A reddish-brown
metal that is an excellent conductor of heat
and electricity. Copper is a chemical element.
adj. Made of or containing copper.

cop·y |kŏp′ ē| *v.* **copied, copying** To
make something that is exactly like an original.

cor·al |kôr′ əl| *n., pl.* **corals** A hard, stony
substance formed by the skeletons of tiny sea
animals massed together in great numbers. It is
often white, pink, or reddish.

cor·ner |kôr′ nər| *n., pl.* **corners** The
place where two lines, walls, or streets meet.

cor·ral |kə răl′| *n., pl.* **corrals** A fenced-in
area or pen for cattle or horses.

cot·tage |kŏt′ ĭj| *n., pl.* **cottages** A small
house in the country.

cottage

couch |kouch| *n., pl.* **couches** A sofa.

coun·try |kŭn′ trē| *n., pl.* **countries** An
area of land; region: *The country near our house
is full of forests.*

cou·ple |kŭp′ əl| *n., pl.* **couples 1.** Two
things of the same kind that are connected
or considered together; pair: *I wrote a couple
of letters.* **2.** Two persons who are closely
associated, especially a man and woman who
are married.

course |kôrs| *n., pl.* **courses 1.** A series
of studies that leads to a degree: *The student
finished the four-year course in high school.*
2. A place where a race is held or a sport is
played: *a golf course.*
♦ *These sound alike* **course, coarse.**

cous·in |kŭz′ ən| *n., pl.* **cousins** A child of
one's aunt or uncle.

cov·er |kŭv′ ər| *n., pl.* **covers** Something
that is put over or on something else.

cra·zy |krā′ zē| *adj.* **crazier, craziest** Not
sensible: *It's crazy to drive too fast.*

creak |krēk| *v.* **creaked, creaking** To make
or move with a squeaking sound: *The rusty gate
creaked. n., pl.* **creaks** A creaking sound.
♦ *These sound alike* **creak, creek.**

creak·i·ness |krē′ kē nĭs| *n.* Squeakiness.

creak·y |krē′ kē| *adj.* **creakier, creakiest**
Giving off a creak or creaks.

cream |krēm| *adj.* **creams** The yellowish
fatty part of milk. Cream can be separated from
milk and is used in cooking. It is also used to
make butter.

creek |krēk| or |krĭk| *n., pl.* **creeks** A small
stream of water, often one that flows into a river.
♦ *These sound alike* **creek, creak.**

crime |krīm| *n., pl.* **crimes** Unlawful activity
in general: *The police fight crime.*

crim·i·nal |krĭm′ ə nəl| *n., pl.* **criminals** A
person who has committed or been convicted of
a crime.

croc·o·dile |krŏk′ ə dīl′| *n., pl.* **crocodiles**
A large reptile with thick skin, sharp teeth, and
long, narrow jaws.
◊ *Idiom* **shed crocodile tears** To cry,
pretending to be sad

crook·ed |krŏŏk′ ĭd| *adj.* Not straight.

crow |krō| *n., pl.* **crows** A large black bird
with a harsh, hoarse call.

cru·el·ty |krŏŏ′ əl tē| *n., pl.* **cruelties**
Lack of kindness.

crumb |krŭm| *n., pl.* **crumbs** A tiny piece
of food, especially of bread or cake.

crum·ble |krŭm′ bəl| *v.* **crumbled,
crumbling** To break or fall into small pieces
or crumbs: *The lump of dirt crumbled into dust.*

cup·board |kŭb′ ərd| *n., pl.* **cupboards**
A cabinet, usually with shelves, for storing
food or dishes.

cure |kyŏŏr| *v.* **cured, curing** To bring
back to good health; heal.

curl |kûrl| *v.* **curled, curling** To twist into
or form ringlets. *n., pl.* **curls** A ring of hair.

cur·rent |kûr′ ənt| *n., pl.* **currents** A mass
of liquid or gas that is in motion: *We paddled
the canoe into the current of the river.*

curve |kûrv| *n., pl.* **curves** A line or surface
that keeps bending smoothly without
sharp angles.

cut·ter |kŭt′ ər| *n., pl.* **cutters** A small,
lightly armed boat used by the Coast Guard.

D

dair·y |dâr′ ē| *n., pl.* **dairies** A farm that
produces milk.

dam·age |dăm′ ĭj| *n., pl.* **damages** Harm
or injury that causes loss or makes something
less valuable. *v.* **damaged, damaging** To
harm or injure.

dance |dăns| *v.* **danced, dancing** To move
with rhythmic steps and motions, usually in
time to music.

dan·ger |dān′ jər| *n., pl.* **dangers** The
chance of harm or destruction; peril: *The
settlers faced danger with courage.*

dare |dâr| *v.* **dared, daring** To be brave or
bold enough: *The explorer dared to sail alone
across the ocean.*

dark |därk| *adj.* **darker, darkest** Without
light or with very little light; shaded.

dark·ness |därk′ nĭs| *n.* Absence of light;
partial or total blackness: *the darkness
before dawn.*

Pronunciation Key

ă	pat	ō	go	th	**th**in
ā	pay	ô	paw, for	hw	**wh**ich
â	care	oi	oil	zh	usual
ä	father	ŏŏ	book	ə	ago,
ĕ	pet	ōō	boot		item,
ē	be	yōō	cute		pencil,
ĭ	pit	ou	out		atom,
ī	ice	ŭ	cut		circus
î	near	û	fur	ər	butter
ŏ	pot	th	the		

dark·room |därk′ rōōm′| or
|därk′ rŏŏm′| *n., pl.* **darkrooms** A room
in which photographic materials are processed,
either in total darkness or under light to which
they are not sensitive.

daugh·ter |dô′ tər| *n., pl.* **daughters** A
female offspring or child.

dawn |dôn| *n., pl.* **dawns** The time each
morning when the sun comes up.

dead·line |dĕd′ līn′| *n., pl.* **deadlines** A
set time by which something must be done.

dear |dîr| *adj.* **dearer, dearest** Much loved;
precious: *You are my dear friend.*
◆ *These sound alike* **dear, deer.**

debt |dĕt| *n., pl.* **debts** Something that is
owed to another: *I always pay my debts.*

dec·i·mal |dĕs′ ə məl| *n., pl.* **decimals**
A fraction in which the denominator is 10 or a
multiple of 10: *The decimal .1 = 1/10, and the
decimal .12 = 12/100. adj.* Of or based on 10.

deck |dĕk| *n., pl.* **decks** One of the floors
dividing a ship into different levels.

de·clare |dĭ klâr′| *v.* **declared, declaring**
To say with emphasis or certainty.

dec·la·ra·tion |dĕk′ lə rā′ shən| *n., pl.*
declarations The act of declaring.

dec·o·rate |dĕk′ ə rāt′| *v.* **decorated,
decorating** To furnish with something
attractive or beautiful; adorn: *We decorated the
room with flowers.*

dec·o·ra·tion |dĕk′ ə rā′ shən| *n., pl.*
decorations An ornament; something that
decorates.

deer |dîr| *n., pl.* **deer** Any of several animals
that have hoofs and chew their cud. The males
usually have antlers.
◆ *These sound alike* **deer, dear.**

Spelling Dictionary

de·fend |dĭ fĕnd′| *v.* **defended, defending** To protect from attack, harm, danger, or challenge.

de·fine |dĭ fīn′| *v.* **defined, defining** To explain the meaning of: *Dictionaries define words.*

def·i·ni·tion |dĕf′ ə nĭsh′ ən| *n., pl.* **definitions** A statement of the meaning of a word or phrase.

de·gree |dĭ grē′| *n., pl.* **degrees** A step or stage in a series or process: *My shyness decreased by degrees.*

de·lay |dĭ lā′| *n., pl.* **delays** The act of delaying or condition of being delayed: *Do your homework without delay.* *v.* **delayed, delaying** To put off; postpone: *We delayed dinner an hour.*

de·liv·er |dĭ lĭv′ ər| *v.* **delivered, delivering** To take and turn over to the proper person or at the proper destination: *The mail carrier delivers packages.*

de·part·ment |dĭ pärt′ mənt| *n., pl.* **departments** A separate division of an organization, as a government or business.

de·pend |dĭ pĕnd′| *v.* **depended, depending** To be determined by something else: *Success depends on hard work.*

de·pos·it |dĭ pŏz′ ĭt| *v.* **deposited, depositing** To put money into a bank account.

de·scent |dĭ sĕnt′| *n., pl.* **descents** A downward slope.

des·ert |dĕz′ ərt| *n., pl.* **deserts** A dry area, usually covered with sand, in which few plants or animals live.

desk |dĕsk| *n., pl.* **desks** A piece of furniture with a top for use in reading or writing, often in a classroom.

de·vel·op |dĭ vĕl′ əp| *v.* **developed, developing** To treat a film with chemicals so that a picture can be seen.

di·a·ry |dī′ ə rē| *n., pl.* **diaries** A daily written record of a person's thoughts, activities, opinions, and experiences.

die·sel |dē zəl| *n.* Something powered by a diesel engine, especially a locomotive. *adj.* Powered by or intended for a diesel engine; oil-burning.

dim |dĭm| *adj.* **dimmer, dimmest** **1.** Somewhat dark. **2.** Giving off little light: *a dim lamp.* **3.** Not clearly seen: *a dim shape.* *v.* **dimmed, dimming** To make or become dim.

din·er |dī′ nər| *n., pl.* **diners** A railroad car in which meals are served or a restaurant that looks like one.

din·ner |dĭn′ ər| *n., pl.* **dinners** The main meal of the day.

dirt·y |dûr′ tē| *adj.* **dirtier, dirtiest** Full of or covered with dirt; not clean.

dis- A prefix that means: **1.** Not; opposite: *dishonest.* **2.** Not having; lack of: *discomfort.*

dis·as·ter |dĭ zăs′ tər| *n., pl.* **disasters** Something, such as a flood, that causes great destruction.

dis·col·or |dĭs kŭl′ ər| *v.* **discolored, discoloring** To spoil the color of; stain.

dis·con·tin·ue |dĭs′ kən tĭn′ yōō| *v.* **discontinued, discontinuing** To bring or come to an end; stop.

dis·ease |dĭ zēz′| *n., pl.* **diseases** A condition that keeps the body from functioning normally; illness.

dis·like |dĭs līk′| *v.* **dislike, disliking** To have a feeling of not liking: *I dislike beans.*

dis·or·der |dĭs ôr′ dər| *n., pl.* **disorders** Lack of order; confusion.

dis·please |dĭs plēz′| *v.* **displeased, displeasing** To make dissatisfied.

dis·trust |dĭs trŭst′| *n.* Lack of trust; suspicion.

dis·turb |dĭ stûrb′| *v.* **disturbed, disturbing** **1.** To trouble or worry: *Your noisy play disturbs me.* **2.** To break in on; interrupt: *The fire sirens disturbed our sleep.*

di·vide |dĭ vīd′| *v.* **divided, dividing** **1.** To separate into two or more parts or groups. **2.** To determine how many times one number contains another: *The teacher told me to divide 20 by 2.*

doc·tor |dŏk′ tər| *n., pl.* **doctors** A physician, dentist, or veterinarian trained in and licensed to practice a healing art.

dodge |dŏj| *v.* **dodged, dodging** To move quickly aside: *The cat dodged the dog.*

dol·lar |dŏl′ ər| *n., pl.* **dollars** A unit of money equal to 100 cents that is used in the United States and Canada.

dol·phin |dŏl′ fĭn| *n., pl.* **dolphins** A sea animal that is related to the whale but is smaller and has a snout that looks like a beak. It can be trained by human beings.

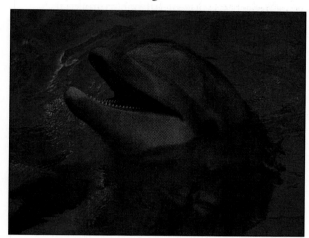

dolphin

done |dŭn| *v.* Past participle of **do:** *Have you done your homework?*

do·nor |dō′ nər| *n., pl.* **donors** A person who gives, donates, or contributes.

dou·ble |dŭb′ əl| *adj.* Twice as much in size, strength, number, or amount.

doubt |dout| *v.* **doubted, doubting** To be uncertain or unsure about; distrust: *I doubt my ability to win the contest.*

drag |drăg| *v.* **dragged, dragging** To draw along the ground or haul by force; to pull.

drag·on |drăg′ ən| *n., pl.* **dragons** An imaginary fire-breathing monster that is usually pictured as a giant lizard or reptile with wings and claws.

drain |drān| *n., pl.* **drains** A pipe or channel by which liquid is drained off: *The water was stopped up in the drain.*

drawn |drôn| *v.* Past participle of **draw:** *The artist has drawn a wonderful picture of my brother.*

dream |drēm| *n., pl.* **dreams** A series of pictures, thoughts, or emotions occurring during sleep.

dress·er |drĕs′ ər| *n., pl.* **dressers** A chest of drawers, usually with a mirror; bureau.

drill |drĭl| *n., pl.* **drills** A tool used to make holes in solid materials.

Pronunciation Key

ă	pat	ō	go	th	**th**in
ā	pay	ô	paw, for	hw	**wh**ich
â	care	oi	oil	zh	usual
ä	father	ŏŏ	book	ə	ago,
ĕ	pet	ōō	boot		item,
ē	be	yōō	cute		pencil,
ĭ	pit	ou	out		atom,
ī	ice	ŭ	cut		circus
î	near	û	fur	ər	butter
ŏ	pot	*th*	**the**		

drink |drĭngk| *n., pl.* **drinks** A kind of liquid for drinking; beverage. *v.* **drank** |drăngk|, **drunk** |drŭngk|, **drinking** To swallow liquid.

drop |drŏp| *v.* **dropped, dropping 1.** To fall or let fall in drops. **2.** To fall or let fall: *I dropped a dish.*

drop·let |drŏp′ lĭt| *n., pl.* **droplets** A small drop.

drought |drout| *n., pl.* **droughts** A period of little or no rain.

due |dōō| or |dyōō| *adj.* Owed or owing as a right or debt: *Please pay the amount that is still due.*

dull |dŭl| *adj.* **duller, dullest** Not interesting; boring: *This story is dull.*

dun·geon |dŭn′ jən| *n., pl.* **dungeons** A dark underground prison.

du·ty |dōō′ tē| or |dyōō′ tē| *n., pl.* **duties 1.** Something that a person ought to do: *We feel it is our duty to help the poor.* **2.** Action that a person's occupation or position requires: *The candidate can perform the duties of a senator.*

E

ea·ger |ē′ gər| *adj.* **eagerer, eagerest** Full of strong desire; impatient: *We're ready and eager to get started.*

ea·gle |ē′ gəl| *n., pl.* **eagles** A large bird with a hooked bill, broad strong wings, and sharp eyesight. Eagles soar high in the air.

ear·ly |ûr′ lē| *adv.* **earlier, earliest** At or near the beginning: *We always get up early in the morning.*

Spelling Dictionary

earn |ûrn| *v.* **earned, earning** **1.** To gain by working or by supplying service: *Computer programmers earn good salaries.* **2.** To deserve as a result of effort or behavior: *They earned good grades by working hard.*
♦ *These sound alike* **earn, urn.**

ear·nest |ûr′ nĭst| *adj.* Not playful or trifling; sincere: *Make an earnest apology for your mistake.*

eas·i·ly |ē′ zə lē| *adv.* Without difficulty or stress.

east |ēst| *n.* The direction in which the sun is seen rising in the morning. *adj.* **1.** Of, in, or toward the east: *We camped on the east side of the lake.* **2.** Coming from the east: *An east wind blew all day. adv.* Toward the east: *We drove east.*

eas·y |ē′ zē| *adj.* **easier, easiest** Needing very little effort or thought; not hard: *The homework was easy.*

ed·dy |ĕd′ ē| *n., pl.* **eddies** A current, as of a liquid or gas, that moves contrary to the direction of a main current, especially in a circular motion.

edge |ĕj| *n., pl.* **edges** The line or point where an object or area ends; rim; border.

e·di·tion |ĭ dĭsh′ ən| *n., pl.* **editions** The entire number of copies of a book, magazine, or newspaper printed at one time: *the morning edition of a newspaper.*

ed·i·tor |ĕd′ ĭ tər| *n., pl.* **editors** A person who prepares material for publication by correcting, revising, or marking directions for a printer.

eel |ēl| *n., pl.* **eels** A long, slippery, snake-like fish.

eel

ei·ther |ē′ thər| or |ī′ thər| *pron.* One or the other of two: *They went a mile before either spoke.*

e·las·tic |ĭ lăs′ tĭk| *n., pl.* **elastics** A tape woven with strands of rubber to make it stretch; rubber band: *The teacher put an elastic around the test papers.*

e·lec·tric |ĭ lĕk′ trĭk| *adj.* **1.** Of, relating to, or produced by electricity: *An electric current runs through the wiring of the house.* **2.** Exceptionally tense; charged with emotion: *an atmosphere electric with suspicion.*

e·lec·tri·cian |ĭ lĕk trĭsh′ ən| *n., pl.* **electricians** A person whose work is installing, repairing, or operating electric equipment.

e·lec·tric·i·ty |ĭ lĕk trĭs′ ĭ tē| or |ē′ lĕk trĭs′ ĭ tē| *n.* Power that is transmitted by electrical means; electric power.

elf |ĕlf| *n., pl.* **elves** A tiny, often mischievous, imaginary creature with magical powers.

em·broi·der·y |ĕm broi′ də rē| *n., pl.* **embroideries** A decorated fabric or design made with a needle and thread.

emp·ty |ĕmp′ tē| *adj.* Containing nothing: *You can fill the empty bottle with orange juice. v.* **emptied, emptying** To make or become empty.

en·chant |ĕn chănt′| *v.* **enchanted, enchanting** To put under a magic spell; bewitch.

end·less |ĕnd′ lĭs| *adj.* Having or seeming to have no end or limit; infinite: *endless stretches of sandy beaches.*

en·e·my |ĕn′ ə mē| *n., pl.* **enemies** A person, animal, or group that hates or wishes harm to another; foe.

en·er·gy |ĕn′ ər jē| *n., pl.* **energies** Strength and vigor in action: *Good food helps give us energy.*

en·gine |ĕn′ jən| *n., pl.* **engines** A machine that uses energy, as that produced by oil or steam, to make something run or move; motor.

en·joy |ĕn joi′| *v.* **enjoyed, enjoying** To receive pleasure from: *We enjoy living in the country.*

e·nor·mous |ĭ nôr′ məs| *adj.* Extremely large; huge.

e·nough |ĭ **nŭf′**| *adj.* Being as much or as many as needed to meet a requirement; adequate: *There is enough food for everybody.*

en·ter |ĕn′ tər| *v.* **entered, entering** To come or to go in or into: *The ship entered the harbor.*

en·vi·ous |ĕn′ vē əs| *adj.* Having a bad feeling toward a competitor: *I was envious of Jake's gold medal in swimming.*

en·vy |ĕn′ vē| *n., pl.* **envies** A feeling of discontent at the advantages or success enjoyed by another together with a strong desire to have them for oneself; jealousy: *I was filled with envy when I saw their new car.*

e·qua·tor |ĭ **kwā′** tər| *n., pl.* **equators** An imaginary line around the middle of the earth at an equal distance from the North and South Poles. The equator divides the earth into the Northern Hemisphere and the Southern Hemisphere.

-er A suffix that forms nouns and means:
1. Something or someone who does: *baker.*
2. Someone who is: *foreigner.* **3.** A person who was born in or lives in a place: *islander.*

es·cape |ĭ **skāp′**| *v.* **escaped, escaping** To get free: *The prisoners escaped by climbing the wall.*

-et A suffix that forms nouns and means "small": *jacket.*

e·vent |ĭ **vĕnt′**| *n., pl.* **events** Something that happens; occurrence: *The town newspaper reports events such as accidents, marriages, and births.*

ev·er |ĕv′ ər| *adv.* At any time: *Have you ever caught a fish?*

eve·ry·thing |ĕv′ rē thĭng′| *pron.* All things: *Everything in the store is for sale.*

eve·ry·where |ĕv′ rē hwâr′| *adv.* In every place; in all places: *I looked everywhere for my lost keys.*

ex·act |ĭg **zăkt′**| *adj.* Accurate in every detail: *It cost me about five dollars—the exact amount was $5.03.*

ex·am·i·na·tion |ĭg zăm′ ə **nā′** shən| *n., pl.* **examinations** A set of questions designed to test knowledge or skills; exam.

ex·am·ine |ĭg **zăm′** ĭn| *v.* **examined, examining** To look at carefully: *The detective examined the tracks to see if they matched the suspect's boot soles.*

Pronunciation Key

ă	pat	ō	go	th	thin
ā	pay	ô	paw, for	hw	which
â	care	oi	oil	zh	usual
ä	father	o͞o	book	ə	ago,
ĕ	pet	o͞o	boot		item,
ē	be	yo͞o	cute		pencil,
ĭ	pit	ou	out		atom,
ī	ice	ŭ	cut		circus
î	near	û	fur	ər	butter
ŏ	pot	*th*	the		

ex·cel·lence |ĕk′ sə lens| *n.* The condition or quality of being excellent or of high quality; superiority.

ex·er·cise |ĕk′ sər sīz′| *n., pl.* **exercises** Physical activity for the good of the body: *We try to get some exercise every day.*

ex·it |ĕg′ zĭt| or |ĕk′ sĭt| *n., pl.* **exits** A way out.

ex·pert |ĕk′ spûrt′| *n., pl.* **experts** A person who has great knowledge or skill in a special area: *My teacher is an expert on American history.* |ĕk′ spûrt′| or |ĭk **spûrt′**| *adj.* Having or displaying special knowledge or skill in a field.

ex·plore |ĭk **splôr′**| *v.* **explored, exploring** To go into or travel through an unknown or unfamiliar place for the purpose of discovery: *The Spanish explored the New World.*

F

face |fās| *n., pl.* **faces** The front part of the head from the forehead to the chin.

faint |fānt| *v.* **fainted, fainting** To lose consciousness for a short time.

false |fôls| *adj.* **falser, falsest 1.** Not true, real, honest, or correct: *a false statement.* **2.** Lacking loyalty: *They turned out to be false friends.*

fam·i·ly |făm′ ə lē| *n., pl.* **families** A group consisting of parents and their children.

fa·mous |fā′ məs| *adj.* Very well known.

Spelling Dictionary

fan·cy |făn′ sē| *adj.* **fancier, fanciest** Not plain or simple; elaborate.

farm·er |fär′ mər| *n., pl.* **farmers** A person who owns or operates a piece of land on which crops or animals are raised.

fast |făst| *adj.* **faster, fastest** Firmly fixed, attached, or fastened: *Keep a fast grip on the rope.*

fas·ten |făs′ ən| *v.* **fastened, fastening** To attach firmly; secure: *We fastened our skis to a rack on the roof of the car.*

fau·cet |fô′ sĭt| *n., pl.* **faucets** A device for controlling the flow of liquid, as from a pipe; tap: *The plumber had to turn off the faucet when he fixed the sink.*

fa·vor |fā′ vər| *n., pl.* **favors** A kind or helpful act. *v.* **favored, favoring** To show preference for.

fear·ful |fîr′ fəl| *adj.* Feeling afraid: *I was fearful of losing my way in the forest.*

feast |fēst| *n., pl.* **feasts** A fancy meal; banquet: *We prepared a feast for the wedding.*

feath·er |fĕth′ ər| *n., pl.* **feathers** One of the light horny structures forming the outer covering of a bird.

fea·ture |fē′ chər| *n., pl.* **features** The part or quality that is most noticeable.

fel·low |fĕl′ ō| *n., pl.* **fellows** A man or boy.

fe·male |fē′ māl′| *adj.* Of or belonging to the sex that can give birth to young or produce eggs. *n., pl.* **females** A female person or animal.

fence |fĕns| *n., pl.* **fences** A structure set up to prevent entry into an area or to mark it off.

fer·ry |fĕr′ ē| *n., pl.* **ferries** A boat or boat service used to carry people, cars, or goods across water.

fes·ti·val |fĕs′ tə vəl| *n., pl.* **festivals** **1.** A day or period of celebrating; holiday. **2.** A series of special cultural events, such as films, concerts, or exhibitions.

fes·tive |fĕs′ tĭv| *adj.* Merry; joyous: *We were in a festive mood after the birthday party.*

fes·toon |fĕ stōōn′| *n., pl.* **festoons** **1.** A string or garland of leaves or flowers hanging in a curve between two points. **2.** A painting or sculpture of such a string or garland. *v.* **festooned, festooning** **1.** To decorate with festoons. **2.** To form or make into festoons.

fe·ver |fē′ vər| *n., pl.* **fevers** A body temperature that is higher than normal.

few |fyōō| *adj.* **fewer, fewest** Amounting to a small number: *The bag held a few apples. n. (used with a plural verb)* A small number: *Most of the kids have a ride, but a few do not. pron. (used with a plural verb)* A small number of persons or things: *Few passed the test.*

field |fēld| *n., pl.* **fields** An area of land where a crop is grown, a natural product is obtained, or a special activity is done.

fier·y |fīr′ ē| *adj.* **fierier, fieriest** Of or glowing like fire: *The fiery sunset lit up the western sky.*

fif·ty |fĭf′ tē| *n., pl.* **fifties** The number, written 50, that is equal to the product of 10 x 5. *adj.* Being equal to ten times five.

fig·ure |fĭg′ yər| *n., pl.* **figures** **1.** A written symbol that stands for a number. **2.** A shape or form: *A tall figure stood in the doorway.*

fil·ly |fĭl′ ē| *n., pl.* **fillies** A young female horse.

film |fĭlm| *n., pl.* **films** A thin strip of material coated with a chemical that changes when light strikes it. Film is used in taking photographs.

fil·ter |fĭl′ tər| *n., pl.* **filters** A sheet of material that changes the colors of light passing through it by blocking certain light waves and letting others pass through.

fi·nal |fī′ nəl| *adj.* **1.** Coming at the end: *We took a final spelling test at the end of the school year.* **2.** Not to be reconsidered; decisive: *The judge's decision is final.*

fi·nal·i·ty |fī năl′ ĭ tē| *n., pl.* **finalities** The quality of being final; decisiveness: *The nurse spoke loudly and with finality.*

fi·nan·cial |fĭ năn′ shəl| or |fī năn′ shəl| *adj.* Of or having to do with the management or use of money: *The store was a financial failure and soon closed.*

fin·ish |fĭn′ ĭsh| *n., pl.* **finishes** The conclusion of; end: *The finish of the race was exciting.*

fire·place |fīr′ plās′| *n., pl.* **fireplaces** A structure for holding a fire for heating or cooking. An indoor fireplace is an opening in the wall of a room with a chimney leading up from it.

firm |fûrm| *adj.* **firmer, firmest 1.** Not giving way when pressed or pushed; solid; hard: *The firm ground of the track was ideal for running.* **2.** Not changing or varying; steady: *Our friendship is firm.* **3.** Strong and sure: *Keep a firm grip on the handlebars.*

first |fûrst| *n., pl.* **firsts 1.** The number in a series that matches the number one. **2.** A person or thing that is first: *Would the first in line come here? adj.* Coming before all others: *the first house on the block.*

fit·ness |fĭt′ nĭs| *n.* The state or quality of being physically sound; healthy: *Jogging is a good way to maintain fitness.*

fix |fĭks| *v.* **fixed, fixing 1.** To place or fasten firmly: *We fixed the lightning rod to the chimney.* **2.** To set right; mend: *I fixed the broken radio.*

flash |flăsh| *n., pl.* **flashes** A short, sudden burst of light: *We were startled by the flash of lightning.*

fla·vor |flā′ vər| *n., pl.* **flavors** The quality that causes something to have a certain taste.

fleece |flēs| *n., pl.* **fleeces** The wool forming the coat of an animal, especially a sheep.

fleet |flēt| *n., pl.* **fleets** A number of boats, ships, or vehicles that form a group: *The company owns a fleet of cars for its sales force to use.*

flight |flīt| *n., pl.* **flights** The act or process of flying: *The bird's flight was almost too swift to see.*

flip |flĭp| *v.* **flipped, flipping** To move or turn by tossing in the air: *Let's flip a coin to decide who goes first.*

flip·per |flĭp′ ər| *n., pl.* **flippers** A wide, flat rubber shoe worn for swimming and skin diving.

flipper

Pronunciation Key

ă	pat	ō	go	th	thin
ā	pay	ô	paw, for	hw	which
â	care	oi	oil	zh	usual
ä	father	ōō	book	ə	ago,
ĕ	pet	ōō	boot		item,
ē	be	yōō	cute		pencil,
ĭ	pit	ou	out		atom,
ī	ice	ŭ	cut		circus
î	near	û	fur	ər	butter
ŏ	pot	th	the		

flood |flŭd| *n., pl.* **floods** A large flow of water over dry land.

folk |fōk| *n., pl.* **folk** *or* **folks** The people who make up a nation or tribe.

fol·low |fŏl′ ō| *v.* **followed, following** To go or come after: *The cat followed me home.*

fool |fōōl| *n., pl.* **fools** A person who lacks judgment or good sense.

foot·wear |fōōt′ wâr′| *n., pl.* **footwear** Coverings for the feet, such as shoes or boots.

for·eign |fôr′ ĭn| *adj.* **1.** Of or from another country: *I tried to learn a foreign language.* **2.** Strange.

for·ev·er |fər ĕv′ ər| *adv.* For all time; always: *I'll be your friend forever.*

for·get |fər gĕt′| *v.* **forgot** |fər gŏt′|, **forgotten** *or* **forgot, forgetting** To be unable to bring to mind; fail to remember: *I forgot my friend's new address.*

for·mal |fôr′ məl| *adj.* Following the usual forms, customs, or rules: *I received a formal wedding invitation.*

for·mal·i·ty |fôr măl′ ĭ tē| *n., pl.* **formalities** Rigorous observance of accepted rules or forms.

fra·grance |frā′ grəns| *n., pl.* **fragrances** A sweet or pleasant scent or odor.

free |frē| *adj.* **freed, freeing** To set at liberty: *We opened the cage and freed the bird.*

fresh |frĕsh| *adj.* **fresher, freshest 1.** Just made, grown, or gathered: *We ate warm, fresh bread with our salad.* **2.** Rested, revived: *I feel fresh as a daisy.*

fresh·ness |frĕsh′ nĭs| *n.* Quality of being fresh.

friend |frĕnd| *n., pl.* **friends** A person one knows, likes, and enjoys being with.

friend·li·ness |frĕnd′ lē nĭs| *n.*
The quality of showing or encouraging friendship.

friend·ly |frĕnd′ lē| *adj.* **friendlier, friendliest** Of or suitable to friend or friends: *friendly cooperation; a friendly letter.*

fright |frīt| *n., pl.* **frights** Sudden strong fear; terror.

fringe |frĭnj| *n., pl.* **fringes** A border or edge of hanging threads or strips. Fringes are used on curtains and bedspreads.

front |frŭnt| *n., pl.* **fronts** The forward part or surface of a thing or place: *The front of a shirt has buttons.*

fron·tier |frŭn tîr′| *n., pl.* **frontiers** A remote area that marks the farthest point of settlement: *The American frontier gradually moved westward.*

frost |frôst| *n., pl.* **frosts** A covering of small ice particles formed from frozen water vapor: *Our windows were covered with frost.*

frost·y |frô′ stē| or |frŏs′ tē| *adj.* **frostier, frostiest** Of or producing frost: *It will be frosty tonight.*

frown |froun| *n., pl.* **frowns** The act of wrinkling the forehead when puzzled, unhappy, or thinking.

fro·zen |frō′ zən| *v.* Past participle of **freeze:** *There are some frozen berries in the freezer.*

fruit |fro͞ot| *n., pl.* **fruit** *or* **fruits** A seed-bearing plant part that is fleshy or juicy, eaten as fruit. Apples, oranges, grapes, strawberries, and bananas are fruits.

fry |frī| *v.* **fried, frying** To cook over direct heat in hot oil or fat: *Fry the chicken lightly in butter.*

-ful A suffix that forms adjectives and means: **1.** Having; having the qualities of: *beautiful.* **2.** Able to; apt to: *forgetful.* **3.** An amount that fills: *cupful.*

full |fo͝ol| *adj.* **fuller, fullest** Holding as much as possible; filled: *Water trickled down the side of the full bucket.*

fun·ny |fŭn′ ē| *adj.* **funnier, funniest** Causing amusement or laughter; humorous.

G

gain |gān| *v.* **gained, gaining 1.** To get or obtain by effort: *We gained experience by working in a number of jobs.* **2.** To develop gradually; pick up: *The movement gained strength.*

gal·ax·y |găl′ ək sē| *n., pl.* **galaxies** A very large group of stars. Our sun and its planets are in a single galaxy called the Milky Way.

gal·ley |găl′ ē| *n., pl.* **galleys** The kitchen of a ship.

game |gām| *n.* Wild birds hunted for food or sport: *The thick underbrush hid the game from the hunter.*

gar·bage |gär′ bĭj| *n.* Food and trash to be thrown away, as from a kitchen.

gar·den |gär′ dn| *n., pl.* **gardens** A piece of land where flowers, vegetables, or fruit are grown.

gas·o·line |găs′ ə lēn′| or |găs′ ə lēn′| *n.* A liquid made from petroleum. Gasoline burns easily and is used as a fuel to make engines run.

gath·er |găth′ ər| *v.* **gathered, gathering** To bring or come together into one place, collect: *I gathered the papers together.*

gear |gîr| *n., pl.* **gears 1.** A wheel with teeth that fit into the teeth of another wheel. **2.** Equipment, such as tools or clothing, used for a particular activity: *I packed our fishing gear.*

gen·u·ine |jĕn′ yo͞o ĭn| *adj.* Not false; real; true.

gi·raffe |jĭ răf′| *n., pl.* **giraffes** A tall African animal with short horns, a very long neck and legs, and a tan coat with brown blotches.

glad |glăd| *adj.* **gladder, gladdest** Pleased; happy.

glance |glăns| *v.* **glanced, glancing** To look quickly: *I glanced at my watch.* *n., pl.* **glances** A quick look.

glass |glăs| *n., pl.* **glasses** A hard, usually clear substance that breaks easily. Glass is used for making windowpanes.

glass·ware |glăs′ wâr′| *n., pl.* **glassware** Objects, especially containers, made of glass.

glid·er |glī′ dər| *n., pl.* **gliders** An aircraft without an engine that glides on currents of air.

globe |glōb| *n., pl.* **globes 1.** Something shaped like a ball; sphere. **2.** A map of the earth or heavens that is shaped like a globe. **3.** The earth.

gloss |glôs| *n., pl.* **glosses** A bright shine on a smooth surface: *The old spoons were polished to give them a beautiful gloss.*

glove |glŭv| *n., pl.* **gloves** A covering for the hand that has a separate section for each finger.

glue |gloo| *n., pl.* **glues** A thick, sticky substance that is used to stick things together. *v.* **glued, gluing** To stick with or as if with glue.

gnaw |nô| *v.* **gnawed, gnawing** To chew or bite on: *The mouse gnawed the cheese.*

goal |gōl| *n., pl.* **goals** Something wanted or worked for; purpose; aim: *My goal in life is to help other people.*

gold |gōld| *n.* A soft, yellow metallic chemical element used in making coins and jewelry.

gorge |gôrj| *n., pl.* **gorges** A deep, narrow passage, as between mountains.

gown |goun| *n., pl.* **gowns** A woman's dress, especially a formal one.

grace·ful |grās′ fəl| *adj.* Showing grace or beauty in movement: *The deer is a graceful animal.*

grand·fa·ther |grănd′ fä′ thər| *n., pl.* **grandfathers** The father of one's father or mother.

grand·moth·er |grănd′ mŭth′ ər| *n., pl.* **grandmothers** The mother of one's father or mother.

grate |grāt| *v.* **grated, grating** To break into fragments or shreds by rubbing against a rough surface: *I grated a little nutmeg on the top of the custard.*

grav·i·ty |grăv′ ĭ tē| *n., pl.* **gravities** The natural force that causes smaller objects to move toward the center of the earth. A ball that is tossed in the air falls back to the ground because of the pull of gravity.

gray |grā| *n., pl.* **grays** A color made by mixing black and white.

greed |grēd| *n.* A selfish desire for more than what one needs or deserves.

Pronunciation Key

ă	pat	ō	go	th	**th**in
ā	pay	ô	paw, for	hw	**wh**ich
â	care	oi	**oi**l	zh	u**s**ual
ä	father	oo	b**oo**k	ə	**a**go,
ĕ	pet	oo	b**oo**t		item,
ē	be	yoo	cute		pencil,
ĭ	pit	ou	**out**		atom,
ī	ice	ŭ	cut		circus
î	near	û	fur	ər	butter
ŏ	pot	*th*	**the**		

grey·hound |grā′ hound′| *n., pl.* **greyhounds** A slender dog with long legs, a smooth coat, and a narrow head. Greyhounds can run very fast.

greyhound

grind |grīnd| *v.* **ground** |ground|, **grinding** To rub, pound, or crush something into powder or very small pieces: *Our grocery store has a machine that grinds coffee beans.*

group |groop| *n., pl.* **groups** A number of persons or things gathered or located together: *A group of people are waiting for the bus.*

grown |grōn| *adj.* Having reached an adult age; mature. *v.* Past participle of **grow.**

guar·an·tee |găr′ ən tē′| *n., pl.* **guarantees** A way of making sure of a certain outcome or result: *Buying a ticket ahead of time is a guarantee of a good seat at the show.* *v.* **guaranteed, guaranteeing** To make certain.

guard |gärd| *n., pl.* **guards** A person or group that keeps watch or protects: *The palace guards stood in line at attention.*

guess |gĕs| *v.* **guessed, guessing** To form an opinion without enough information to be sure of it; estimate: *I'd guess there were 6,000 people at the concert.* *n., pl.* **guesses** An opinion or estimate arrived at by guessing: *If you're not sure of the answer, at least make a guess.*

guest |gĕst| *n., pl.* **guests** A person who is at another person's home for a visit or a meal; visitor: *Our parents cooked a special meal for their dinner guests.*

guide |gīd| *n., pl.* **guides** Someone or something that shows the way, directs, leads, or teaches: *Our guide led us safely out of the woods.*

guilt |gĭlt| *n.* A feeling of responsibility or deep shame for having done something bad or illegal: *I felt guilt for having quarreled with my friend.*

gym |jĭm| *n., pl.* **gyms** A gymnasium.

gym·na·si·um |jĭm **nā**′ zē əm| *n., pl.* **gymnasiums** A room or building with equipment for physical exercises and training and for indoor sports; gym.

H

hab·it |hăb′ ĭt| *n., pl.* **habits** An activity or action done so often that one does it without thinking: *I have a habit of getting up early every morning.*

hail |hāl| *n.* Small round pieces of frozen rain that fall to the earth, often during thunderstorms.

hair·y |hâr′ ē| *adj.* **hairier, hairiest** Having much hair or covered with hair: *Gorillas are hairy animals.*

hall |hôl| *n., pl.* **halls** 1. A passageway or corridor in a house, hotel, or other building. 2. A building or room to meet in.
♦ *These sound alike* **hall, haul.**

ham·bur·ger |hăm′ bûr′ gər| *n., pl.* **hamburgers** A patty of ground beef, fried or broiled and usually served in a roll or bun.

ham·mer |hăm′ ər| *n., pl.* **hammers** A hand tool with a metal head and a long handle, used especially for driving nails.

hand·ker·chief |hăng′ kər chĭf| *n., pl.* **handkerchiefs** A small square of cloth used to wipe the nose or face.

han·dle |hăn′ dl| *n., pl.* **handles** The part of a tool, door, or container that is made to be held or pulled with the hand.

hand·saw |hănd′ sô′| *n., pl.* **handsaws** A saw used with one hand for cutting hard material.

handsaw

hand·some |hăn′ səm| *adj.* **handsomer, handsomest** Pleasing in appearance; good-looking.

hang |hăng| *v.* **hung** *or* **hanged, hanging** To fasten or be attached at the upper end only: *Hang the clothes on the line.*

han·gar |hăng′ ər| *n., pl.* **hangars** A building in which aircraft are kept and repaired.

hap·pen |hăp′ ən| *v.* **happened, happening** To take place; occur: *Tell me everything that happened today.*

hap·py |hăp′ ē| *adj.* **happier, happiest** Showing or feeling pleasure or joy: *I'm happy that we're all home safe.*

har·bor |här′ bər| *n., pl.* **harbors** A sheltered place along a coast where ships can safely anchor or dock; port.

hard |härd| *adj. and adv.* **harder, hardest** 1. Not bending or yielding when pushed; firm. 2. Difficult to solve or understand: *There were some hard questions on the test.*

hard·ware |härd′ wâr′| *n., pl.* **hardware** 1. Articles made of metal and used for making and repairing other things. Tools, nails, bolts, and hinges are hardware. 2. The physical parts of a computer system, including the keyboard, video display screen, memory storage devices, and printer.

har·vest |här′ vĭst| *v.* **harvested, harvesting**
To gather a crop: *We harvested the corn.*
haste |hāst| *n.* Speed in moving or acting:
We ate with great haste to get to school on time.
has·ten |hā′ sən| *v.* **hastened, hastening**
To move or act swiftly; hurry: *I hastened home to tell my family the good news.*
haul |hôl| *v.* **hauled, hauling** To pull, drag, or carry; tug: *We hauled the sled up the hill.*
◆ *These sound alike* **haul, hall.**
haz·ard |hăz′ ərd| *n., pl.* **hazards**
Something that may cause injury or harm; a danger: *Piles of oily rags are a fire hazard.*
haz·y |hā′ zē| *adj.* **hazier, haziest** Marked by or covered with fine dust, smoke, or water vapor in the air: *It was a humid day with a hazy sun.*
head |hĕd| *n., pl.* **heads** *or* **head 1.** The top part of the body, containing the brain, eyes, ears, nose, mouth, and jaws. **2.** The uppermost part of something; top: *Place the label at the head of each column.*
head·line |hĕd′ līn′| *n., pl.* **headlines**
A group of words that is printed in large type over a newspaper article. Headlines tell what the articles are about.
head·wear |hĕd′ wâr′| *n., pl.* **headwear** A hat or other covering for the head.
heal |hēl| *v.* **healed, healing** To make or become healthy and sound.
◆ *These sound alike* **heal, heel.**
health |hĕlth| *n.* Freedom from disease or injury: *We wish you a speedy return to health.*
heart |härt| *n., pl.* **hearts 1.** The hollow, muscular organ that pumps blood throughout the body. **2.** The part of a person's mind that feels emotions, such as love: *These words come from the heart.*
◇ *Idioms* **wear your heart on your sleeve**
To show one's feelings so that everyone sees them. **heart-to-heart** Honest, personal, and deep talk. **heart of stone** Being cruel and without feelings. **to lose heart** To feel without hope. **by heart** From memory.
hearth |härth| *n., pl.* **hearths** The floor of a fireplace and the area in front of it, usually made of stone or brick.
heav·y |hĕv′ ē| *adj.* **heavier, heaviest**
Weighing a lot; not light.

Pronunciation Key

ă	pat	ō	go	th	**th**in
ā	pay	ô	paw, for	hw	**wh**ich
â	care	oi	**oi**l	zh	usual
ä	father	ŏŏ	b**oo**k	ə	**a**go,
ĕ	pet	ōō	b**oo**t		item,
ē	be	yōō	cute		pencil,
ĭ	pit	ou	**ou**t		atom,
ī	ice	ŭ	c**u**t		circus
î	near	û	f**u**r	ər	butt**er**
ŏ	pot	th	**th**e		

heel |hēl| *n., pl.* **heels** The rounded rear portion of the human foot, under and behind the ankle.
◆ *These sound alike* **heel, heal.**
heir |âr| *n., pl.* **heirs** A person who receives or has the right to receive the property or title of another when the other person dies.
hel·i·cop·ter |hĕl′ ĭ kŏp′ tər| *n., pl.*
helicopters An aircraft without wings that is kept in the air by horizontal propellers that rotate above the craft.
hel·i·port |hĕl′ ə pôrt′| *n., pl.* **heliports**
A place for helicopters to take off and land.
hel·lo |hĕ lō′| *or* |hə lō′| *interj.* An expression that is used as a greeting or to attract attention.
hel·met |hĕl′ mĭt| *n., pl.* **helmets** A head covering made of a hard material such as metal. A helmet is worn to protect the head, as in some sports.
help |hĕlp| *v.* **helped, helping** To give assistance or support to; aid: *She helped him with the farming. n., pl.* **helps** The act or an example of helping: *We appreciate your help.*
help·er |hĕlp′ ər| *n., pl.* **helpers** Someone who helps or assists.
hike |hīk| *v.* **hiked, hiking** To go on a long walk for pleasure or exercise. *n., pl.*
hikes A long walk.
hint |hĭnt| *n., pl.* **hints** A piece of useful information; clue: *Here are some hints to help you solve the riddle.*
hoarse |hôrs| *adj.* **hoarser, hoarsest** Low, rough, or harsh in sound: *The cry of the crow is hoarse.*
◆ *These sound alike* **hoarse, horse.**

Spelling Dictionary

hob·by |hŏb′ ē| *n., pl.* **hobbies** An activity done for pleasure in one's spare time: *Building airplane models is my favorite hobby.*

hock·ey |hŏk′ ē| *n.* A game played by two teams who try to drive a puck or ball through a goal with curved sticks. Hockey is played on ice with a puck or on a field with a ball.

hol·low |hŏl′ ō| *adj.* **hollower, hollowest** Having a space or opening inside: *The squirrel hid in a hollow log.*

home·sick |hōm′ sĭk′| *adj.* Unhappy and longing for home and family.

home·stead |hōm′ stěd′| *n., pl.* **homesteads** A piece of land that is given by the government to a settler who claims it and builds a home on it.

hom·o·graph |hŏm′ ə grăf′| or |hō′ mə grăf′| *n., pl.* **homographs** A word that has the same spelling as another word but differs in meaning, origin, and sometimes in pronunciation. For example, **ring** (circle) and **ring** (sound).

hom·o·phone |hŏm′ ə fōn′| or |hō′ mə fōn′| *n., pl.* **homophones** A word that has the same sound as another word but differs in spelling, meaning, and origin. For example, **steel** and **steal.**

hon·est |ŏn′ ĭst| *adj.* Not lying, stealing, or cheating.

hon·ey |hŭn′ ē| *n., pl.* **honeys** A sweet, thick, syrupy substance made by bees from the nectar of flowers and used as food.

hon·or |ŏn′ ər| *n., pl.* **honors** **1.** Special respect or high regard: *We display the flag to show honor to the United States.* **2.** High moral standards.

hook |hŏŏk| *n., pl.* **hooks** A curved or bent object, often of metal, that is used to catch, hold, fasten, or pull something: *I put a hook on my fishing line.*

hope·ful |hōp′ fəl| *adj.* Feeling or showing hope.

hope·less |hōp′ lĭs| *adj.* Having no hope: *The lost hikers felt hopeless.*

horse |hôrs| *n., pl.* **horses** A large hoofed animal that has a long mane and tail. Horses are used for riding, pulling vehicles, and carrying loads.

♦ *These sound alike* **horse, hoarse.**

hos·pi·tal |hŏs′ pĭ təl| *n., pl.* **hospitals** A medical institution that treats sick and injured people.

host |hōst| *n., pl.* **hosts** A person or group that receives or entertains guests.

hour |our| *n., pl.* **hours** A unit of time that is equal to sixty minutes: *There are twenty-four hours in a day.*

how·ev·er |hou ěv′ ər| *conj.* In spite of that; yet; nevertheless: *It was growing very dark; however, we were not worried.*

howl |houl| *n., pl.* **howls** A long, wailing cry, such as the one made by a dog, wolf, or coyote.

huge |hyōōj| *adj.* **huger, hugest** Very big; enormous; not small or tiny.

hull |hŭl| *n., pl.* **hulls** The body or frame of a ship or boat, including only its sides and bottom.

hu·man |hyōō′ mən| *adj.* Of or characteristic of people: *Many people can't afford basic human comforts, like food, shelter, and clothing.* *n., pl.* **humans** A person.

hu·man·i·ty |hyōō măn′ ĭ tē| *n.* The human race; people.

hu·mor·ous |hyōō′ mər əs| *adj.* Funny, amusing, or comical.

hun·gry |hŭng′ grē| *adj.* **hungrier, hungriest** Wanting food.

hur·dle |hûr′ dl| *n., pl.* **hurdles** A barrier, usually consisting of a horizontal bar held in place by two upright supports. Hurdles are used in certain track and field events. *v.* **hurdled, hurdling** To jump over: *The horse hurdled the fence with ease.*

hur·ri·cane |hûr′ ĭ kān′| *n., pl.* **hurricanes** A very powerful storm with extremely strong winds over 75 miles per hour and heavy rains.

hur·ry |hûr′ ē| *v.* **hurried, hurrying** To act or move quickly: *Don't hurry through your work.*

hurt |hûrt| *v.* **hurt, hurting** To cause pain or injury to: *I fell and hurt my wrist.*

husk·y |hŭs′ kē| *n., pl.* **huskies** A dog with a thick, furry coat. Huskies are used for pulling sleds in the far north.

I

ic·y |ī′ sē| *adj.* **icier, iciest** Covered with ice; frozen: *I slid on the icy sidewalk.*

i·den·ti·fy |ī děn′ tə fī| *v.* **identified, identifying** To acknowledge as being a certain person or thing: *We could not identify the person in the old snapshot.*

ill·ness |ĭl′ nĭs| *n., pl.* **illnesses** A sickness or disease: *Pneumonia is a serious illness.*

i·mag·i·nar·y |ĭ măj′ ə něr′ ē| *adj.* Existing only in the imagination; not real: *Ghosts are imaginary creatures.*

im·por·tant |ĭm pôr′ tnt| *adj.* Strongly affecting the course of events or the nature of things; significant: *This is an important message about safety.*

inch |ĭnch| *n., pl.* **inches** A unit of length equal to 1/12 of a foot.

in·dus·tri·al |ĭn dŭs′ trē əl| *adj.* Of or having to do with industry: *Steel and gasoline are industrial products.*

in·ex·pen·sive |ĭn′ ĭk spěn′ sĭv| *adj.* Not expensive; low-priced; cheap.

in·fect |ĭn fěkt′| *v.* **infected, infecting** To cause to come in contact with germs or bacteria that cause disease.

in·fect·ed |ĭn fěkt′ əd| *adj.* Being contaminated with germs or bacteria.

in·flex·i·ble |ĭn flěk′ sə bəl| *adj.* Not bending; stiff: *The leather belt was so old and dry that it had become inflexible.*

in·sect |ĭn′ sěkt′| *n., pl.* **insects** Any of a large group of animals that have six legs, a body with three main divisions, and usually wings. Flies, bees, grasshoppers, butterflies, and moths are insects.

in·side |ĭn′ sīd′| or |ĭn sīd′| *n., pl.* **insides** The inner part, side, or surface; interior: *The inside of the house looked better than the outside.*

in·spect |ĭn spěkt′| *v.* **inspected, inspecting** To look over carefully; examine: *Supervisors inspected the rivets to be sure the jet would be safe to fly.*

in·ter·view |ĭn′ tər vyoo′| *n., pl.* **interviews** **1.** A meeting of people face to face: *The principal asked the new student to report for an interview.* **2.** A conversation between a reporter and a person during which the reporter asks for facts, information, or statements.

i·ron |ī′ ərn| *n., pl.* **irons** A hard, gray metal that can be magnetized. It is used to make steel. Iron is used in making many tools and machines.

is·land |ī′ lənd| *n., pl.* **islands** A piece of land that is encircled by water.

island

its |ĭts| *adj.* Relating or belonging to **it**: *Everything was in its place.*
◆ *These sound alike* **its, it's.**

it's |ĭts| Contraction of "it is" or "it has": *It's a very good book.*
◆ *These sound alike* **it's, its.**

i·vy |ī′ vē| *n., pl.* **ivies** A climbing vine with evergreen leaves and black berries that grows on houses and walls.

J

jack·et |jăk′ ĭt| *n., pl.* **jackets** A short coat.

jail |jāl| *n., pl.* **jails** A place for keeping persons who are serving sentences for crimes.

Pronunciation Key

ă	pat	ō	go	th	thin	
ā	pay	ô	paw, for	hw	which	
â	care	oi	oil	zh	usual	
ä	father	oo	book	ə	ago,	
ě	pet	oo	boot		item,	
ē	be	yoo	cute		pencil,	
ĭ	pit	ou	out		atom,	
ī	ice	ŭ	cut		circus	
î	near	û	fur	ər	butter	
ŏ	pot	th	the			

Spelling Dictionary

jaw |jô| *n., pl.* **jaws** One of a pair of structures that hold the teeth and form the framework and shape of the mouth. The jaws are made of bone and cartilage.

jeal·ous |jĕl′ əs| *adj.* Having a bad feeling toward another person who is a competitor; envious: *I was jealous of my friend's new skates.*

joke |jōk| *v.* **joked, joking** To say or do something as a joke: *I was only joking when I said that.*

jour·nal·ist |jûr′ nə lĭst| *n., pl.* **journalists** A person who gathers and reports news, especially a reporter or editor.

joust |joust| *v.* **jousted, jousting** To take part in a combat with lances between two knights on horses.

joust

joy·ous |joi′ əs| *adj.* Feeling, showing, or causing great happiness or delight.

judge |jŭj| *n., pl.* **judges** A public official who listens to and makes decisions about cases in a court of law.

juice |jōōs| *n., pl.* **juices** A liquid contained in meats or in the fruit, stem, or roots of plants: *Orange juice is rich in vitamins.*

juic·y |jōō′ sē| *adj.* **juicier, juiciest** Full of juice.

June |jōōn| *n.* The sixth month of the year. June has thirty days.

jun·gle |jŭng′ gəl| *n., pl.* **jungles** A heavy growth of tropical trees and plants or land that is covered with such growth.

junk |jŭngk| *n.* Materials, such as rags or machine parts, that are thrown away but can be used again in some way.

K

kept |kĕpt| *v.* Past tense and past participle of **keep.** Held and not given away: *Neva kept her money in the bank for five years.*

kin·dle |kĭn′ dl| *v.* **kindled, kindling** To start a fire: *Kindle a fire with these matches, please.*

kin·dling |kĭnd′ lĭng| *n.* Material such as dry sticks of wood used for building a fire.

kind·ness |kīnd′ nĭs| *n., pl.* **kindnesses** The quality or condition of being helpful, considerate, or gentle; generosity: *The teacher's kindness made her popular.*

knead |nēd| *v.* **kneaded, kneading** To mix and work a substance, as by folding, rolling, or pressing it: *We helped to knead the bread dough.*

kneel |nēl| *v.* **knelt** |nĕlt| *or* **kneeled, kneeling** To rest or get down on a bent knee or knees: *We knelt around the campfire.*

knew |nōō| *or* |nyōō| *v.* Past tense of **know:** *I knew you when you were a baby.*

knife |nīf| *n., pl.* **knives** |nīvz| A device made of a sharp blade attached to a handle. A knife is used for cutting or carving.

knight |nīt| *n., pl.* **knights** A soldier in the Middle Ages who served and pledged loyalty to a king or lord. In return, the knight was given the right to hold land.

knit |nĭt| *v.* **knit** *or* **knitted, knitting** To make a fabric or garment by interlocking yarn or thread in connected loops with special needles: *I am knitting a sweater.*

knob |nŏb| *n., pl.* **knobs** A rounded dial or handle, as for operating a television or stereo or for opening a drawer or door.

knock |nŏk| *v.* **knocked, knocking** To make a loud noise by hitting a hard surface; rap: *I knocked and knocked, but nobody came to the door.*

knoll |nōl| *n., pl.* **knolls** A small, rounded hill.

know |nō| *v.* **knew** |nōō| *or* |nyōō|, **known, knowing** To understand or have the facts about: *Do you know what causes thunder?*

L

la·bor |lā′ bər| *n., pl.* **labors** Hard work: *It took months of labor to dig the tunnel.*

lab·o·ra·tor·y |lăb′ rə tôr′ ē| *n., pl.* **laboratories** A room or building with special equipment for doing scientific tests and experiments.

lad·der |lăd′ ər| *n., pl.* **ladders** A device for climbing, made of two long side pieces joined by short rods or bars that serve as steps.

la·goon |lə goon′| *n., pl.* **lagoons** A shallow body of water along a coast or shore.

lamb |lăm| *n., pl.* **lambs** A young sheep.

land |lănd| *v.* **landed, landing** To come or bring to shore: *The boat landed at the dock.*

land·mark |lănd′ märk| *n., pl.* **landmarks** A familiar or easily seen object or building that marks or identifies a place: *The Golden Gate Bridge is a landmark of San Francisco.*

lan·tern |lăn′ tərn| *n., pl.* **lanterns** A portable container for holding a light, with sides that let the light shine through.

large |lärj| *adj.* **larger, largest** Bigger than average size or amount: *The zoo has large animals such as elephants.*

las·so |lăs′ ō| or |lăs soo′| *n., pl.* **lassos or lassoes** A long rope with a noose at one end that is used to catch horses or cattle.

last |lăst| *adj.* Coming, being, or placed after all others; final: *We won the last game of the season.*

latch |lăch| *n., pl.* **latches** A movable bar that is used to hold a door, gate, or window closed.

lat·i·tude |lăt′ ĭ tood′| or |lăt′ ĭ tyood| *n., pl.* **latitudes** Distance north or south of the equator measured in degrees.

launch |lônch| *v.* **launched, launching** To set afloat: *The new ship was launched.*

lawn |lôn| *n., pl.* **lawns** A piece of ground, as near a house or in a park, planted with grass.

la·zy |lā′ zē| *adj.* **lazier, laziest** Not willing to work or be active: *Lazy students usually receive poor grades.*

lead¹ |lēd| *v.* **led** |lĕd|, **leading** **1.** To show

Pronunciation Key

ă	pat	ō	go	th	thin
ā	pay	ô	paw, for	hw	which
â	care	oi	oil	zh	usual
ä	father	oo	book	ə	ago,
ĕ	pet	oo	boot		item,
ē	be	yoo	cute		pencil,
ĭ	pit	ou	out		atom,
ī	ice	ŭ	cut		circus
î	near	û	fur	ər	butter
ŏ	pot	th	the		

or direct along the way, as by going with or ahead of: *The ranger will lead us to the top of the mountain.* **2.** To be or go at the head of: *The color guard will lead the parade.*

lead² |lĕd| *n., pl.* **leads** **1.** A soft, heavy, gray metal that is easy to bend, melt, and shape. Lead is a chemical element. **2.** A thin piece of graphite used as the writing substance in pencils.
◆ *These sound alike* **lead², led.**

learn |lûrn| *v.* **learned** or **learnt, learning** To get knowledge of or skill in through study or instruction: *The third-graders are learning Spanish.*

learn·er |lûr′ nər| *n., pl.* **learners** One who learns.

least |lēst| *adj.* Smallest in degree or size: *Don't let the least criticism upset you.* *adv.* In the smallest or lowest degree: *I like tennis best and baseball least.* *n.* The smallest amount or degree: *The least you can do is offer to help.*

led |lĕd| *v.* Past tense and past participle of **lead¹**: *The captain led us to victory.*
◆ *These sound alike* **led, lead².**

left¹ |lĕft| *n.* The side from which a person begins to read a line of English: *The number 9 is on the left of a clock's face.*

left² |lĕft| *v.* Past tense of **leave.**

lens |lĕnz| *n., pl.* **lenses** A combination of two or more lenses used to form or magnify an image, as in a camera or telescope.

-less A suffix that forms adjectives and means "not having" or "without": *harmless.*

les·son |lĕs′ ən| *n., pl.* **lessons** Something to be learned or taught.

-let A suffix that forms nouns and means "small": *droplet.*

Spelling Dictionary

li·brar·y |lī′ brĕr′ ē| *n., pl.* **libraries**
A place where books, magazines, records, and reference materials are kept for reading or borrowing.

li·cense |lī′ səns| *n., pl.* **licenses** Legal permission to do or own something.

lift |lĭft| *v.* **lifted, lifting** To raise from a lower to a higher position or condition: *The suitcase is too heavy to lift.*

light·ning |līt′ nĭng| *n.* The flash of light in the sky when electricity passes between clouds.

limb |lĭm| *n., pl.* **limbs 1.** A paired and jointed animal part, such as a leg, arm, wing, or flipper. **2.** One of the larger branches of a tree.

◇ *Idiom* **out on a limb** In a dangerous or risky position.

lim·ber |lĭm′ bər| *adj.* Moving easily; agile: *a limber athlete.*

lim·it |lĭm′ ĭt| *n., pl.* **limits** A point beyond which someone or something cannot go: *The speed limit is 55 miles per hour.*

lis·ten |lĭs′ ən| *v.* **listened, listening** To try to hear something: *If you listen, you can hear the ocean.*

lit·tle |lĭt′ l| *adj.* **littler** or **less, littlest** or **least** Small in size or quantity: *Dolls look like little people. We have little food to waste.*

live¹ |lĭv| *v.* **lived, living** To be alive; exist: *Fish cannot live long out of water.*

live² |līv| *adj.* **1.** Having life; living: *The zoo has live animals.* **2.** Carrying an electric current: *Don't touch that live wire.*

lo·cate |lō′ kāt| *v.* **located, locating** To find by searching.

lo·ca·tion |lō′ kā′ shən| *n., pl.* **locations** A place where something is located; position: *We finally found the location of the airport.*

lock·et |lŏk′ ĭt| *n., pl.* **lockets** A small ornamental case for a picture or other keepsake. A locket is often worn on a chain around the neck.

lodge |lŏj| *n., pl.* **lodges** A cottage or cabin, especially one used as a temporary place to stay.

lone·ly |lōn′ lē| *adj.* **lonelier, loneliest** Sad at being alone: *The lonely child had no friends.*

lon·gi·tude |lŏn′ jĭ tōōd′| or |lŏn′ jĭ tyōōd′| *n., pl.* **longitudes** Distance measured in degrees east or west of the meridian at Greenwich, a city in southeastern England.

lord |lôrd| *n., pl.* **lords 1.** A man of noble rank in Great Britain. **2.** An owner of an estate.

lose |lōōz| *v.* **lost** |lôst|, **losing** To fail to win or gain.

loud |loud| *adj.* **louder, loudest** Having a high volume of sound; noisy: *We heard a loud crash.*

love |lŭv| *n., pl.* **loves** Strong affection and warm feelings for another.

luck |lŭk| *n.* The chance happening of good or bad events; fortune: *Good luck seemed to favor the other team, and we lost the game.*

lum·ber |lŭm′ bər| *n.* Timber sawed into boards and planks. *v.* To cut down and prepare timber for market.

lump·y |lŭm′ pē| *adj.* **lumpier, lumpiest** Full of or covered with lumps.

lu·nar |lōō′ nər| *adj.* Of, on, or having to do with the moon: *The spacecraft made a perfect lunar landing.*

lunch |lŭnch| *n., pl.* **lunches** A meal eaten at midday. *v.* **lunched, lunching**

M

ma·chine |mə shēn′| *n., pl.* **machines** A combination of mechanical parts that operate together to perform a certain task: *Vacuum cleaners are useful machines.*

Mad·i·son |măd′ ĭ sən| The capital of Wisconsin.

mag·a·zine |măg′ ə zēn′| or |măg′ ə zēn′| *n., pl.* **magazines** A publication that is issued regularly, as every week or month.

History

Magazine comes from an Arabic word meaning "storehouse." A magazine is a "storehouse" of information.

mag·ic |**măj**′ ĭk| *n.* The pretended art of controlling natural forces by using charms or spells.

ma·gi·cian |mə **jĭsh**′ ən| *n., pl.* **magicians** A person who uses magic; wizard.

make-be·lieve |**māk**′ bĭ lēv′| *n.* A playful pretending: *Elves live only in the world of make-believe. adj.* Pretended; imaginary.

man·age |**măn**′ ĭj| *v.* **managed, managing** To have control over; direct: *Who will manage the business while you are away?*

man·or |**măn**′ ər| *n., pl.* **manors** A lord's estate in the Middle Ages.

map |măp| *n., pl.* **maps** A drawing or chart of all or part of the earth's surface that shows features such as rivers and mountains.

ma·ple |**mā**′ pəl| *n., pl.* **maples** A tree that has leaves with deep notches, seeds that grow in pairs and look like wings, and hard wood. One kind of maple has sap that is boiled to produce syrup and sugar.

maple

mare |mâr| *n., pl.* **mares** A female horse or a related animal, such as a zebra.

ma·rine |mə **rēn**′| *adj.* Of, relating to, or living in the sea: *We studied marine plants and animals.*

mar·ket |**mär**′ kĭt| *n., pl.* **markets** A public place where people buy and sell goods: *We took our fruits and vegetables to market.*

Pronunciation Key

ă	pat	ō	go	th	**th**in
ā	pay	ô	paw, for	hw	**wh**ich
â	care	oi	**oi**l	zh	u**s**ual
ä	father	ŏŏ	b**oo**k	ə	**a**go,
ĕ	pet	ōō	b**oo**t		**i**tem,
ē	be	yōō	c**u**te		penc**i**l,
ĭ	pit	ou	**ou**t		at**o**m,
ī	ice	ŭ	c**u**t		circ**u**s
î	near	û	f**ur**	ər	butt**er**
ŏ	pot	*th*	**the**		

ma·roon |mə **rōōn**′| *v.* **marooned, marooning** To be abandoned on a deserted shore or island with little hope of escaping or of being rescued.

mar·riage |**măr**′ ĭj| *n., pl.* **marriages** The condition of living together as husband and wife.

mar·ry |**măr**′ ē| *v.* **married, marrying** To take as husband or wife: *He married my sister.*

mar·vel |**mär**′ vəl| *adj.* **marveled, marveling** To be filled with surprise, astonishment, or wonder: *We marveled at the beauty of the mountain scenery.*

mar·vel·ous |**mär**′ və ləs| *adj.* Of the highest or best kind or quality.

mask |măsk| *n., pl.* **masks** A covering worn over the face to protect: *The mask kept water out of the swimmer's eyes.*

mast |măst| *n., pl.* **masts** A tall upright pole that supports the sails and rigging of a ship or boat.

mas·ter |**măs**′ tər| *n., pl.* **masters** A person who has power, control, or authority over another: *The dog ran to its master.*

math·e·ma·ti·cian |**măth**′ ə mə **tĭsh**′ ən| *n., pl.* **mathematicians** A person who specializes in mathematics.

math·e·mat·ics |**măth**′ ə **măt**′ ĭks| *n.* (used with a singular verb) The study of numbers, shapes, and measurements; math. Arithmetic, algebra, and geometry are branches of mathematics.

mean·while |**mēn**′ hwīl′| *adv.* During the time between; meantime.

meas·ure |**mĕzh**′ ər| *v.* **measured, measuring** To find the size, amount, capacity, or degree of: *We measured the room twice.*

Spelling Dictionary

meat |mēt| *n., pl.* **meats** The flesh of an animal eaten as food.
♦ *These sound alike* **meat, meet.**

med·al |mĕd′ l| *n., pl.* **medals** A small, flat, often circular piece of metal with a design. A medal may be awarded to honor a person, an action, an accomplishment, or an event.

me·dal·lion |mə dăl′ yən| *n., pl.* **medallions** A large medal.

med·i·cine |mĕd′ ĭ sĭn| *n., pl.* **medicines** A substance used to treat a disease or relieve pain.

med·ley |mĕd′ lē| *n., pl.* **medleys** A piece of music made up of different songs or melodies.

meet |mēt| *v.* **met** |mĕt|, **meeting** To come face to face; encounter: *The two friends shook hands when they met.*
♦ *These sound alike* **meet, meat.**

mel·low |mĕl′ ō| *adj.* **mellower, mellowest** Soft and sweet to the taste; fully ripened: *We ate the juicy, mellow peaches.*

mem·ber |mĕm′ bər| *n., pl.* **members** A person or thing belonging to a group or organization: *The lion is a member of the cat family. My club has six members.*

-ment A suffix that forms nouns and means: **1.** Action; process: *government.* **2.** Condition: *amazement.*

men·u |mĕn′ yōō| *n., pl.* **menus** A list of foods and drinks available for a meal.

mer·cu·ry |mûr′ kyə rē| *n.* A silvery-white metal that is a liquid at room temperature. Mercury is one of the chemical elements. It is used in thermometers.

mer·cy |mûr′ sē| *n., pl.* **mercies** Kindness that goes beyond what can be expected.

met·al |mĕt′ l| *n., pl.* **metals** A substance, such as copper, iron, silver, or gold, that is usually shiny and hard, conducts heat and electricity, and can be hammered or cast into a desired shape. *adj.* Made of a metal or metals.

me·tal·lic |mə tăl′ ĭk| *adj.* Of or like metal.

meth·od |mĕth′ əd| *n., pl.* **methods** A regular or deliberate way of doing something.

mid·dle |mĭd′ l| *n., pl.* **middles** A point or part that is the same distance from each side or end; center: *A deer stood in the middle of the road.*

mince |mĭns| *v.* **minced, mincing** To cut or chop into very small pieces.

mind |mīnd| *n., pl.* **minds** The part of a human being that thinks, feels, understands, remembers, and reasons: *The mathematician has a brilliant mind.* *v.* **minded, minding** To object to or to dislike: *Would you mind if I sat down?*

min·ute¹ |mĭn′ ĭt| *n., pl.* **minutes** A unit of time equal to sixty seconds.

mi·nute² |mī nōōt′| or |mī nyōōt′| *adj.* Very, very small; tiny: *The wind blew a minute speck of dirt into her eye.*

mir·ror |mĭr′ ər| *n., pl.* **mirrors** A surface, as of glass, that reflects the image of an object placed in front of it.

mis·take |mĭ stāk′| *n., pl.* **mistakes** Something that is thought up, done, or figured out in an incorrect way: *I made a mistake in arithmetic.*

mix |mĭks| *v.* **mixed, mixing** To blend or combine into a single mass or substance: *Mix the flour, water, and eggs together.*

mod·el |mŏd′ l| *n., pl.* **models** **1.** A small copy: *I built a model of a sailboat.* **2.** A person or thing that is a good example: *The farm is a model of efficient management.*

mod·ern |mŏd′ ərn| *adj.* Advanced, as in style; up-to-date: *My parents work in a modern office building.*

mo·ment |mō′ mənt| *n., pl.* **moments** A very short period of time; instant: *Wait a moment while I wash my hands.*

mon·ey |mŭn′ ē| *n.* Coins and bills issued by a government for use in buying or paying for goods and services; currency.

mon·key |mŭng′ kē| *n., pl.* **monkeys** Any of a group of animals that have long arms and legs, and hands and feet that are adapted for climbing and grasping objects. Monkeys, and especially the smaller ones, have long tails.

mon·soon |mŏn sōōn′| *n., pl.* **monsoons** A wind in southern Asia that changes direction with the seasons. The monsoon brings on the rainy season.

month |mŭnth| *n., pl.* **months** One of the twelve periods that make up a year.

mo·ped |**mō′** pĕd| *n., pl.* **mopeds** A lightweight motorized bicycle that can be pedaled.

moped

most |mōst| *adj.* Greatest, as in number, size, extent, or degree: *The player with the most skill won the game.*

mo·tel |mō tĕl′| *n., pl.* **motels** A hotel for motorists with rooms usually next to parking spaces.

mo·tion |mō′shən| *n., pl.* **motions** The act or process of moving; movement or gesture.

motion picture *n., pl.* **motion pictures** A series of pictures projected on a screen so quickly that the objects in the pictures seem to move as they would in life; movie.

mo·tor |mō′ tər| *n., pl.* **motors** A device that provides the power to make something move or run; engine: *An electric motor drives the fan.*

mo·tor·cy·cle |mō′ tər sī′ kəl| *n., pl.* **motorcycles** A vehicle with two wheels that is driven by an engine.

mount |mount| *v.* **mounted, mounting** To go up; climb: *We mounted the stairs.*

move |mōōv| *v.* **moved, moving**
1. To change or cause to change position: *Don't move while I take your picture.* **2.** To change the place where one lives or works: *My grandparents moved to Florida.*

move·ment |mōōv′ mənt| *n., pl.* **movements** The act or process of moving: *Jay grabbed the ball in a quick movement.*

mov·ie |mōō′ vē| *n., pl.* **movies** A motion picture.

muf·fin |mŭf′ ĭn| *n., pl.* **muffins** A small, cup-shaped bread.

mu·sic |myōō′ zĭk| *n.* **1.** The art of combining tones or sounds in a pleasing or meaningful way. **2.** Vocal or instrumental

Pronunciation Key

ă	pat	ō	go	th	thin
ā	pay	ô	paw, for	hw	which
â	care	oi	oil	zh	usual
ä	father	ŏŏ	book	ə	ago,
ĕ	pet	ōō	boot		item,
ē	be	yōō	cute		pencil,
ĭ	pit	ou	out		atom,
ī	ice	ŭ	cut		circus
î	near	û	fur	ər	butter
ŏ	pot	*th*	the		

sounds with rhythm, melody, and harmony.

mu·si·cian |myōō zĭsh′ ən| *n., pl.* **musicians** A person skilled in music, especially as a professional composer or performer.

mus·tang |mŭs′ tăng′| *n., pl.* **mustangs** A small wild horse of the plains of western North America.

N

nar·rate |năr′ āt′| *v.* **narrated, narrating** To tell the story of in speech or writing.

nar·row |năr′ ō| *adj.* **narrower, narrowest** Small or slender in width: *The road was long and narrow.*

na·tion |nā′ shən| *n., pl.* **nations** A group of people sharing the same territory and organized under a single government; country.

na·tion·wide |nā′ shən wīd′| *adj.* Throughout a whole nation.

nat·u·ral |năch′ ər əl| *adj.* Found in or produced by nature; not artificial or man-made.

na·ture |nā′ chər| *n., pl.* **natures** The world of living things and the outdoors; wildlife and natural scenery: *We campers enjoy nature.*

na·vy |nā′ vē| *n., pl.* **navies** A dark blue color.

near |nîr| *adv.* To, at, or within a short distance or time: *The deer ran off as we came near. adj.* **nearer, nearest** Close in distance or time: *I'll see you in the near future. prep.* Close to: *Stay near me when we explore the cave. v.* **neared, nearing** To draw near; approach: *The ship neared the port.*

need |nēd| *n., pl.* **needs** A lack of something required or desirable: *Their crops are in need of water.* *v.* **needed, needing 1.** To have to: *I need to return the book today.* **2.** To have need of; require: *This toaster needs repair.*

neigh·bor |nā′ bər| *n., pl.* **neighbors** A person who lives next door to or near another.

nerv·ous |nûr′ vəs| *adj.* Tense, anxious, or fearful.

-ness A suffix that forms nouns and means "condition" or "quality": *kindness.*

nev·er |nĕv′ ər| *adv.* At no time; not ever: *I have never been here before.*

news·cast |nōōz′ kăst′| or |nyōōz′ kăst′| *n., pl.* **newscasts** A broadcast of news on radio or television.

news·pa·per |nōōz′ pā′ pər| or |nyōōz′ pā′ pər| *n., pl.* **newspapers** A printed paper that is usually issued every day and contains news, articles, and advertisements.

nice |nīs| *adj.* **nicer, nicest** Pleasing; agreeable: *It was a nice party. You look nice in your new outfit.*

nick·el |nĭk′ əl| *n., pl.* **nickels** A United States or Canadian coin worth five cents.

nine·ty-nine |nīn′ tē nīn′| *n.* A number, written 99 in Arabic numerals, that is equal to the sum of 98 + 1. It is the positive integer that comes after 98.

nois·y |noi′ zē| *adj.* **noisier, noisiest** Making a lot of sound; not quiet: *The audience was restless and noisy.*

noth·ing |nŭth′ ĭng| *pron.* Not anything: *I have nothing to say.*

No·vem·ber |nō vĕm′ bər| *n.* The eleventh month of the year. November has thirty days.

numb |nŭm| *adj.* **number, numbest** Deprived of the power to feel or move normally: *toes numb with cold.*

num·ber |nŭm′ bər| *n., pl.* **numbers** A numeral given to something to identify it: *What is your house number?*

numb·ness |nŭm′ nĭs| *n.* The condition of lacking the power to feel or move.

nurse |nûrs| *n., pl.* **nurses** A person who cares for or is trained to care for sick people.

oar |ôr| *n., pl.* **oars** A long pole with a blade at one end that is used to row or steer a boat; a paddle.

o·cean |ō′ shən| *n., pl.* **oceans** The great mass of salt water that covers about 72 percent of the earth's surface.

Oc·to·ber |ŏk tō′ bər| *n.* The tenth month of the year. The month of October has thirty-one days.

oc·to·pus |ŏk′ tə pəs| *n., pl.* **octopuses** A sea animal that has a large head, a soft, rounded body, and eight arms. The undersides of the arms have sucking disks.

odd |ŏd| *adj.* **odder, oddest 1.** Not ordinary or usual; peculiar; strange: *The car is making an odd noise.* **2.** Being the only one left of a set or pair: *I found an odd mitten in the drawer.*

of·fer |ô′ fər| *v.* **offered, offering** To put forward to be accepted or refused: *They offered us some soup.*

of·fice |ô′ fĭs| *n., pl.* **offices** A place, as a room or series of rooms, in which the work of a business is carried on.

of·ten |ô′ fən| *adv.* Many times, frequently: *I often read before going to sleep.*

O·lym·pi·a |ō lĭm′ pē ə| The capital of the state of Washington.

om·ni·bus |ŏm′ nĭ bŭs′| *n., pl.* **omnibuses** A large motor vehicle used for carrying passengers; bus.

once |wŭns| *adv.* One time only: *We feed our dog once a day.*

o·pen |ō′ pən| *adj.* Not shut, closed, fastened, or sealed: *An open book lay on the desk. The door is open.*

op·er·ate |ŏp′ ə rāt′| *v.* **operated, operating** To work or run: *This machine operates well.*

op·er·a·tion |ŏp′ ə rā′ shən| *n., pl.* **operations** The act, process, or way of operating: *We are learning the operation of a computer.*

-or A suffix that forms nouns and means "something or someone who does": *operator.*

or·ange |ôr′ ĭnj| *n., pl.* **oranges** A round, juicy fruit with a reddish-yellow rind. Oranges grow in warm regions on evergreen trees that have fragrant white flowers.

or·bit |ôr′ bĭt| *n., pl.* **orbits** The path of a heavenly body or manmade satellite as it circles around another body. The earth is in orbit around the sun: *The spacecraft went into orbit.*

ore |ôr| *n., pl.* **ores** A mineral from which a metal, such as gold, can be mined.

or·gan |ôr′ gən| *n., pl.* **organs** A musical instrument with one or more keyboards that control the flow of air to pipes. The pipes sound tones when supplied with air.

oth·er |ŭth′ ər| *adj.* Different: *Call me some other time.*

our·selves |our sĕlvz′| *pron.* Our own selves: *Let's keep our plans to ourselves.*

-ous A suffix that forms adjectives and means "full of" or "having": *famous.*

out·side |out sīd′| *n., pl.* **outsides** An outer surface, side, or part; exterior: *I wrote my friend's name on the outside of the envelope.*

ov·en |ŭv′ ən| *n., pl.* **ovens** An enclosed chamber, as in a stove, used for baking, heating, or drying.

owl |oul| *n., pl.* **owls** Any of several birds of prey that usually fly at night and that have a large head, a short, hooked bill, and a flat, disklike face.

oy·ster |oi′ stər| *n., pl.* **oysters** A sea animal that lives in shallow waters and has an edible soft body with a shell made up of two hinged parts. Some kinds produce pearls inside their shells.

P

pack·age |păk′ ĭj| *n., pl.* **packages** A bundle of things packed together; parcel.

pack·et |păk′ ĭt| *n., pl.* **packets** A small package or bundle, as of mail.

pad·dle |păd′ l| *n., pl.* **paddles** A short oar with a flat blade at one or both ends, used to move and steer a small boat or canoe.

page |pāj| *n., pl.* **pages** One side of a printed or written sheet of paper, as in a book.

pail |pāl| *n., pl.* **pails** A round container with a handle that is used especially for carrying water and sand; bucket: *The horse drank a pail of water.*

Pronunciation Key

ă	pat	ō	go	th	thin
ā	pay	ô	paw, for	hw	which
â	care	oi	oil	zh	usual
ä	father	ōō	book	ə	ago,
ĕ	pet	ōō	boot		item,
ē	be	yōō	cute		pencil,
ĭ	pit	ou	out		atom,
ī	ice	ŭ	cut		circus
î	near	û	fur	ər	butter
ŏ	pot	*th*	the		

pain |pān| *n., pl.* **pains** Physical suffering caused by injury or sickness.

pain·ful |pān′ fəl| *adj.* **1.** Causing or full of pain; hurtful: *a painful injury.* **2.** Causing suffering or anxiety; distressing: *a painful decision.*

pain·less |pān′ lĭs| *adj.* Without pain.

paint |pānt| *n., pl.* **paints** A mixture of solid coloring matter and a liquid put onto surfaces to protect or decorate them.

pal·ace |păl′ ĭs| *n., pl.* **palaces** A ruler's official residence.

palm |päm| *n., pl.* **palms** The inner surface of the hand between the wrist and the fingers. ◇ *Idiom* **an itchy palm** A greedy desire for money.

pa·per |pā′ pər| *n., pl.* **papers** **1.** A material made in thin sheets from pulp. **2.** A single sheet of paper. *v.* **papered, papering** To cover with wallpaper.

par·a·chute |păr′ ə shōōt′| *n., pl.* **parachutes** A folding device shaped like an umbrella that is used to slow the fall of persons or objects from the sky.

parachute

Spelling Dictionary

pa·rade |pə **rād'**| *n., pl.* **parades** A festive public event in which people or vehicles pass by spectators: *Fourth of July parade.*

par·ent |**păr'** ənt| *n., pl.* **parents** A father or mother.

par·ka |**pär'** kə| *n., pl.* **parkas** A warm jacket with a hood.

pass·book |**păs'** book'| or |**päs'** book'| *n., pl.* **passbooks** A bankbook in which deposits and withdrawals are recorded.

past |păst| *adj.* Expressing a time gone by: *a past event. n., pl.* **pasts** A time before the present: *happy memories of the past.*

pas·ture |**păs'** chər| *n., pl.* **pastures** Ground where animals graze.

pa·tient |**pā'** shənt| *n., pl.* **patients** A person who is receiving medical treatment.

pa·trol |pə **trōl'**| *n., pl.* **patrols** The act of moving about an area in order to watch or guard.

peace |pēs| *n.* The absence of war or other hostilities.

peace·ful |**pēs'** fəl| *adj.* **1.** Not likely to go to war or to fight: *We live in a peaceful nation.* **2.** Marked by peace and calmness.

peach |pēch| *n., pl.* **peaches** A sweet, round, juicy fruit with fuzzy yellow or pink skin and a pit with a hard shell.

peak |pēk| *n., pl.* **peaks** The top of a mountain.
♦ *These sound alike* **peak, peek.**

peas·ant |**pĕz'** ənt| *n., pl.* **peasants** A small farmer or farm laborer in Europe.

pe·cu·liar |pĭ **kyool'** yər| *adj.* **1.** Not usual. **2.** Belonging to a particular person or place: *music peculiar to Asia.*

peek |pēk| *v.* **peeked, peeking** To glance or look quickly or secretly.
♦ *These sound alike* **peek, peak.**

pen·cil |**pĕn'** səl| *n., pl.* **pencils** A thin stick of black or colored material used for writing or drawing.

pen·ny |**pĕn'** ē| *n., pl.* **pennies** A coin used in the United States and Canada; cent. One hundred pennies equal one dollar.

per·fect |**pûr'** fĭkt| *adj.* Having no flaws, mistakes, or defects: *My drawing is a perfect copy of yours.*

per·fec·tion |pər **fĕc'** shən| *n.* The quality or condition of being perfect.

per·form |pər **fôrm'**| *v.* **performed, performing** To carry out; do: *We will perform an experiment in class.*

per·il |**pĕr'** əl| *n., pl.* **perils** **1.** The condition of being in danger: *The diver's life is in peril.* **2.** Something dangerous.

per·son |**pûr'** sən| *n., pl.* **persons** A human being; individual: *Any person who wants to can come.*

pheas·ant |**fĕz'** ənt| *n., pl.* **pheasants** A large, brightly colored game bird with a long tail: *Pheasants often were hunted for their beautiful feathers.*

pheasant

phone |fōn| *v.* **phoned, phoning** To telephone.

pho·to·graph |**fō'** tə grăf'| *n., pl.* **photographs** An image formed on film by a camera and developed by chemicals to produce a print.

pi·an·o·for·te |pē ăn' ō **fôr'** tā| or |pē ăn' ō **fôr'** tē| *n., pl.* **pianofortes** A musical instrument with a keyboard that moves hammers that strike wire strings, producing tones; piano.

pic·nic |**pĭk'** nĭk'| *n., pl.* **picnics** A party in which those taking part carry their food with them and then eat it outdoors. *adj:* *We have a new picnic basket.*

pic·ture |**pĭk'** chər| *n., pl.* **pictures** A painting, drawing, or photograph.

piece |pēs| *n., pl.* **pieces** Something considered as a part of a larger quantity or group; a portion: *a piece of wood.*
◆ *These sound alike* **piece, peace.**

pig·let |pĭg′ lĭt| *n., pl.* **piglets** A small, young pig.

pil·low |pĭl′ ō| *n., pl.* **pillows** A case filled with soft material and used to cushion a person's head during rest or sleep.

pi·lot |pī′ lət| *n., pl.* **pilots** A person who operates an aircraft inflight.

pi·o·neer |pī′ ə nîr′| *n., pl.* **pioneers** A person who is first to settle in a region.

place |plās| *v.* **placed, placing** To put in a particular place or order: *I placed cups and saucers on the table. n., pl.* **places** An area or region: *We visited many places.*

plan·et |plăn′ ĭt| *n., pl.* **planets** A heavenly body that moves in an orbit around a star, such as the sun.

plank |plăngk| *n., pl.* **planks** A long board.

plant |plănt| *n., pl.* **plants** A living thing, as a flower, tree, fern, or mushroom, that is not an animal, that cannot usually move from place to place, but can usually make its own food. *v.* **planted, planting** To put in the ground or in soil to grow.

plas·tic |plăs′ tĭk| *n., pl.* **plastics** Any of a large number of materials that are made from chemicals. Plastic can be formed into films, molded into objects, or made into fibers.

pleas·ant |plĕz′ ənt| *adj.* **pleasanter, pleasantest** Pleasing; agreeable; delightful: *A pleasant aroma came from the bakery.*

please |plēz| *v.* **pleased, pleasing** To give (someone or something) pleasure or satisfaction.

pleas·ing |plē′ zĭng| *adj.* Giving pleasure; agreeable: *Her smile was pleasing.*

pleas·ure |plĕzh′ ər| *n., pl.* **pleasures** A feeling of happiness or enjoyment; delight: *She smiled with pleasure.*

plen·ty |plĕn′ tē| *n.* A full supply or amount: *Children need plenty of exercise. adj.* More than enough; not few.

pli·ers |plī′ ərz| *pl. n.* A tool consisting of a pair of pivoted jaws and a pair of handles, used for holding, bending, or cutting wire.

Pronunciation Key

ă	pat	ō	go	th	**th**in
ā	pay	ô	paw, for	hw	**wh**ich
â	care	oi	**oi**l	zh	u**s**ual
ä	father	ōō	b**oo**k	ə	**a**go,
ĕ	pet	ōō	b**oo**t		it**e**m,
ē	be	yōō	c**u**te		penc**i**l,
ĭ	pit	ou	**ou**t		at**o**m,
ī	ice	ŭ	c**u**t		circ**u**s
î	near	û	f**u**r	ər	butt**er**
ŏ	pot	th	**th**e		

poach |pōch| *v.* **poached, poaching** To cook in gently boiling liquid.

pock·et |pŏk′ ĭt| *n., pl.* **pockets** A small pouch, open at the side or top, that is sewn into or onto a garment for carrying small items.

pock·et·book |pŏk′ ĭt bōōk′| *n., pl.* **pocketbooks** A container used to hold money, papers, cosmetics, and other small articles; handbag; purse.

poke |pōk| *n., pl.* **pokes** A large bag for holding many objects. *See* **sack.**

po·lice |pə lēs′| *pl. n.* The members of a police department. The police keep order, see that laws are obeyed, and try to solve crimes.

pol·ish |pŏl′ ĭsh| *v.* **polished, polishing** To make smooth and shiny, especially by rubbing: *We polish the marble floor regularly. n., pl.* **polishes** A smooth and shiny surface; gloss: *We admired the polish on the new car.*

po·lite |pə līt′| *adj.* **politer, politest** Having or showing good manners; courteous.

History

Polite comes from the Latin word *polītus,* meaning "polished."

pon·cho |pŏn′ chō| *n., pl.* **ponchos** **1.** A cloak like a blanket with a hole in the center for the head. **2.** A waterproof poncho worn as a raincoat.

poo·dle |pōōd′ l| *n., pl.* **poodles** A dog with thick, curly hair.

por·cu·pine |**pôr′** kyə pīn′| *n., pl.*
porcupines An animal whose back and sides
are covered with long, sharp quills.

History

Porcupine comes from an Old French
phrase that meant "spiny pig."

---

port |pôrt| *n., pl.* **ports** A place along a body
of water where ships can dock or anchor.

por·trait |**pôr′** trĭt′| *n., pl.* **portraits**
A picture of someone's face or sometimes of the
whole person.

pose |pōz| *n., pl.* **poses** A position taken,
especially for a portrait.

post·script |**pōst′** skrĭpt′| *n., pl.* **postscripts**
A message added at the end of a letter after the
writer's signature.

pot·ter·y |**pŏt′** ə rē| *n.* Objects, such as
pots, vases, or dishes, that are shaped from moist
clay and hardened by heat in a kiln or oven.

pounce |pouns| *v.* **pounced, pouncing**
To seize by or as if by swooping: *The kitten
pounced on the ball. n., pl.* **pounces** The act
of seizing with a swoop.

pound¹ |pound| *n., pl.* **pounds** A unit of
weight and mass equal to 16 ounces.

pound² |pound| *n., pl.* **pounds** An enclosed
place for keeping stray animals.

pow·er·ful |**pou′** ər fəl| *adj.* Having power,
authority, or influence; mighty: *The United States
of America is a powerful nation.*

prai·rie |**prâr′** ē| *n., pl.* **prairies** A wide area
of flat or rolling land with tall grass and few trees.

prairie

pray |prā| *v.* **prayed, praying** To hope very
much.

pre·fix |**prē′** fĭks′| *n., pl.* **prefixes** A word
part added to the beginning of a base word to
change the meaning of the word. For example,
the word parts **dis-** in *dislike,* **re-** in *repeat,* and
un- in *unable* are prefixes.

pre·scrip·tion |prĭ **skrĭp′** shən| *n., pl.*
prescriptions A written instruction from a
doctor indicating the medicine or treatment
a patient is to receive.

press |prĕs| *n., pl.* **presses** A printing
press that prints letters, words, and designs
by pressing sheets of paper onto an inked
surface.

pret·ty |**prĭt′** ē| *adj.* **prettier, prettiest**
Pleasing, attractive, or appealing to the eye
or ear.

pride |prīd| *n.* Pleasure or satisfaction in
accomplishments or possessions: *My parents
take pride in their children.*

prince |prĭns| *n., pl.* **princes** The son of a
king or queen.

prin·cess |**prĭn′** sĭs| or |**prĭn′** sĕs′| *n., pl.*
princesses The daughter of a king or queen.

pris·on |**prĭz′** ən| *n., pl.* **prisons** A
place where persons convicted of crimes are
confined.

prop·er |**prŏp′** ər| *adj.* Right for a
purpose or occasion; appropriate: *I don't have
the proper tools for mending the roof.*

proud |proud| *adj.* **prouder, proudest**
Feeling pleased and satisfied over something
one owns, makes, does, or is a part of.

prove |prōōv| *v.* **proved, proved** *or*
proven, proving To show to be true by or as
if by producing evidence or using convincing
arguments: *The police could not prove that the
person was guilty.*

prowl |proul| *v.* **prowled, prowling** To
move about secretly and quietly as if looking
for prey: *The cat prowled in the alley.*

pub·lic |**pŭb′** lĭk| *adj.* Supported by, used
by, or open to all people; not private: *I used a
public telephone to make the call.*

pull |pōōl| *v.* **pulled, pulling** To apply
force to in order to draw someone or
something in the direction of the force;
tug at: *A team of horses pulled the wagon.*

pump |pŭmp| *n., pl.* **pumps** A device used to move a liquid or gas from one place or container to another: *I filled the balloons with a small air pump.*

punc·tu·ate |pŭngk′ chōō āt′| *v.* **punctuated, punctuating** To mark written or printed material with punctuation.

punc·tu·a·tion |pŭngk′ chōō ā′ shən| *n.* Marks, such as periods, commas, and semicolons, that are used to make the meaning of written or printed material clear.

pun·ish |pŭn′ ĭsh| *v.* **punished, punishing** To cause to suffer for a crime, fault, or misbehavior.

pu·pil |pyōō′ pəl| *n., pl.* **pupils** A young person who is being taught in a school or by a private teacher.

pure |pyŏŏr| *adj.* **purer, purest** Not mixed with anything else: *a cup of pure silver.*

pur·ple |pûr′ pəl| *n., pl.* **purples** A color between blue and red. *adj.* Of the color purple.

purse |pûrs| *n., pl.* **purses** A bag or pouch used to carry money, papers, cosmetics, and other small items; handbag, pocketbook.

push |pŏŏsh| *v.* **pushed, pushing** To press against so as to move away: *I pushed the rock, but it wouldn't budge.*

put |pŏŏt| *v.* **put, putting** To cause to be in a particular position or condition: *Put the bowl on the table. Put the papers in order.*

Q

qual·i·ty |kwŏl′ ĭ tē| *n., pl.* **qualities** A property or feature that makes someone or something what it is: *I used vinegar in the dressing because of its sour quality.*

quar·an·tine |kwôr′ ən tēn′| *n., pl.* **quarantines** The prevention or tight control of the movement of people, animals, plants or goods out of a place or region to keep pests or disease from spreading.

quar·ter |kwôr′ tər| *n., pl.* **quarters** One fourth of a year; three months: *Sales were up in the second quarter.*

Pronunciation Key

ă	pat	ō	go	th	thin
ā	pay	ô	paw, for	hw	which
â	care	oi	oil	zh	usual
ä	father	ŏŏ	book	ə	ago,
ĕ	pet	ōō	boot		item,
ē	be	yōō	cute		pencil,
ĭ	pit	ou	out		atom,
ī	ice	ŭ	cut		circus
î	near	û	fur	ər	butter
ŏ	pot	*th*	**the**		

ques·tion |kwĕs′ chən| *n., pl.* **questions** Something that is asked: *I don't understand your question.*

quick |kwĭk| *adj.* **quicker, quickest** Very fast; rapid: *I turned on the light with a quick motion of my hand.*

quilt |kwĭlt| *v.* **quilted, quilting** To stitch together two layers of fabric with an inner padding of cotton, wool, down, or feathers.

quiv·er |kwĭv′ ər| *v.* **quivered, quivering** To shake with a slight vibrating motion; tremble: *My voice quivered with fear. n., pl.* **quivers** The act or motion of quivering.

R

race |rās| *v.* **raced, racing** **1.** To try to beat in a contest of speed. **2.** To rush at top speed: *I raced home when I heard the news.*

ra·dar |rā′ där′| *n.* A device for finding the location and measuring the speed of distant objects, such as airplanes.

ra·di·o |rā′ dē ō| *n., pl.* **radios** The equipment used to send or receive signals transmitted by radio.

raft |răft| *n., pl.* **rafts** A floating platform made of material such as logs or rubber.

rail·road |rāl′ rōd′| *n., pl.* **railroads** A system of transportation consisting of a railroad and the equipment and property, such as stations, land, and trains, that are needed for its operation.

ranch |rănch| *n., pl.* **ranches** A large farm where cattle, sheep, or horses are raised.

rap·ids |**răp′** ĭdz| *pl. n.* A place in a river where the water flows very fast.

ras·cal |**răs′** kəl| *n., pl.* **rascals 1.** A person who misbehaves in a playful way. **2.** A scoundrel.

rath·er |**ră***th***′** ər| *adv.* **1.** To a certain extent; somewhat: *I'm feeling rather sleepy.* **2.** More willingly: *I'd rather read.*

rat·tle·snake |**răt′** l snāk′| *n., pl.* **rattlesnakes** A poisonous American snake that has dry, horny rings at the end of its tail. When the snake shakes its tail, the rings make a rattling sound.

rattlesnake

re- A prefix that means: **1.** Again: *replay.* **2.** Back; backward: *recall.*

reach |rēch| *v.* **reached, reaching 1.** To go as far as; arrive at: *We managed to reach the house before it rained.* **2.** To stretch out; extend: *Nerves reach to every part of the body.* **3.** To touch or try to touch by extending a part of the body, as the hand: *I reached for a cup. n., pl.* **reaches 1.** An act of reaching. **2.** The distance or extent of reaching: *The grapes were within reach.*

read·y |**rĕd′** ē| *adj.* **readier, readiest** Prepared for action or use: *Are you getting ready for school?*

re·al |**rē′** əl| or |rēl| *adj.* **1.** Not artificial; genuine: *A real cat was sitting next to a picture of one.* **2.** Actual, not made up: *This is a story about real people.*

re·ar·range |rē′ ə **rānj′**| *v.* **rearranged, rearranging** To arrange in a different way or order; reorganize.

rea·son |**rē′** zən| *n., pl.* **reasons** An explanation for an act or belief: *These are my reasons for being late. v.* **reasoned, reasoning** To use the ability to think clearly and sensibly.

re·build |rē **bĭld′**| *v.* **rebuilt** |rē **bĭlt′**|, **rebuilding** To build again; reconstruct.

re·call |rĭ **kôl′**| *v.* **recalled, recalling** To bring back to mind; remember: *I can't recall their telephone number.*

re·ceive |rĭ **sēv′**| *v.* **received, receiving** To take or acquire something given, offered, or sent: *I receive an allowance every week.*

rec·og·nize |**rĕk′** əg nīze′| *v.* **recognized, recognizing** To know and remember from past experience: *I recognized my old friend right away.*

re·count |rĭ **kount′**| *v.* **recounted, recounting** To tell in detail; narrate.

re·dec·o·rate |rē **dĕk′** ə rāt′| *v.* **redecorated, redecorating** *tr. v.* To change the decor of, as by painting. *intr. v.* To change the decor of a room, building, etc.

re·do |rē **dōō′**| *v.* **redid** |rē **dĭd′**|, **redoing** To do again.

reef |rēf| *n., pl.* **reefs** A strip or ridge of rock, sand, or coral that rises to or close to the surface of a body of water.

re·fill |rē **fĭl′**| *v.* **refilled, refilling** To fill again: *I used all the ice cubes and forgot to refill the tray. n., pl.* **refills** |**rē′** fĭlz| A replacement for something that has been used up.

re·flect |rĭ **flĕkt′**| *v.* **reflected, reflecting** To give back an image of, as a mirror does.

re·fresh |rĭ **frĕsh′**| *v.* **refreshed, refreshing** To make fresh again with food or rest.

re·fresh·ment |rĭ **frĕsh′** mənt| *n., pl.* **refreshments** A light meal or snack.

re·heat |rē **hēt′**| *v.* **reheated, reheating** To heat again.

reign |rān| *n., pl.* **reigns** The power or rule of a monarch. *v.* **reigned, reigning** To rule as a monarch.

♦ *These sound alike* **reign, rein.**

rein |rān| *n., pl.* **reins** A long, narrow, leather strap attached to the bit of a bridle and held by the rider or driver to control an animal.

♦ *These sound alike* **rein, reign.**

re·late |rĭ **lāt′**| *v.* **related, relating 1.** To tell or narrate: *I related the story of our trip.* **2.** To have a relationship or connection to: *Family members are related.*

re·la·tion |rĭ lā′ shən| *n., pl.* **relations** A connection or association between two or more things.

rel·a·tive |rĕl′ ə tĭv| *n., pl.* **relatives** A person related to another by family.

re·lay |rē′ lā′| or |rĭ lā′| *v.* **relayed, relaying** To pass or send along: *The principal relayed the message to the teacher.*

re·make |rē māk′| *v.* **remade** |rē mād′|, **remaking** To make anew; reconstruct.

re·mem·ber |rĭ mĕm′ bər| *v.* **remembered, remembering 1.** To bring back to the mind; think of again; recall: *I could not remember how to stop the machine.* **2.** To keep carefully in one's memory; not to forget: *Remember that we have to leave early tonight.*

re·paint |rē pānt′| *v.* **repainted, repainting** To paint again.

re·port·er |rĭ pôr′ tər| *n., pl.* **reporters** A person who gathers and reports news for a newspaper or magazine or for a radio or television station.

re·read |rē rēd′| *v.* **reread** |rē rĕd′|, **rereading** To read again.

res·cue |rĕs′ kyōō| *v.* **rescued, rescuing** To save from danger or harm: *Lifeguards learn how to rescue swimmers. n., pl.* **rescues** An act of rescuing or saving.

re·source·ful |rĭ sôrs′ fəl| or |rĭ sōrs′ fəl| *adj.* Clever and imaginative, especially in finding ways to deal with a difficult situation.

res·tau·rant |rĕs′ tər ənt| or |rĕs′ tər änt′| *n., pl.* **restaurants** A place where meals are served to the public.

rest·less |rĕst′ lĭs| *adj.* Unable to rest, relax, or be still: *The baby is restless.*

re·ward |rĭ wôrd′| *n., pl.* **rewards** Something that is offered, given, or received in return for a worthy act, service, or accomplishment.

re·wind |rē wīnd′| *v.* **rewound** |rē wound′|, **rewinding** To wind again.

re·write |rē rīt′| *v.* **rewrote** |rē rōt′|, **rewritten** |rē rĭt′ n|, **rewriting** To write again, especially in a different or improved form.

rhyme |rīm| *n., pl.* **rhymes** A poem that has the same or similar sounds at the ends of lines.

Pronunciation Key

ă	pat	ō	go	th	thin
ā	pay	ô	paw, for	hw	which
â	care	oi	oil	zh	usual
ä	father	ōō	book	ə	ago,
ĕ	pet	ōō	boot		item,
ē	be	yōō	cute		pencil,
ĭ	pit	ou	out		atom,
ī	ice	ŭ	cut		circus
î	near	û	fur	ər	butter
ŏ	pot	*th*	*the*		

---

ridge |rĭj| *n., pl.* **ridges** A long, narrow peak or crest of something: *the ridge of a roof.*

rig·ging |rĭg′ ĭng| *n.* The system of ropes, chains, and tackle used to support and control the masts, sails, and yards of a sailing vessel.

rig·id |rĭj′ ĭd| *adj.* Not bending; stiff; inflexible: *When you salute, keep your arm rigid.*

ring¹ |rĭng| *n., pl.* **rings** A circular band that is worn on a finger or is used to encircle or hold something.
◆ *These sound alike* **ring, wring.**

ring² |rĭng| *n., pl.* **rings** The clear piercing sound made by a bell.
◆ *These sound alike* **ring, wring.**

rink |rĭngk| *n., pl.* **rinks** An area with a smooth surface for skating.

ripe |rīp| *adj.* **riper, ripest** Fully grown and developed: *We ate ripe peaches and berries for dessert.*

risk |rĭsk| *n., pl.* **risks** The possibility of suffering harm or loss.

ri·val |rī′ vəl| *n., pl.* **rivals** Someone who tries to do as well as or better than another; competitor.

rob·in |rŏb′ ĭn| *n., pl.* **robins** A North American songbird with a rust-red breast and a dark gray back.

rock·et |rŏk′ ĭt| *n., pl.* **rockets** A device that is driven through the air by an explosive or by rapidly burning liquid or solid fuel. A rocket is tube-shaped, with one end open. Gases from the explosive or fuel escape from the open end. Large rockets carry space capsules into space. *v.* **rocketed, rocketing** To travel very fast in or as if in a rocket: *The train rocketed by.*

317

ro·de·o |rō′ dē ō′| or |rō **dā′** ō| *n., pl.* **rodeos** A show in which cowboys and cowgirls display their skill in riding horses and bulls and compete in events such as roping cattle.

roof |ro͞of| or |ro͝of| *n., pl.* **roofs** The outside top covering of a building.

route |ro͞ot| or |rout| *n., pl.* **routes** A road or course of travel between two places.

rou·tine |ro͞o **tēn′**| *n., pl.* **routines** A series of regular or usual activities; standard procedure: *a daily routine.*

rub |rŭb| *v.* **rubbed, rubbing** To put or spread on by rubbing: *Rub some stain on the boards. n., pl.* **rubs** An act of rubbing.

rub·ber band |rŭb′ ər bănd| *n., pl.* **rubber bands** An elastic loop of rubber used to hold objects together; elastic.

run·way |rŭn′ wā′| *n., pl.* **runways** A strip of level ground, usually paved, on which aircraft take off and land.

S

sack |săk| *n., pl.* **sacks** A bag of strong material for carrying many objects: *The clerk put the groceries in the sack.*

Sac·ra·men·to |săk rə **mĕn′** tō| The capital of California.

sad·dle |săd′ l| *n., pl.* **saddles** A seat for a rider, as of a horse or bicycle. *v.* **saddled, saddling** To put a saddle on.

sad·ly |săd′ lē| *adv.* Sorrowfully; with regret: *She spoke sadly about her loss.*

safe |sāf| *adj.* **safer, safest 1.** Secure or free from danger, risk, or harm. **2.** Providing protection: *Let's put the silver in a safe place.* **3.** Showing caution; careful: *His sister is a safe driver. n., pl.* **safes** A metal container in which valuable things are kept for protection.

safe·ly |sāf′ lē| *adv.* Without harm.

safe·ty |sāf′ tē| *n., pl.* **safeties** Being safe; freedom from danger, accident, injury, or threat of harm.

sail·or |sā′ lər| *n., pl.* **sailors** A person who sails, especially as a member of a ship's crew.

Saint Ber·nard |sānt bər **närd′**| *n., pl.* **Saint Bernards** A large, strong dog that was originally used to rescue lost travelers in the mountains of Switzerland.

Saint Bernard

sal·ad |săl′ əd| *n., pl.* **salads** A cold dish of raw vegetables or fruit, often served with a dressing.

sale |sāl| *n., pl.* **sales 1.** The act of selling. **2.** A sale of goods at reduced prices.

salt·y |sôl′ tē| *adj.* **saltier, saltiest** Of, containing, tasting of, or full of salt.

sat·el·lite |săt′ l īt′| *n., pl.* **satellites** An object launched by a rocket in order to orbit and perhaps study a heavenly body.

sauce |sôs| *n., pl.* **sauces** A liquid dressing or relish served with food.

sav·ing |sā′ vĭng| *n., pl.* **savings** Money saved.

say |sā| *v.* **said** |sĕd|, **saying, says** |sĕz| To utter aloud; speak: *I said hello.*

scar |skär| *v.* **scarred, scarring** To mark with or form a scar from a healed wound.

scarce |skârs| *adj.* **scarcer, scarcest 1.** Not enough to meet a demand: *Food is scarce in some countries.* **2.** Not often found; rare: *Scarce supplies of coal.*

scare |skâr| *v.* **scared, scaring 1.** To frighten or become frightened. **2.** To frighten or drive away. *n., pl.* **scares** A sense of fear.

scarf |skärf| *n., pl.* **scarfs** or **scarves** |skärvz| A piece of cloth that is worn around the neck or head.

school |sko͞ol| *n., pl.* **schools** A place for teaching and learning. *adj.: a school bus.*

schoo·ner |sko͞o′ nər| *n., pl.* **schooners** A ship with two or more masts and sails that are set lengthwise.

schwa |shwä| *n.* A weak vowel sound found in unstressed syllables in words. The symbol for the schwa sound is |ə|. Different vowel letters can spell the schwa sound.

score |skôr| *n., pl.* **scores** The number of points made by each participant in a game, contest, or test.

scout |skout| *v.* **scouted, scouting** To observe or explore carefully for information.

scraw·ni·ness |skrô′ nē nĭs| *n.* Condition of being scrawny.

scraw·ny |skrô′ nē| *adj.* **scrawnier, scrawniest** Thin and bony; skinny.

scream |skrēm| *v.* **screamed, screaming** To make a long, loud, piercing cry.

screw·driv·er |skro͞o′ drī′ vər| *n., pl.* **screwdrivers** A tool that is used to turn screws.

scu·ba |sko͞o′ bə| *n.* One or more tanks of compressed air, worn on the back by divers for breathing underwater.

scu·ba di·ver |sko͞o′ bə dī′ vər| *n., pl.* **scuba divers** One who uses scuba gear in underwater swimming.

sea·coast |sē′ kōst| *n., pl.* **seacoasts** Land along the sea.

search |sûrch| *v.* **searched, searching** **1.** To look thoroughly and carefully: *We searched for fossils in the rocks.* **2.** To look over or go through carefully to find something. *n., pl.* **searches** An act or example of searching.

sea·son |sē′ zən| *n., pl.* **seasons 1.** One of the four equal natural divisions of the year. The seasons are spring, summer, autumn, and winter. **2.** A period of the year marked by a certain activity or event: *Winter in New England is the skiing season.*

seat belt |sēt bĕlt| *n., pl.* **seat belts** A safety strap or harness that is designed to hold a person securely in a seat, as in a car or airplane.

sec·ond |sĕk′ ənd| *n., pl.* **seconds** The number in a series that matches the number two.

Pronunciation Key

ă	pat	ō	go	th	**thin**
ā	pay	ô	paw, for	hw	**which**
â	care	oi	**oil**	zh	u**s**ual
ä	father	o͞o	book	ə	**a**go,
ĕ	pet	o͞o	boot		item,
ē	be	yo͞o	cute		pencil,
ĭ	pit	ou	**out**		atom,
ī	ice	ŭ	cut		circus
î	near	û	fur	ər	butter
ŏ	pot	*th*	**the**		

se·cret |sē′ krĭt| *adj.* Hidden from general knowledge or view.

seek |sēk| *v.* **sought** |sôt|, **seeking** To try to find; search.

seem |sēm| *v.* **seemed, seeming** To give the impression of being; appear to be: *You seem worried.*

see·saw |sē′ sô| *n., pl.* **seesaws** A long plank balanced so that with a person riding on either end, one end goes up as the other goes down: *The playground has a new seesaw.*

sel·dom |sĕl′ dəm| *adv.* Not often; rarely.

set·tle |sĕt′ l| *v.* **settled, settling** To make a home or place to live in: *Pioneers settled the West.*

sev·en |sĕv′ ən| *n., pl.* **sevens** The number, written 7, that is equal to the sum of 6 + 1. *adj.* Being one more than six.

sev·er·al |sĕv′ ər əl| *adj.* More than two but not many: *We live several miles away.* *n.* More than two people or things.

shall |shăl| *helping v., past tense* **should** Used to show: **1.** Something that will take place or exist in the future: *We shall arrive tomorrow.* **2.** The will to do something or make something happen: *I shall not cry.*

shape |shāp| *n., pl.* **shapes 1.** The outer form of an object; outline: *We drew circles, triangles, and other shapes.* **2.** Proper physical condition or mechanical order: *Athletes must stay in shape.*

shark |shärk| *n., pl.* **sharks** A large, fierce ocean fish that has a big mouth and sharp teeth.

sharp |shärp| *adj.* **sharper, sharpest** **1.** Having a thin edge that cuts or a fine point that pierces. **2.** Not rounded or blunt; pointed. *adv.* Exactly; precisely: *It's three o'clock sharp.*

Spelling Dictionary

shel·ter |shĕl′ tər| *n., pl.* **shelters**
Something that protects or covers.

sher·iff |shĕr′ ĭf| *n., pl.* **sheriffs** A
county official who is in charge of enforcing
the law.

shine |shīn| *v.* **shone** |shōn|, **shining**
To give off light or reflect light; glow.

ship·wreck |shĭp′ rĕk′| *n., pl.*
shipwrecks A wrecked ship.

shirt |shûrt| *n., pl.* **shirts** A garment for
the upper part of the body. A shirt usually
has a collar, sleeves, and an opening in the
front.

shock |shŏk| *n., pl.* **shocks 1.** A mental
or emotional upset caused by something that
happens suddenly; a bad surprise. **2.** The
feeling caused by the passage of an electric
current through the body.

shoe |shōo| *n., pl.* **shoes** An outer
covering for the foot. A typical shoe has a
stiff sole and heel and a flexible upper part.

shook |shŏok| *v.* Past tense of **shake:** *The
puppy shook with fear.*

shoot |shōot| *v.* **shot** |shŏt|, **shooting**
To send or be sent forth with great force or
speed: *They shot a rocket into outer space.*

shout |shout| *v.* **shouted, shouting** To
cry out or say loudly; yell. *n., pl.* **shouts** A
loud cry or yell.

show·er |shou′ ər| *n., pl.* **showers** A
brief fall of rain.

shown |shōn| *v.* A past participle of
show: *We have shown our pictures to the
travel club.*

shut |shŭt| *v.* **shut, shutting** To move
into a closed position: *Shut the door.*

shut·ter |shŭt′ ər| *n., pl.* **shutters**
A movable cover over a camera lens that
opens for an instant to let in light.

shy |shī| *adj.* **shier** *or* **shyer, shiest** *or*
shyest 1. Feeling uneasy around people or
with strangers; bashful. **2.** Easily frightened;
timid. **3.** Less than a certain amount; short:
I am three inches shy of five feet. v. **shied,
shying** To move suddenly, as if startled: *The
horse shied away from the children.*

sick·ness |sĭk′ nĭs| *n., pl.* **sicknesses** The
condition of being sick or without health;
illness.

sift |sĭft| *v.* **sifted, sifting** To remove
lumps or large chunks from by shaking or
pushing through a sieve.

sigh |sī| *v.* **sighed, sighing** To let out a
long, deep breath because of fatigue, sorrow,
or relief. *n., pl.* **sighs** The act or sound of
sighing.

sight |sīt| *n., pl.* **sights** The ability to see;
vision.

si·lent |sī′ lənt| *adj.* **1.** Making or having
no sound; quiet. **2.** Saying little or nothing.
3. Not spoken or expressed out loud: *We sat
in silent thought.* **4.** Not pronounced or
sounded: *The "k" in "knife" is silent.*

sil·ver |sĭl′ vər| *n.* A soft shiny white
metal that is one of the chemical elements.
Silver is used to make coins, jewelry, and
table utensils.

sil·ver·ware |sĭl′ vər wâr′| *n., pl.*
silverware Utensils made of or coated with
silver or another shiny metal.

sim·mer |sĭm′ ər| *v.* **simmered,
simmering** To cook below or just at the
boiling point: *The soup simmered on the stove.*

sim·ple |sĭm′ pəl| *adj.* **simpler, simplest**
Not complicated; easy: *simple directions.*

since |sĭns| *adv.* Before now; ago: *I've long
since forgotten.*

sing·er |sĭng′ ər| *n., pl.* **singers** Someone
who performs songs, especially someone who
has had special training.

sink |sĭngk| *n., pl.* **sinks** A basin with a
drain and faucets for turning on and off a
water supply.

si·ren |sī′ rən| *n., pl.* **sirens** A device that
makes a loud whistling or wailing sound as a
signal or warning.

skate |skāt| *n., pl.* **skates** A boot, shoe,
or metal frame having a metal blade used for
gliding on ice. *v.* **skated, skating** To move
along on skates.

ski |skē| *v.* **skied, skiing** To move along
over snow on skis.

skill |skĭl| *n., pl.* **skills** The ability to do
something well.

skil·let |skĭl′ ĭt| *n., pl.* **skillets** A frying
pan: *We cooked the fish in the skillet.*

skip |skĭp| *v.* **skipped, skipping** To jump
lightly over: *I like to skip rope.*

skunk |skŭngk| *n., pl.* **skunks** An animal that has black and white fur and a bushy tail. A skunk can spray a bad-smelling liquid when it is attacked.

sled |slĕd| *v.* **sledded, sledding** To ride on a sled.

sleep·wear |slēp' wâr'| *n., pl.* **sleepwear** Nightclothes, such as night gowns or pajamas.

sleigh |slā| *n., pl.* **sleighs** A vehicle on runners that is usually pulled by a horse over ice or snow.

slope |slōp| *v.* **sloped, sloping** To slant upward or downward. *n., pl.* **slopes** 1. A slanting line, surface, or direction. 2. A sloping stretch of ground.

slow |slō| *adj.* **slower, slowest** Not moving or able to move quickly; proceeding at a low speed: *a slow car.*

slow·ly |slō' lē| *adv.* Proceeding at a low speed: *I drove slowly down the street.*

slum·ber |slŭm' bər| *v.* **slumbered, slumbering** To sleep; doze. *n., pl.* **slumbers** Sleep.

small |smôl| *adj.* **smaller, smallest** Little in size, amount, or extent.

smell |smĕl| *v.* **smelled** *or* **smelt, smelling** To detect the odor of by using sense organs in the nose; to sniff: *I smell smoke.*

smell·y |smĕl' ē| *adj.* **smellier, smelliest** Having an unpleasant odor.

smile |smīl| *n., pl.* **smiles** A pleased or happy expression on the face formed by curving the corners of the mouth upward.

smog |smôg| *n.* Fog mixed with smoke: *The city is filled with smog because of the weather and the traffic.*

smoke |smōk| *n.* The mixture of gases and particles of carbon that rises from burning material.

smok·y |smō' kē| *adj.* **smokier, smokiest** Filled with or giving off much smoke.

smooth |smōōth| *adj.* **smoother, smoothest** Having a surface that is not rough or uneven.

snap |snăp| *v.* **snapped, snapping** To make or cause to make a sharp cracking sound.

Pronunciation Key

ă	pat	ō	go	th	**th**in
ā	pay	ô	paw, for	hw	**wh**ich
â	care	oi	**oi**l	zh	usual
ä	father	ŏŏ	b**oo**k	ə	**a**go,
ĕ	pet	ōō	b**oo**t		item,
ē	be	yōō	c**u**te		pencil,
ĭ	pit	ou	**ou**t		atom,
ī	ice	ŭ	c**u**t		circus
î	near	û	f**u**r	ər	butt**er**
ŏ	pot	*th*	**th**e		

snow |snō| *n., pl.* **snows** Soft white crystals of ice that form from water vapor in the upper air and fall to earth.

snow·mo·bile |snō' mō bēl'| *n., pl.* **snowmobiles** A vehicle like a sled with a motor, used for traveling over snow.

snowmobile

soap |sōp| *n., pl.* **soaps** A substance that is usually made from fat and lye and is used for washing. *v.* **soaped, soaping** To treat, rub, or cover with soap.

sock |sŏk| *n., pl.* **socks** A short, knitted or woven covering for the foot that reaches above the ankle and ends below the knee.

soft |sôft| *adj.* **softer, softest** Not hard or firm.

sof·ten |sô' fən| *v.* **softened, softening** To make or become soft or softer.

soft·ware |sôft' wâr'| *n., pl.* **software** Written or printed data, such as programs, that are used in operating computers.

Spelling Dictionary

so·lar |sō′ lər| *adj.* Of or relating to the sun.

some·times |sŭm′ tīmz′| *adv.* Now and then: *I see them sometimes but not often.*

song·fest |sông′ fĕst| *n., pl.* **songfests** A casual gathering for group singing.

soot |sŏŏt| *n.* A fine, black powder produced when something, such as wood or coal, burns.

sor·ry |sŏr′ ē| *adj.* **sorrier, sorriest** Feeling sorrow, sympathy, pity, or regret: *I'm sorry I'm late.*

sound |sound| *n., pl.* **sounds** A kind of vibration that travels through a substance, such as air, and can be heard.

soup |sōōp| *n., pl.* **soups** A liquid food prepared from meat, fish, or vegetable broth, often with various solid ingredients added.

south |south| *adv.* Toward the direction to the left of a person who faces the sunset: *We drove south to the camp. adj.* Of, in, or toward the south: *the south side.*

south·ern |sŭth′ ərn| *adj.* Of, in, or toward the south: *We drove through the southern states.*

space shut·tle |spās′ shŭt′ l| *n., pl.* **space shuttles** A space vehicle designed to carry astronauts back and forth between the earth and an orbiting space station.

span·iel |spăn′ yəl| *n., pl.* **spaniels** A dog of small or medium size with drooping ears, short legs, and a silky wavy coat.

spare |spâr| *v.* **spared, sparing** To show mercy or consideration to: *I tried to spare your feelings by not telling you about the problem. adj.* **sparer, sparest** Beyond what is needed; extra: *Do you have any spare change?*

speak |spēk| *v.* **spoke** |spōk|, **spoken, speaking** To utter words; talk.

spear |spîr| *n., pl.* **spears** A weapon with a long shaft and a sharply pointed head.

spe·cial |spĕsh′ əl| *adj.* Different from what is common or usual; exceptional: *Birthdays are special occasions.*

speck·led |spĕk′ əld| *adj.* Dotted or covered with small spots, especially a natural marking.

speed |spēd| *n., pl.* **speeds** The condition of moving or acting rapidly; quickness: *You work with amazing speed.*

spent |spĕnt| *v.* Past tense and past participle of **spend:** *I saved my allowance, but Jolen spent hers.*

spic·y |spī′ sē| *n., pl.* **spicier, spiciest** Flavored with a spice or spices.

spi·der |spī′ dər| *n., pl.* **spiders 1.** An animal with eight legs and a body divided into two parts that spins webs to catch insects. **2.** A frying pan; skillet.

spig·ot |spĭg′ ət| *n., pl.* **spigots** A faucet: *The kitchen spigot needs to be repaired.*

spoke |spōk| *v.* Past tense of **speak.** Said: *We spoke to her by phone.*

sponge |spŭnj| *n., pl.* **sponges** A water animal that has a soft skeleton with many small holes that absorb water.

spong·y |spŭn′ jē| *adj.* **spongier, spongiest** Resembling a sponge; soft, porous, and elastic.

spoon |spōōn| *n., pl.* **spoons** A utensil with a shallow bowl at the end of its handle. Spoons are used in measuring, serving, or eating food.

spruce |sprōōs| *n., pl.* **spruces** An evergreen tree with short needles and soft wood.

square |skwâr| *n., pl.* **squares** A rectangle having four equal sides.

squeak·y |skwē′ kē| *adj.* **squeakier, squeakiest** Tending to squeak.

squid |skwĭd| *n., pl.* **squids** or **squid** A sea animal that is related to the octopus and has a long body and ten arms.

squire |skwĭr| *n., pl.* **squires** A young man of noble birth who served a knight.

squir·rel |skwûr′ əl| *n., pl.* **squirrels** Any of several animals with gray, reddish-brown, or black fur and a bushy tail. Squirrels climb trees.

stage |stāj| *n., pl.* **stages** The raised platform in a theater on which entertainers perform.

stage·coach |stāj′ kōch′| *n., pl.* **stagecoaches** A coach with four wheels that is drawn by horses. Stagecoaches were once used to carry mail, baggage, and passengers.

stair |stâr| *n., pl.* **stairs 1. stairs** A series or flight of steps; staircase. **2.** One of a flight of steps.

stam·pede |stăm **pēd′**| *n., pl.* **stampedes**
A sudden rush of startled animals, such as
cattle. *v.* **stampeded, stampeding** To take
or cause to take part in a stampede.

star |stär| *n., pl.* **stars** A heavenly body that
appears as a very bright point in the sky at night.

stare |stâr| *n., pl.* **stared, staring** To look
with a steady, often wide-eyed gaze. *n., pl.*
stares A staring gaze.

start |stärt| *v.* **started, starting** To begin
to move, go, or act.

star·tle |stär′ tl| *v.* **startled, startling**
1. To cause to make a sudden movement, as
of surprise: *A thud on the roof startled us.*
2. To fill with sudden alarm.

starve |stärv| *v.* **starved, starving** **1.** To
suffer or die from lack of food. **2.** To suffer
or cause to suffer from a lack of something
necessary: *The plants are starving for water.*

state·ment |stāt′ mənt| *n., pl.* **statements**
Something expressed in words; a declaration.

steak |stāk| *n., pl.* **steaks** A slice of meat,
as beef or fish, that is usually broiled or fried.

steal |stēl| *v.* **stole** |stōl|, **stolen, stealing**
1. To take without right or permission:
Someone stole my bicycle. **2.** To move very
quietly: *A big cat stole through the garden.*
♦ *These sound alike* **steal, steel.**

stealth |stĕlth| *n.* The act of moving in a
quiet, secret way so as to avoid notice.

steel |stēl| *n.* A metal made from iron and
carbon.
♦ *These sound alike* **steel, steal.**

stee·ple |stē′ pəl| *n., pl.* **steeples** A tall
tower that rises from the roof of a building,
especially one on a church or courthouse.

steeple

Pronunciation Key

ă	pat	ō	go	th	**th**in
ā	pay	ô	paw, for	hw	**wh**ich
â	care	oi	**oi**l	zh	u**s**ual
ä	father	o͝o	b**oo**k	ə	**a**go,
ĕ	pet	o͞o	b**oo**t		it**e**m,
ē	be	yo͞o	c**u**te		penc**i**l,
ĭ	pit	ou	**ou**t		at**o**m,
ī	ice	ŭ	c**u**t		circ**u**s
î	near	û	f**u**r	ər	butt**er**
ŏ	pot	*th*	**the**		

steer |stîr| *v.* **steered, steering** To direct the
course of: *The pilot steered the ship to the dock.*

stel·lar |stĕl′ ər| *adj.* Of or consisting of
a star or stars.

sten·cil |stĕn′ səl| *v.* **stenciled** *or* **stencilled,**
stenciling *or* **stencilling** To apply ink or paint to
a sheet of material, such as paper, out of which
letters or designs have been cut. When ink is
applied, the patterns appear on the surface
beneath.

stern |stûrn| *n., pl.* **sterns** The rear part of
a ship or boat.

still |stĭl| *adj.* **stiller, stillest** Without motion;
calm: *The air was still before the storm.*

sting |stĭng| *v.* **stung** |stŭng|, **stinging**
1. To prick or wound with a small, sharp point:
A bee stung me on the foot. **2.** To feel or cause to
feel a sharp, burning pain: *My ears stung with the
cold.* *n., pl.* **stings** The act of stinging.

stir·rup |stûr′ əp| *n., pl.* **stirrups** A ring or
loop hanging by a strap from a saddle to support
a rider's foot.

stock |stŏk| *n., pl.* **stocks** **1.** A supply for
future use: *The farmer had a stock of grain for
winter.* **2.** Animals, such as cows, sheep, or pigs,
that are raised on a farm or ranch; livestock. *v.*
stocked, stocking To provide with, keep, or lay
in a supply of: *We stocked the cupboards with food.*
adj. Kept regularly on hand for sale.

sto·len |stō′ lən| *v.* Past participle of **steal**:
My lunch was stolen.

stom·ach |stŭm′ ək| *n., pl.* **stomachs** The
large muscular pouch into which food passes
when it leaves the mouth and esophagus and in
which digestion takes place.

Spelling Dictionary

ston·y |stō′ nē| *adj.* **stonier, stoniest**
Of, full of, or covered with stones.

stood |stŏŏd| *v.* Past tense and past participle of **stand:** *I stood on a footstool.*

stool |stōōl| *n., pl.* **stools** **1.** A seat without arms or a back. **2.** A low support to rest the feet on while sitting; footstool.

storm |stôrm| *n., pl.* **storms** A strong wind with rain, hail, sleet, or snow. *v.* **stormed, storming** To blow with a strong wind and rain, hail, sleet, or snow.

sto·ry |stôr′ ē| *n., pl.* **stories** A tale made up to entertain people: *I just read an adventure story.*

straight |strāt| *adj.* **straighter, straightest** Not curving, curling, or bending: *I have straight hair.*

strange |strānj| *adj.* **stranger, strangest** Not ordinary; unusual.

strength·en |strĕngk′ thən| *v.* **strengthened, strengthening** To make or become strong.

stretch |strĕch| *v.* **stretched, stretching** To flex the muscles: *It feels good to stretch after a long drive.*

strip |strĭp| *v.* **stripped, stripping** To remove the covering from.

stripe |strīp| *n., pl.* **stripes** A long, narrow band of color material that is different from its background.

striped |strīpt| *adj.* Having long, narrow lines of different colors.

strive |strīv| *v.* **strove** |strōv|, **striven** |strĭv′ ən|, *or* **strived, striving** **1.** To exert much effort or energy; to reach a goal: *We must strive to improve working conditions.* **2.** To struggle; contend: *The pioneers had to strive against great odds.*

struck |strŭk| *v.* Past tense and past participle of **strike:** *The batter struck the ball.*

stud·y |stŭd′ ē| *v.* **studied, studying** To try to learn: *We study Spanish.*

style |stīl| *n., pl.* **styles** A way of dressing or acting that is fashionable: *My clothes are out of style.*

sub·ma·rine |sŭb′ mə rēn′| or |sŭb′ mə rēn′| *n., pl.* **submarines** A ship that can operate both underwater and on the surface; sub.

sub·merge |səb mûrj′| *v.* **submerged, submerging** To cover with water: *Huge waves submerged the pier.*

sud·den |sŭd′ n| *adj.* Happening or arriving without warning: *We were caught in a sudden snowstorm.*

suf·fer |sŭf′ ər| *v.* **suffered, suffering** To feel pain or distress: *The dog was suffering in the hot weather.*

sug·ar |shŏŏg′ ər| *n., pl.* **sugars** A sweet substance gotten mainly from sugar beets or sugar cane. Sugar sweetens food.

sug·ges·tion |səg jĕs′ chən| *n., pl.* **suggestions** Something offered for consideration: *At the train conductor's suggestion we moved to a seat that had a better view.*

suit |sōōt| *n., pl.* **suits** A set of clothes to be used together: *We put on our gym suits.*

sum |sŭm| *n., pl.* **sums** **1.** The result of the operation of addition: *The sum of 2 + 2 is 4.* **2.** The whole amount: *The sum of my knowledge is very small.*

sum·mer |sŭm′ ər| *n., pl.* **summers** The hottest season of the year, between spring and autumn.

sun·ny |sŭn′ ē| *adj.* **sunnier, sunniest** Full of sunshine: *Let's hope for a sunny day.*

su·perb |sōō pûrb′| *adj.* Being the very best; excellent; magnificent: *Your grades are superb.*

sup·ply |sə plī′| *n., pl.* **supplies** Necessary materials kept and used or given out when needed: *After three months, the explorers' supplies ran out.*

sup·port |sə pôrt′| *v.* **supported, supporting** To keep from falling; hold in position: *Two steel towers support the bridge.*

sup·pose |sə pōz′| *v.* **supposed, supposing** To be inclined to think; assume: *I suppose you're right.*

sup·po·si·tion |sŭp′ ə zĭsh′ ən| *n., pl.* **suppositions** The mental process of supposing; guesswork: *The idea that the cat broke the vase is pure supposition.*

sur·ger·y |sûr′ jə rē| *n., pl.* A branch of medicine in which injury and disease are treated by cutting into and removing or repairing parts of the body.

sur·vive |sər vīv′| *v.* **survived, surviving** To stay alive or in existence.

sweet |swēt| *adj.* **sweeter, sweetest**
1. Having a pleasing taste like that of sugar.
2. Not sour: *This milk is still sweet.*
swift |swĭft| *adj.* **swifter, swiftest** Moving or able to move very fast.
swim·wear |swĭm' wâr'| *n., pl.*
swimwear Clothing designed to be worn for swimming or with swimsuits.
syl·la·ble |sĭl' ə bəl| *n., pl.* **syllables** A word or a word part that has one vowel sound.
syn·o·nym |sĭn' ə nĭm| *n., pl.* **synonyms** A word having the same or similar meaning as that of another word.

T

tal·ent |tăl' ənt| *n., pl.* **talents** A natural ability to do something well: *If you give up music, you'll waste your talent.*
talk |tôk| *v.* **talked, talking** To say words.
tan |tăn| *v.* **tanned, tanning** To make or become brown from the sun.
tank |tăngk| *n., pl.* **tanks** A large container for holding compressed air, worn on the back by divers for breathing underwater.
tap |tăp| *v.* **tapped, tapping** To strike gently with a light blow: *I tapped my friend on the shoulder.*
tax·i·me·ter cab |tăk' sē mē' tər căb| *n., pl.* **taximeter cabs** An automobile that carries passengers for a price or fare. The fare is usually calculated by a taximeter, an instrument that measures distance and time; taxicab; taxi; cab.

taximeter cab

Pronunciation Key

ă	pat	ō	go	th	thin
ā	pay	ô	paw, for	hw	which
â	care	oi	oil	zh	usual
ä	father	o͝o	book	ə	ago,
ě	pet	o͞o	boot		item,
ē	be	yo͞o	cute		pencil,
ĭ	pit	ou	out		atom,
ī	ice	ŭ	cut		circus
î	near	û	fur	ər	butter
ŏ	pot	*th*	**the**		

teach·er |tē' chər| *n., pl.* **teachers** A person who gives instructions or provides knowledge, usually in a school.
tear[1] |târ| *v.* **tore** |tôr| or |tōr|, **torn** |tôrn| or |tōrn|, **tearing** To pull or divide into pieces; split; rip.
tear[2] |tîr| *n., pl.* **tears** A drop of the clear liquid secreted by glands of the eyes.
tee·ter-tot·ter |tē' tər tŏt' ər| *n., pl.*
teeter-totters *See* **seesaw.**
tel·e·phone |tĕl' ə fōn'| *n., pl.*
telephones An instrument that sends and receives sound, especially speech, by wires or radio waves; phone.
tem·per |tĕm' pər| *n., pl.* **tempers** A person's usual state of mind or emotions; disposition.
ten·der |tĕn' dər| *adj.* **tenderer, tenderest 1.** Fragile. **2.** Not tough. **3.** Painful; sore. **4.** Gentle; loving.
tent |tĕnt| *n., pl.* **tents** A portable shelter, as of canvas, usually supported by poles.
ter·mi·nal |tûr' mə nəl| *n., pl.* **terminals** A station at the end of a railway, bus line, or airline.
ter·ri·er |tĕr' ē ər| *n., pl.* **terriers** A small, active dog that was once used for hunting small animals in their burrows.
thank·ful |thăngk' fəl| *adj.* Showing or feeling gratitude; grateful.
thatch |thăch| *v.* **thatched, thatching** To cover with plant material, such as straw or reeds: *a thatched roof.*
their |*th*âr| *adv.* Relating or belonging to them: *They put their boots in the closet.*
◆ *These sound alike* **their, there, they're.**

Spelling Dictionary

there |*thâr*| *adv.* At or in that place: *Set the package there on the table.*
◆ *These sound alike* **there, their, they're.**

they're |*thâr*| Contraction of "they are."
◆ *These sound alike* **they're, their, there.**

third |thûrd| *n., pl.* **thirds 1.** The number in a series that matches the number three. **2.** One of three equal parts, written 1/3. *adj.* Coming after the second.

thir·teen |thûr′ tēn′| *n., pl.* **thirteens** The number, written 13, that is equal to the sum of 12 + 1. *adj.* Being one more than twelve.

thir·ty |thûr′ tē| *n., pl.* **thirties** The number, written 30, that is equal to the product of 10 x 3. *adj.* Being equal to ten times three.

thor·ough·bred |thûr′ ō brĕd′| or |thûr′ ə brĕd′| or |thûr′ brĕd′| *n.* An animal bred of pure or pedigreed stock.

threat·en |thrĕt′ n| *v.* **threatened, threatening** To be a threat to; endanger: *Landslides threatened the village.*

three |thrē| *n., pl.* **threes** The number, written 3, that is equal to the sum of 2 + 1. *adj.* Being one more than two.

threw |thrōō| *v.* Past tense of **throw.**
◆ *These sound alike* **threw, through.**

through |thrōō| *prep.* In one side and out the other side of: *We walked through the park.*
◆ *These sound alike* **through, threw.**

thumb |thŭm| *n., pl.* **thumbs** A short, thick first finger of the human hand.

thun·der |thŭn′ dər| *n.* The deep, rumbling noise that goes with or comes after a flash of lightning.

tick·et |tĭk′ ĭt| *n., pl.* **tickets** A paper slip or card that gives a person the right to a service, such as a bus ride or entrance to a theater.

ti·ger |tī gər| *n., pl.* **tigers** A large animal of Asia that belongs to the cat family. A tiger has light brown fur with black stripes.

tight |tīt| *adj.* **tighter, tightest** Not letting water or air pass through: *We were warm that night in our tight little cabin.*

tin |tĭn| *n., pl.* **tins** A soft, shiny metal that hardly rusts at all and is used to coat other metals. Tin is a chemical element.

ti·ny |tī′ nē| *adj.* **tinier, tiniest** Extremely small.

tire |tīr| *v.* **tired, tiring** To make or become weak from work or effort; weary: *The long walk tired me.*

tis·sue |tĭsh′ ōō| *n., pl.* **tissues 1.** Often **tissue paper** Light, thin paper used for wrapping. **2.** A piece of soft, absorbent paper used as a handkerchief.

ti·tle |tīt′ l| *n., pl.* **titles 1.** An identifying name given to a book, painting, song, or other work. **2.** A word or name given to a person to show his or her rank, office, or occupation. Some titles are Mr., Ms., Dr., Senator, and Judge.

to·bog·gan |tə bŏg′ ən| *n., pl.* **toboggans** A long, narrow sled without runners. A toboggan curves upward at the front.

toboggan

to·day |tə dā′| *adv.* During or on the present day. *n.* The present day, time, or age: *Are the athletes of today better than those of the past?*

to·geth·er |tə gĕth′ ər| *adv.* In or into a single group or place; with each other; not apart: *Many people were crowded together.*

to·mor·row |tə môr′ ō| *n.* The day after today.

tool |tōōl| *n., pl.* **tools** A device, such as a hammer or an axe, that is especially made or shaped to help a person do work. *v.* **tooled, tooling** To shape or decorate with tools.

tooth |tōōth| *n., pl.* **teeth** |tēth| One of a set of hard, bony parts in the mouth that are used to chew and bite.

To·pe·ka |tə pē′ kə| The capital of Kansas.

top·ic |tŏp′ ĭk| *n., pl.* **topics** A subject treated in a speech, conversation, or piece of writing: *Name the main topic of your paragraph.*

to·tal |tōt′ l| *adj.* Absolute; complete: *Our play was a total success.*

to·tal·i·ty |tō tăl´ ĭ tē| *n., pl.* **totalities**
A total amount; a sum.

tour·na·ment |tûr´ nə mənt| *n., pl.*
tournaments A medieval contest between
jousting knights.

tow·el |tou´ əl| *n., pl.* **towels** A piece
of cloth or paper used for wiping or drying
something that is wet.
◇ *Idiom* **throw in the towel** To admit defeat.

trace |trās| *v.* **traced, tracing** **1.** To
follow the track, course, or trail of: *The post
office traced the lost letter.* **2.** To copy by
following lines seen through transparent paper.

track |trăk| *n., pl.* **tracks** A rail or set of
rails for vehicles such as trains to run on.

trav·el |trăv´ əl| *v.* **traveled, traveling**
To go from one place to another; journey:
The whole family traveled around the world.

treat·ment |trēt´ mənt| *n., pl.* **treatments**
The use of something to relieve or cure a
disease.

trem·ble |trĕm´ bəl| *v.* **trembled,
trembling** To shake or shiver: *A slight breeze
made the leaves on the tree tremble.*

Tren·ton |trĕn´ tən| The capital of New
Jersey.

tribe |trīb| *n., pl.* **tribes** A group of people
sharing a common ancestry, language, and
culture.

tri·fle |trī´ fəl| *n., pl.* **trifles** **1.** Something
unimportant or worthless. **2.** A small amount.

trou·ble |trŭb´ əl| *n., pl.* **troubles** A
difficult, dangerous, or upsetting situation:
The damaged ship was in trouble.

true |trōō| *adj.* **truer, truest** **1.** Being
in agreement with fact or reality; accurate.
2. Faithful and loyal; not false or disloyal:
You are a true friend.

trunk |trŭngk| *n., pl.* **trunks** **1.** The often
tall, thick, woody main stem of a tree. **2.** The
covered compartment of an automobile, used
for storage.

truth |trōōth| *n., pl.* **truths** **1.** The quality
or condition of being true or accurate: *There
was truth in what she said.* **2.** Something that
is true: *I told him the truth.*

tube |tōōb| or |tyōōb| *n., pl.* **tubes** A
flexible container from which substances such
as toothpaste can be squeezed out.

Pronunciation Key

ă	pat	ō	go	th	thin
ā	pay	ô	paw, for	hw	which
â	care	oi	oil	zh	usual
ä	father	ŏŏ	book	ə	ago,
ĕ	pet	ōō	boot		item,
ē	be	yōō	cute		pencil,
ĭ	pit	ou	out		atom,
ī	ice	ŭ	cut		circus
î	near	û	fur	ər	butter
ŏ	pot	*th*	the		

tu·na |tōō´ nə| or |tyōō´ nə| *n., pl.* **tuna**
or **tunas** An often large ocean fish caught in
great numbers for food. Some tuna can be as
long as 14 feet and can weigh 1,600 pounds.

tune |tōōn| or |tyōōn| *n., pl.* **tunes** A
melody, especially one that is simple and easy
to remember.

tur·key |tûr´ kē| *n., pl.* **turkeys** A large
North American bird that is raised for food.

twice |twīs| *adv.* Two times: *He saw the
movie twice.*

twirl |twûrl| *v.* **twirled, twirling** To rotate
quickly; spin.

type |tīp| *n., pl.* **types** A group, kind, or
class sharing common traits or characteristics:
What type of sailboat is that? v. **typed, typing**
To write with a typewriter.

U

ug·ly |ŭg´ lē| *adj.* **uglier, ugliest** Not
pleasing to look at; not beautiful or attractive:
I think the hat is ugly.

un- A prefix that means: **1.** Not: *unable;
unbecoming.* **2.** Lack of: *unemployment.*
3. To do the opposite of: *unlock.*

un·cle |ŭng´ kəl| *n., pl.* **uncles** The
brother of one's mother or father.

un·clear |ŭn klîr´| *adj.* Not clear.

un·der·stand |ŭn´ dər stănd´| *v.*
understood |ŭn dər stŏŏd´|, **understanding**
1. To get the meaning of: *Do you understand
my question?* **2.** To be familiar with; know
well: *I wish I could understand Spanish.*

Spelling Dictionary

un·der·wa·ter |ŭn' dər wô' tər| *adj.*
Located, living, done, or used under the surface
of the water: *The company drilled for underwater
oil. adv.* Under the surface of the water:
to swim underwater.

un·do |ŭn doo'| *v.* **undid** |ŭn dĭd'|, **undoing**
To do away with or reverse the result or effect of:
They wished they could undo their mistake.

un·e·ven |ŭn ē' vən| *adj.* **unevener,**
unevenest Not level, smooth, or straight: *The
surface of coral is uneven.*

un·fair |ŭn fâr'| *adj.* **unfairer, unfairest** Not
fair or just: *an unfair punishment.*

un·fa·mil·iar |ŭn' fə mĭl' yər| *adj.* Not
known; strange: *We saw an unfamiliar face at the
door.*

un·hap·py |ŭn hăp' ē| *adj.* **unhappier,**
unhappiest Not happy; sad.

u·ni·form |yoo' nə fôrm'| *n., pl.* **uniforms**
Clothing that identifies those who wear it as
members of a certain group, such as a police force.

un·kind |ŭn kīnd'| *adj.* **unkinder,**
unkindest Harsh or cruel.

un·learn |ŭn lûrn'| *v.* **unlearned,**
unlearning To learn not to do or respond to
something learned previously: *Sometimes we
must unlearn a bad habit.*

un·load |ŭn lōd'| *v.* **unloaded, unloading**
To remove a load from: *We unloaded the truck.*

un·luck·y |ŭn lŭk' ē| *adj.* **unluckier,**
unluckiest Having or bringing bad luck.

un·pack |ŭn păk'| *v.* **unpacked, unpacking**
To remove the contents of a container or vehicle,
such as a suitcase or car: *I unpacked the old trunk.*

un·paid |ŭn pād'| *adj.* Not yet paid: *an
unpaid bill.*

un·safe |ŭn sāf'| *adj.* Not safe; dangerous.

un·sure |ŭn shoor'| *adj.* Not sure; uncertain.

un·ti·dy |ŭn tī' dē| *adj.* **untidier, untidiest**
Not tidy or neat; sloppy; messy: *Jeff cleaned up
his untidy room.*

un·til |ŭn tĭl'| *prep.* Up to the time of: *They
studied until dinner.*

un·u·su·al |ŭn yoo' zhoo əl| *adj.* Not usual,
common, or ordinary: *It's unusual for me not to
eat; I must be sick.*

urge |ûrj| *v.* **urged, urging** To try to
convince; plead with: *My parents urged me
to study harder.*

urn |ûrn| *n., pl.* **urns** A metal container
with a spigot used for making and serving tea
or coffee.
◆ *These sound alike* **urn, earn.**

use·ful |yoos' fəl| *adj.* Being of use or
service; helpful: *Our map of Chicago was useful
when we visited there.*

use·less |yoos' lĭs| *adj.* Being of no use
or service; worthless: *We threw out the broken
radio because it was useless.*

V

vac·cine |văk sēn'| *n., pl.* **vaccines** A
preparation of weak or dead germs that are
injected into a person or animal as a protection
against the disease caused by those germs: *The
children were given a vaccine against polio.*

vain |vān| *adj.* **vainer, vainest** Having no
success: *Firefighters made a vain attempt to save
the burning building.*
◆ *These sound alike* **vain, vane, vein.**

val·ley |văl' ē| *n., pl.* **valleys** A long,
narrow area of low land between mountains
or hills, often with a river running along the
bottom.

vane |vān| *n., pl.* **vanes** A thin, flat piece
of wood or metal, often having the shape of
an arrow or a rooster, that turns on a vertical
pivot to show the direction of the wind. Vanes
are often placed on top of buildings.
◆ *These sound alike* **vane, vain, vein.**

vane

va·nil·la |və **nĭl'** ə| *n.* A flavoring made from the seed pods of a tropical plant: *The recipe called for a teaspoon of vanilla.*

vein |vān| *n.* **1.** A blood vessel through which blood returns to the heart. **2.** A long, regularly shaped deposit of mineral in rock: *a vein of gold ore.*
♦ *These sound alike* **vein, vain, vane.**

ven·ture |**vĕn'** chər| *n., pl.* **ventures** A task or activity that is risky or dangerous: *Our first venture to the moon was a great success.* *v.* **ventured, venturing** To travel, undertake a project, etc., despite danger: *We ventured into the swirling waters.*

ves·sel |**vĕs'** əl| *n., pl.* **vessels** A ship or large boat.

vi·brate |**vī'** brāt'| *v.* **vibrated, vibrating** To move or cause to move back and forth rapidly: *Plucking a guitar string causes it to vibrate and produce a sound.*

vic·tim |**vĭk'** tĭm| *n., pl.* **victims** A person or animal that is harmed, killed, or made to suffer.

vic·to·ri·ous |vĭk' **tôr'** ē əs| *adj.* Having won a victory.

vic·to·ry |**vĭk'** tə rē| *n., pl.* **victories** The defeat of an opponent or enemy; success.

vil·lage |**vĭl'** ĭj| *n., pl.* **villages** A group of houses that make up a community smaller than a town.

vis·it |**vĭz'** ĭt| *n., pl.* **visits** A short stay or call: *I paid a visit to my former teacher.*

viv·id |**vĭv'** ĭd| *adj.* Bright and strong; brilliant: *The coat was a vivid blue.*

vol·un·teer |vŏl' ən **tîr'**| *v.* **volunteered, volunteering** To give or offer, usually without being asked: *I volunteered to lead the younger children on an overnight hike.*

W

wag·on |**wăg'** ən| *n., pl.* **wagons** A four-wheeled vehicle for carrying loads or passengers.

wait |wāt| *v.* **waited, waiting** To do nothing or stay in a place until something expected happens: *Wait for me here.*
♦ *These sound alike* **wait, weight.**

Pronunciation Key

ă	pat	ō	go	th	thin
ā	pay	ô	paw, for	hw	which
â	care	oi	oil	zh	usual
ä	father	o͝o	book	ə	ago,
ĕ	pet	o͞o	boot		item,
ē	be	yo͞o	cute		pencil,
ĭ	pit	ou	out		atom,
ī	ice	ŭ	cut		circus
î	near	û	fur	ər	butter
ŏ	pot	*th*	the		

walk |wôk| *v.* **walked, walking** To move or cause to move on foot at an easy, steady pace. *n., pl.* **walks 1.** An act of walking: *We took a walk on the beach.* **2.** A place, such as a path, that is set apart or designed for walking.

ware |wâr| *n.* **1.** Manufactured articles or goods of the same general kind, such as glassware or hardware. **2. wares** Goods for sale: *At the fair all the merchants displayed their wares.*
♦ *These sound alike* **ware, wear.**

waste |wāst| *v.* **wasted, wasting** To spend or use foolishly or needlessly: *Don't waste the whole day watching television.*

wa·ter·proof |**wô'** tər pro͞of'| *adj.* Capable of keeping water from coming through: *Raincoats should be made of waterproof material.*

wave·let |**wāv'** lĭt| *n., pl.* **wavelets** A small wave or ripple.

wa·ver |**wā'** vər| *v.* **wavered, wavering** To be uncertain; falter: *I never wavered in my choice.*

wealth |wĕlth| *n.* A great amount of money or valuable possessions.

wear |wâr| *v.* **wore** |wôr|, **worn, wearing** To have on the body: *All the students wear school uniforms.*
♦ *These sound alike* **wear, ware.**

wea·ry |**wîr'** ē| *adj.* **wearier, weariest** Needing rest; tired: *The weary children went straight to bed.*

weath·er |**wĕth'** ər| *n.* The condition or activity of the atmosphere with respect to whether it is hot or cold, sunny or cloudy, windy or calm, or wet or dry.
♦ *These sound alike* **weather, whether.**

Spelling Dictionary

weave |wēv| *v.* **wove** |wōv| *or* **weaved,** **woven** |wō′ vən|, **weaving** To make something, such as cloth or a basket, by passing something, such as threads or twigs, over and under one another. Weaving is often done on a loom.

week |wēk| *n., pl.* **weeks** A period of seven days: *We'll be there in a week.*
♦ *These sound alike* **week, weak.**

weight |wāt| *n., pl.* **weights** The measure of how heavy something is: *The weight of the box is 100 pounds.*
♦ *These sound alike* **weight, wait.**

weird |wîrd| *adj.* **weirder, weirdest** Strange, odd, or unusual: *Purple trousers, an orange shirt, and a pointed hat make a weird outfit.*

wel·come |wĕl′ kəm| *v.* **welcomed,** **welcoming** To greet with pleasure, hospitality, or special ceremony: *We stood to welcome our guests. n., pl.* **welcomes** The act of welcoming. *adj.* Greeted, received, or accepted with pleasure: *You are always a welcome visitor.*

west |wĕst| *n.* The direction in which the sun is seen setting in the evening. *adj.* Of, in, or toward the west: *We camped on the west side of the large lake. adv.* Toward the west: *We drove west.*

whale |hwāl| *n., pl.* **whales** An often very large sea animal that looks like a fish but is a mammal that breathes air.

when·ev·er |hwĕn ĕv′ ər| *adv.* At whatever time: *Come whenever possible. conj.* At whatever time that: *We can start whenever you're ready.*

wheth·er |hwĕth′ ər| *conj.* If: *Ask whether the museum is open.*
♦ *These sound alike* **whether, weather.**

whirl·pool |hwûrl′ pōol′| *n., pl.* **whirlpools** A current of water that rotates very rapidly.

whirlpool

whit·tle |hwĭt′ l| *v.* **whittled, whittling** To cut small bits or shavings from wood with a knife.

wick·ed |wĭk′ ĭd| *adj.* **wickeder, wickedest** Bad, evil, or mean.

wind¹ |wĭnd| *n., pl.* **winds** Air that is in motion.

wind² |wīnd| *v.* **wound** |wound|, **winding** To tighten the spring of: *I forgot to wind my watch.*

wind·y |wĭn′ dē| *adj.* **windier, windiest** Having much wind.

with·draw |wĭth drô′| *v.* **withdrew** |wĭth drōo′|, **withdrawn, withdrawing** To take back or away; remove: *I withdrew my money from the bank.*

wiz·ard |wĭz′ ərd| *n., pl.* **wizards** A man thought to have magical powers; magician.

wom·an |wŏŏm′ ən| *n., pl.* **women** |wĭm′ ĭn| A fully grown female human being.

won·der |wŭn′ dər| *v.* **wondered, wondering** To be curious about; want to know: *I wonder what went wrong.*

wood |wŏŏd| *n., pl.* **woods** The hard material beneath the bark of trees and shrubs that makes up the trunk and branches. Wood is used as fuel and for building.

wood·y |wŏŏd′ ē| *adj.* **woodier, woodiest** Consisting of or containing wood.

wool |wŏŏl| *n., pl.* **wools** **1.** The soft, thick, curly or wavy hair of animals such as sheep. **2.** Yarn, cloth, or clothing made of wool.

wool·en |wŏŏl′ ən| *adj.* Made of wool.

wool·ly |wŏŏl′ ē| *adj.* **woollier, woolliest** Made of or covered with wool or a material like wool.

word root |wôrd rōot| *or* |wôrd rŏŏt| *n., pl.* **word roots** A word part from which other words are formed. It adds meaning to the words. For example, *pedal* includes the word root *ped,* meaning "foot."

work |wûrk| *n., pl.* **works** **1.** The physical or mental effort that is required to do something; labor: *Cleaning the house is hard work.* **2.** An activity by which a person earns money; job: *Our neighbor is looking for work as a teacher. v.* **worked,** **working** **1.** To put or cause to put out effort to do or make something: *We work hard to get good grades. The teacher works the sixth graders hard.* **2.** To have a job: *My parents work in a hospital.*

work·out |wûrk′ out′| *n.* A period of exercise, especially in athletics: *Mark had a good workout in the gym.*

world |wûrld| *n., pl.* **worlds** The earth: *The world is round.*

worm |wûrm| *n., pl.* **worms** Any of several kinds of animals that have soft bodies and no backbone. Worms have no legs and move by crawling. *v.* **wormed, worming** To move by or as if by crawling: *We wormed our way through the crowd.*

worn |wôrn| *v.* Past participle of **wear.** *adj.* Very tired; exhausted.

wor·ry |wûr′ ē| *v.* **worried, worrying** To feel or cause to feel uneasy: *Your bad cough worries me.*

would |wŏŏd| *helping v.* Past tense of **will.** Used to show or express something that is likely: *They would be here if they had left on time.*

wound |wŏŏnd| *n., pl.* **wounds** An injury in which body tissue is cut or broken.

wrap |răp| *v.* **wrapped, wrapping** To wind or fold as a covering: *I wrapped a shawl around my shoulders.*

wrench |rĕnch| *n., pl.* **wrenches** A tool that has jaws for gripping nuts, bolts, or pieces of pipe so that they can be turned.

wres·tle |rĕs′ əl| *v.* **wrestled, wrestling** To struggle with and try to force or throw an opponent to the ground.

wring |rĭng| *v.* **wrung** |rŭng|, **wringing** **1.** To twist or squeeze so as to force out liquid: *Wring out the wet clothes.* **2.** To force out by or as if by twisting or squeezing: *Wring the water from the towel.*

◆ *These sound alike* **wring, ring.**

wrin·kle |rĭng′ kəl| *n., pl.* **wrinkles** A small fold or crease.

wrist |rĭst| *n., pl.* **wrists** The joint between the hand and the arm.

wrong |rông| *adj.* Not correct or true: *You gave the wrong answer.*

wrote |rōt| *v.* Past tense of **write:** *He wrote a letter with his new pen.*

Pronunciation Key

ă	pat	ō	go	th	thin
ā	pay	ô	paw, for	hw	which
â	care	oi	oil	zh	usual
ä	father	ŏŏ	book	ə	ago,
ĕ	pet	ŏŏ	boot		item,
ē	be	yŏŏ	cute		pencil,
ĭ	pit	ou	out		atom,
ī	ice	ŭ	cut		circus
î	near	û	fur	ər	butter
ŏ	pot	*th*	the		

Y

-y A suffix that forms adjectives and means: **1.** Like a: *bushy.* **2.** Full of: *juicy.*

year |yîr| *n., pl.* **years** **1.** The period of time in which the earth makes one complete trip around the sun. **2.** A period of 365 days, or 366 days in a leap year, divided into 52 weeks or 12 months, beginning January 1 and ending December 31. **3.** A period of 12 months: *We plan to return a year from now.*

yeast |yēst| *n., pl.* **yeasts** A substance that is used to make bread dough rise. Yeast consists of tiny one-celled plants that grow quickly.

yell |yĕl| *v.* **yelled, yelling** To shout or cry out loudly, as in anger, fear, or warning.

yel·low |yĕl′ ō| *n., pl.* **yellows** The color of ripe lemons or of dandelions.

yes·ter·day |yĕs′ tər dā′| *n.* The day before today: *Yesterday was windy.*

Z

zinc |zĭngk| *n.* A shiny bluish-white metal, used as a coating for iron and in electric batteries. Zinc is one of the chemical elements.

Content Index

Numbers in **boldface** indicate pages on which a skill is introduced as well as references to the Capitalization and Punctuation Guide.

Content Index

Credits

Illustration   86 Rita Lascaro 88 Annie Gusman
106 Fred Schrier 109 Lehner & Whyte 112 Rita Lascaro
118 Garth Williams 122 Fred Schrier 124 Jennifer Harris
148 Rita Lascaro 160 Fred Schrier 184 Annie Gusman

Assignment Photography   20 (br), 51 (b) Petrisse Briel
49 (mr), 56 (br, bl), 62 (b), 104 (br), 107 (br), 117 (b), 119
(bl), 130 (br), 133 (mr, ml), 134 (b), 157, 158, 163 (br),
202, 206 Allan Landau 47 (br), 83 (br), 191 (mr), 206 (br),
227 (bm) Parker/Boone Productions 14 (b), 19, 25 (m, ml,
mr), 28 (bl), 32 (br), 34 (m), 38 (tl), 46–47, 123 (t), 153
(tr), 154–155, 159 (br), 161 (l), 169 (br), 171 (m, br), 173
(bl), 175 (br), 181 (tr, bl), 182 (m), 183 (br), 184 (m) Tony
Scarpetta 22 (m) Tracey Wheeler

Photography   5 Image Copyright © 1997 PhotoDisc,
Inc. 6 (l) R. Stuart Cummings, 1994/Southern Stock/PNI 6
(r) Joan Teasdale/The Stock Market 7 (t) © Van/Photo
Researchers, Inc. 7 (m) Scott Nielson/Bruce Coleman/PNI
10 Allan Landau 17 (b) Karl Weatherly/Corbis 25 (b)
Image Copyright © 1997 PhotoDisc, Inc. 28 (r) Frederic
Stein/FPG International 29 (b) F. Stuart Westmorland/
Corbis 33 John Warden/Tony Stone Images 35 (m) The
Granger Collection 35 (r)(l) Image Copyright © 1997
PhotoDisc, Inc. 38 David Carriere/Tony Stone Images 41
Michael Rosenfeld/Tony Stone Images 53 Mitch Kezar/Tony
Stone Images 59 (b) Dick Durrance II/The Stock Market 65
(t) Jeff Schultz/Alaska Stock 65 (l) The Granger Collection
65 (r) Jack Daniels/Tony Stone Images 70 © Richard
Hutchings/PhotoEdit/PNI 73 (b) Image Copyright © 1997
PhotoDisc, Inc. 76 (l) Tony Stone Images 76 (r) Ken
Biggs/Tony Stone Images 77 (t) Image Copyright © 1997
PhotoDisc, Inc. 77 (b) Corbis-Bettmann 81 Image
Copyright © 1997 PhotoDisc, Inc. 82 (l) © Jasmine,
1996/PNI 85 (t) Thomas Zimmermann/FPG International
85 (b) Image Copyright © 1997 PhotoDisc, Inc. 89 (t) John
Terence Turner/FPG International 89 (b) Rich
Iwasaki/Allstock/PNI 91 Adam Woolfitt/Corbis 95 (b) The
Granger Collection 99 (b) Image Copyright © 1997
PhotoDisc, Inc. 100 Dave G. Houser/Corbis 101 (b) Image
Copyright © 1997 PhotoDisc, Inc. 105 (b) Images
Copyright © 1997 PhotoDisc, Inc. 113 The Granger
Collection 117 (t) Tony Garcia/Tony Stone Images 121 R.
Stuart Cummings, 1994/Southern Stock/PNI 125 (t)
Cynthia Matthew/The Stock Market 125 (b) Stephen
Frink/Tony Stone Images 128 Richard Hamilton
Smith/Corbis 129 (tr) ©1996 Joe Sohm/Chromsohm/Stock
Connection 129 (mr) ©1993 Chromsohm/Joe Sohm/The
Stock Market 129 (bl) Wes Thompson/The Stock Market
129 (br) Peter Pearson/Tony Stone Images 130 (l) © Jan
Halaska/Photo Researchers, Inc. 131 Scott Dietrich/Tony
Stone Images 137 Steve Elmore/Tony Stone Images 139
Image Copyright © 1997 PhotoDisc, Inc. 143 © The City
of Oakland, The Oakland Museum, California. 1983 145
Joan Teasdale/The Stock Market 149 (t) Ted Wood/Tony
Stone Images 149 (b) John Beatty/Tony Stone Images 159
Classic PIO Partners 161 Frank Oberle/Tony Stone Images
167 © Van/Photo Researchers, Inc. 169 (l) Tim
Davis/Allstock/PNI 169 (m) Scott Nielson/Bruce
Coleman/PNI 169 (r) Joseph Van Wormer/Bruce
Coleman/PNI 170 Images Copyright © 1997 PhotoDisc,
Inc. 173 Lee Kuhn/FPG International 177 Peter Cade/Tony
Stone Images 179 The Granger Collection 183 Robert
Holmes/Corbis 184 (b) Library of Congress/Corbis 184 (r)
Image Copyright © 1997 PhotoDisc, Inc. 185 (t) (b) NASA
197 Image Copyright © 1997 PhotoDisc, Inc. 199 Art
Wolfe/Tony Stone Images 201 Mark
Newman/Phototake/PNI 203 The Granger Collection 208
© George Mattei/Envision 215 (r) Sovfoto/Eastfoto,
1994/PNI 215 (b) Corbis-Bettmann 220 Ken Biggs/Tony
Stone Images 226 Philip Bailey/The Stock Market 281
Adam Woolfitt/Corbis 285 Tom Walker/Allstock/PNI 287
Dave Bartnuff, 1995/Stock, Boston/PNI 288 Art Wolfe,
1989/Allstock/PNI 289 © Sovfoto/Eastfoto/PNI 290 David
Paterson/Corbis 293 Jonathan Wright, Bruce Coleman/PNI
294 Patrice Ceisel/Stock, Boston/PNI 299 Jack Daniels/Tony
Stone Images 300 Image Copyright © 1997 PhotoDisc,
Inc. 303 David Hiser/Tony Stone Images 304 Cary
Wolinsky/Stock, Boston/PNI 307 Jan Halaska/Photo
Researchers, Inc. 309 Roy Morsch/The Stock Market 311
R. Campillo/The Stock Market 312 Roger Wilmhurst; Frank
Lane Pictures/Corbis 314 James P. Rowan/Tony Stone
Images 316 John Cancalosi/Stock, Boston/PNI 318 Kathi
Lamm/Tony Stone Images 321 Bill Bachmann/Stock,
Boston/PNI 323 Cosmo Candina/Tony Stone Images 325
Joseph Sohm/ChromoSohm Inc./Corbis 326 Ariel
Skelley/The Stock Market 328 Greg L. Ryan: Sally A.
Beyer/Allstock/PNI 330 Norman O. Tomalin/Bruce
Coleman/PNI

Handwriting Models

a b c d e f g h i
j k l m n o p q r
s t u v w x y z

A B C D E F G H I
J K L M N O P Q R
S T U V W X Y Z

Words Often Misspelled

You probably use many of the words on this list when you write. If you cannot think of the spelling of a word, you can always check this list. The words are in alphabetical order.

A
again
a lot
also
always
another
anyone
anyway
around

B
beautiful
because
before
brought
buy

C
cannot
can't
caught
coming
could

D
didn't
different
don't

E
enough
every
everybody
everyone

F
family
finally
friend

G
getting
girl
goes
going
guess

H
happened
haven't
heard
here

I
I'd
I'll
I'm
instead
into
its
it's

K
knew
know

L
letter

M
might
morning
mother's
myself

O
o'clock
off
once
other

P
people
pretty
probably

R
really
right

S
Saturday
school
someone
stopped
sure
swimming

T
than
that's
their
then
there
there's

they
they're
thought
through
to
tonight
too
tried
two

U
usually

W
we're
where
whole
would
wouldn't
write

Y
your
you're